COUNSELING
FAMILIES
AFTER DIVORCE

**CONTEMPORARY CHRISTIAN
COUNSELING**

COUNSELING
FAMILIES
AFTER DIVORCE

DAVID R. MILLER, Ph. D.

CONTEMPORARY CHRISTIAN
COUNSELING

General Editor
GARY R. COLLINS, PH.D.

COUNSELING FAMILIES AFTER DIVORCE
Contemporary Christian Counseling
Copyright © 1994 by Word, Incorporated

Library of Congress Cataloging-in-Publication Data:

Miller, David R., 1941–
　　Counseling families after divorce/David R. Miller.
　　p.　cm.—(Contemporary Christian Counseling)
　　Includes bibliographical references and index.
　　ISBN 0–8499–1062–5:
　　　1. Single parents—Pastoral counseling of—United States.
　　2. Divorced parents—Pastoral counseling of—United States.　3. Single-parent family—United States.　4. Children of single divorced parents—Pastoral counseling of—United States.　5. Children of divorced parents—Pastoral counseling of—United States.　6. Church work with divorced people.　I. Title.　II. Series.
　　BV4438.7.M55　1994
　　259'.1—dc20
　　　　　　　　　　　　　　　　　　　　　　　　　　　　93–46347
　　　　　　　　　　　　　　　　　　　　　　　　　　　　CIP

456789 LBM 7654321

Printed in the United States of America

To Linda, God's gift to me
and the enabler of my ministry
to parents and families.

Contents

Preface

The "traditional" family system composed of mother and father married to each other while living with and raising their own biological children is fast becoming a situation that is not the norm. What has been nontraditional is fast becoming the norm, and what has been traditional is slowly disappearing from the family scene. We may lament this change, but it has arrived! We may fret and worry and preach about the changing family landscape, but there had better be some within the Christian community who are trained and ready to assist the growing percentage of nontraditional, nonnuclear Christian families arriving on the church steps and asking for ministry and help.

Christian counselors are called on to do what we can to try and stem the tide moving away from the traditional nuclear family, and we are happy and willing to respond. But the tide will not be turned. The nontraditional family tide continues to swell and move forward.

We must respond to the changes happening in our families by tearing down obstacles to the tidal flow of family change and replacing them with new channels of ministry. We must open our church doors wide to the never-marrieds with children, the divorced or separated families, and stepfamilies. If we are truly interested in ministry, we will not hesitate to do this. Church leadership will welcome the nonnuclear families into fellowship and be prepared to meet their needs as they have met the needs of traditional church families.

It is in the area of ministry to nontraditionals that Christian counselors find great fulfillment. Separated, divorced, step, and never-marrieds with children can be expected to draw from the body of believers as no other segment of the church. Christian counselors able to respond with nonjudgmental compassion to such challenged families will find their greatest sense of reward and accomplishment as a result.

But the task is daunting! There is much already developed in the knowledge base for counselors working with this population, and study is a necessity. We must know what is really going on in the changing family scene, what needs are developing, and how to respond in a Christian *and* therapeutic manner. This book is an attempt to provide the Christian counselor with essential information, strategies, and processes for working with nonnuclear families in need.

I could not have done this on my own. I am indebted to Dr. Gary Collins for trusting me with such an undertaking. To Copyeditor Lois Stück, Project Manager Terri Gibbs, and others at Word, I am truly grateful for their patience and willingness to expend their energies to help me communicate to Christian counselors. And most of all, I want to thank my wife, Linda, for encouraging me to spend the necessary countless hours down in the study sitting before the word processor while she was alone upstairs. This project could not have been completed without the help of so many!

Chapter 1

The Rise of the Nontraditional American Family

Never in my wildest dreams did I think I would be a single parent! Unimaginable! Unthinkable! But here I am, talking with a counselor who specializes in single-parent families, and I know that I have to come to grips with my reality. I am a divorced mother and a single parent. And I don't like it one bit!"

Sue Craig, a thirty-seven-year-old mother of four was facing this bitter reality because her husband, Ron, had decided to leave her and the children for another woman—a woman several years younger than Sue and without children. This other woman, Sue felt, was offering her husband something more than he could receive at home with her and the children, and her self-concept was at an all-time low. Sue desperately did not want the divorce but had come to realize that the more she begged Ron to reconsider, the farther away he moved.

The marriage of Sue and Ron Craig was finished. It was as unrecoverable as any relationship could be, as irreconcilable as any once strong marriage could become, and more tragic in its developing consequences than either Ron or Sue could realize at this point in the divorce process.

Sue had been to see her pastor for advice, and although the advice was appropriate and well-intentioned, she felt that he did not really understand what she was telling him or the depth of her despair. The pastor was, after all, Ron's pastor as well as a man, and as Sue would learn, pastors sometimes do not accept reality very well.

Thinking about the end of her marriage plagued Sue. It was over! It would not be healed. Ron's decision to leave and begin another marriage was final and beyond Sue's control. No amount of work would restore this marriage. No amount of prayer and supplication had proven powerful enough to change Ron's mind. The decision was made; it was irreversible. Finished! What Sue needed now was help in picking up the pieces of her broken family.

Sue Craig is a divorcée, a single mother, a statistic. But she is a Christian statistic, one of a growing number of believers witnessing the collapse of their marriages. Once thought relatively safe from the plagues of the world, the Christian community now finds itself deeply involved in the world of divorce. As with so many others, Sue Craig believed her Christianity and conservative lifestyle would protect her and her family from the growing trend of divorce. While eventually she would see that her faith would support her and bring her through the darkest days, she would also feel a developing empathy with *all* divorced women and single mothers, regardless of religious affiliation or belief.

THE DECLINE OF THE AMERICAN FAMILY

The United States is clearly one of the most religious of the developed nations of the world. Fully 57 percent of Americans say they belong to a church or a religious organization. This compares to 31 percent in Ireland, the second most religious nation, and Sweden at the low end with only 9 percent. Eighty-five percent of Americans say they believe in the power of prayer compared to 81 percent in Ireland and 33 percent in

Sweden. For a belief in a literal heaven and hell, Americans rank first in the developed world.[1]

So Americans rank first in the world in believing in God, prayer, heaven, and hell and all the other correlates of what has come to be known as "mainstream Christianity," but we have also taken first place in the divorce statistics. In his study of "Christiantown" (Wheaton, Illinois), Richard Stellway found no connection between religious belief and either marital happiness or adjustment to the marriage and concluded that religious beliefs cannot be assumed to positively impact a marriage.[2] Perhaps there is a difference between religiosity and Christian spirituality!

Sue Craig is typical of those believers Stellway studied, and her confusion and need for counsel was not lessened by her lifelong acceptance of God's ordination of the family as stated in Genesis 1:27–28.

> So God created man in his own image, in the image of God he created him; male and female he created them. God blessed them and said to them, "Be fruitful and increase in number; fill the earth. . . ."

The Craig family exemplifies the trends apparent in the developed nations around the world. Marriage is threatened; the family is under siege; what God has ordained is growing weaker in at least five ways.

1. *The family is experiencing deinstitutionalization.* This process involves a gradual loss of the functions of a typical family, which results in the family being replaced by other institutions such as school, civil government, media, and even the church. Deinstitutionalization leads to a family that is less cohesive and together, more oriented to doing things outside the home without the involvement of other family members.[3]

The parenting roles subsumed by extra-family entities include the socialization of children through transmission of values as taught in values clarification classes—as early as kindergarten in some areas. Also common is the teaching of children's rights that, while desirable at one level, can lead to a breakdown of parental authority. The inclusion of rock music stars and heroes from the athletic world as replacement for parents as role models for school children is a concern as well.

In spite of the continued acceptance of and belief in the "normal nuclear family,"[4] the realistic family approaching the turn of the next century is composed of individual members growing increasingly autonomous and independent and needing one another less and less. In societies still retaining a strong family core, we find not independence but *interdependence*, not deinstitutionalization but coordination of family activities to assure the inclusion of all willing members.

One factor that is spurring changes in the family leading to a de-emphasis on family cohesion is two-parent income. In a society where the majority of women with children under six years of age are working full-time outside the home, it should surprise no one that there is less time for and interest in family activities. As an ever greater proportion of American wives and mothers work outside the home, an equal proportion of American women will decide that economic cooperation within the family might not be in the wife's best interest any longer. Financial independence is a quality with many advantages, but there is little doubt that it is a factor in the destabilization of the American family.

When the marriage relationship weakens, the marriage becomes more vulnerable to divorce, parental authority slips, and there is less effective discipline. Family counselors working with people from both secular and religious backgrounds agree on the common problems causing families to seek counseling. In support of the concern being expressed, the National Association of Evangelicals (N.A.E.) put together a task force on the family in the early 1980s and found that surveyed pastors were nearly unanimous in their belief that the problems coming to them from church families were increasingly similar to those of the unchurched community.[5]

2. The American family is weakening in carrying out many of its traditional social functions. As we see more and more of the responsibilities once reserved for parents and the family passed on to entities outside the home, we can expect an increase in rebellion to authority by children who come to believe they no longer need their parents to survive. In fact, the pattern is set. A twelve-year-old boy in Florida successfully sued his single mother for divorce on the grounds that she could not meet his needs as well as the foster family with whom he had been living. The boy won his case, and permanent custody was granted to the foster parents. Those of us who think the excesses of Sweden, Denmark, and other European countries related to limiting parents in what they can and cannot do with their children are radical had better step back and reevaluate. We are nearly there!

Not only are American families barely producing enough children to replace the older generation, but the family is also surrendering its function as a unit of controlled sexual expression. Witness the acceptance of sexual promiscuity in all its forms promoted hourly through television. Fewer and fewer couples, including Christian couples, are entering marriage with a commitment to the permanence of their vows. Glenn conducted a comprehensive study of marital attitudes and found that "it has become considerably less likely that Americans who marry will attain and maintain marital success."[6] He further proposes that the decline in the "ideal of marital permanence" will become increasingly evident in succeeding years and will be manifested in what he termed "permanent availability" of married people based on their expectation that the marriage will probably not succeed. Acceptance of the possibility of divorce leads to an attitude of "tentative availability," making the marriage partners susceptible to being lured out of their present marriage and into another relationship.

In addition to procreation, the family has traditionally assumed responsibility for several other functions, including the physical maintenance of the family, allocation of resources, division of labor, socialization of family members, discipline of family members, placement of family members into the larger society, and the maintenance of motivation and morale. In each area we see parents doing an increasingly less effective job, revealing a discouraging downward spiral for childrearing.

Of particular concern is the issue of socializing children. Christian parents have a tradition of raising reasonably well-behaved children and adolescents. Historically, it was a black eye for the family when a young person got into trouble. In fact, in past years many families would discipline a child *again* after he or she had been disciplined at school. Today, however, parents (including professing Christian parents) are often the *primary* obstacle preventing the school from exercising reasonable discipline. "Don't touch my child!" is the oft-heard challenge of the modern parent. As the school tries to deal with normal child and adolescent misbehavior without overt discipline, the only avenue open to overwhelmed school personnel is to convince youngsters that the school is on their side, even when it comes to disputes with parents. Thus, parents who at one point were interested in asserting their independence from the school have, in fact, relinquished most of their authority to the school. The school has replaced parents, in many cases, as the primary socializing agent for children.

3. *The family is weakening in its relationship to governmental power.* A historical perspective demonstrates that families were primary, and government was established in part to assure that primacy by limiting the power of government and other forces to impact the family. Today, a family dispute is as likely to be resolved in a courtroom as a living room. Family and Domestic Relations judges have stepped in where others have feared to tread. Once a couple decides to separate or divorce, the issue of child custody, financial support for dependent children, and visitation by the noncustodial parent are settled by a court official rather than the parents. True, if there is no disagreement between the parents, the court will usually try to facilitate their decision. But if there is no agreement, the court's decision stands as law.

In so many cases, when a family tries to stand up for itself and make decisions for the child's best interests in opposition to what the state or local government has decreed, the government comes out the winner. Prayer in school, keeping a Bible in one's desk, reading religious literature during lunch, using school facilities for religious activities such as a Bible club have all fallen one by one at the first sign of a complaint from a parent or challenge from a civil libertarian group.

The family loses these battles because so many of those in positions of power have lost confidence in the American family to know what is best for children. Parents are seen more and more as obstacles to free thought, roadblocks to developing a true democracy for the future, and handicaps for their children rather than ladders to success. It has almost become the rule that the family loses all battles with government.

4. *The family is weakened by shrinking size and instability.* Individual family groups are getting smaller and smaller with each generation, and families are becoming more unstable with shorter duration due to separation and divorce. When I grew up in the Detroit area, I lived within walking distance of every relative I knew about, and at least as far as I knew at the time, none of my elders was divorced.

Today, children are surrounded by divorced people; the example of marital failure has become the norm rather than being abnormal. Some research has emphasized the point that while the public in general prefers to think of the normal family as two parents and biological or adopted children living in the same home, nearly half the American population lives in a situation different from that norm. This variance between perception and reality leads to the unpleasant factor of an unattainable standard. Normal has become exceptional, the mother-father-two-children ideal is a reality for less than 5 percent of Americans.[7]

As the family weakens and declines in influence, children are spending less and less time at home during a normal day and moving out of the home psychologically at increasingly younger ages. We know that more children are remaining at home physically for more years, but that does not mean there is continuing influence by the parents. In many families, children and adolescents are allowed to live and behave as if they were simply renting a room (but without paying for it), free to come and go as they wish, rarely taking a meal together, and never choosing to spend time with one another. Many modern American families have become nonaffiliative in that the members seem to express little desire to be with one another, resulting in reduction in parent-to-child influence.

5. *The family is losing its influence spiritually.* How else can we explain the incongruity of the majority of Americans saying they believe in God and attend church on a regular basis while seeing a rise in all aspects of evil. Pornography, sexual immorality,

divorce, and family violence have continued to escalate, yet church attendance statistics climb.

Fathers in two-parent homes are working more hours than ever before, and more than 52 percent of married couples with children have both partners working outside the home, committed as much to career as to family.[8] More working hours leads to less time for spiritual matters. Wednesday evening services are rapidly becoming a historical remnant of a bygone age. Many churches that once saw active and well-attended Sunday evening services have been forced to convert Sunday evening into a fellowship hour rather than a time of preaching and teaching. Speakers on the family have abandoned calls for family devotions because they know their pleas are falling on deaf ears of busy and overworked parents.

Children are placed in day care so mother can work. Although some mothers must work, this deprives children of the invaluable experience of spending time day by day with a Christian mom who teaches Bible stories and prays with the children before meals.

When divorce invades the safety and security of the family, children are at risk for learning negative lessons about how parents can fail them. Such lessons are difficult to contradict in later years. For Christian couples, it seems that a very high percentage of divorces are the result of a moral failure. An even sadder truth is that children will almost certainly learn of the real causes for the divorce, further tarnishing an already dulled parent-image.

So the battle is joined for Christian parents. The challenge lies before us, and the battle plan is spelled out in the writings of Moses, "Love the LORD your God with all your heart and with all your soul and with all your strength. These commandments that I give you today are to be upon your hearts. Impress them on your children. Talk about them when you sit at home and when you walk along the road, when you lie down and when you get up" (Deut. 6:5–7).

THE IMPACT OF FAMILY DECLINE ON CHILDREN

I recommend to my students that they establish a "So what!" column in their notebook to serve as a repository for comments made in class that bear no relevance to what they are studying. The question "So what?" may also be asked about family change and decline in America. Most households in America are better off financially than ever before; a higher standard of living is apparent in superior nutrition, clothing, and money for recreation; medical care is the best in the world; and many families have two cars in their garage and a television in every room!

But the decline in family influence has significant negative consequences for American children. These detriments are based on changes that have come during the previous few generations, bringing us to the present generation of decline. What has changed, and how have these changes impacted our children?

FAMILY SIZE

First, families are becoming smaller with each succeeding generation. American parents are barely replacing themselves with the average American family made up of two parents and slightly more than two children. Stepfamilies aside, the average child today is being raised with just one sibling, which limits opportunities for socialization.

Siblings in larger families are more likely to become confidants for each other, to be the bearer and keeper of deep secrets, thereby learning to trust and be trusted. Multiple-sibling families provide greater opportunity to develop special relationships with one brother or sister, and this opens up opportunities for companionship. Children learn about cooperative play from siblings more than from playmates, because brothers and sisters cannot go home when feelings get hurt. Brothers and sisters can also find ways to get even when Mom is not looking. Older brothers and sisters usually become role models for younger children and may also serve as temporary caregivers when parents are otherwise occupied. All of these advantages are lost or reduced as families get smaller.

FAMILY ACTIVITIES

Nostalgia is a wonderful human trait. It allows us to forget the unpleasant aspects of our growing-up years and remember only the good parts. Talk to a family whose children are grown about their favorite memories of childhood, and you will hear about family activities. Picnics, vacations, sporting events attended together, things done *together* make the difference. Rarely do people reminisce about things done alone. What we remember fondly is what we do with others, especially our families.

But ask those same grown children who are now raising their own children and you will notice that this modern family does not seem to be engaging in the activities so happily remembered. The things we do together today allow us to be solitary even when we are with others. Riding to and from dance class, school activities, sports practice, even going to church and returning are largely solitary, each person alone with his or her thoughts in the car. Rather than talk with one another, everyone puts on their Walkman™ headsets.

Where are the *fun* activities that the modern family does together? Picnics are a rare occurrence. Everybody, kids as well as adults, is just too busy. Many of our kids are becoming activity-holics who need activities outside the home to feel popular and accepted.

We adults will look at old family photographs and sigh about the simple life once experienced, oblivious to the fact that we are not allowing our own children to have the same activities that we happily remember. Failing to create memorable family events *now* prevents grown children from having fond family memories.

PARENT/CHILD, ADULT/CHILD INTERACTION

Children learn to be adults by being children, but children must have adults as role models. In addition to learning how to be adults, children also learn to be husbands and wives and even authority figures. Youngsters learn how to be grownups *appropriately* by having the opportunity to observe, on a regular basis, adults living out their appropriate lives within the child's view.

Today's typical child is a media offspring, attached to the electronic umbilical cord and dependent upon it for psychological nourishment and pleasure. This came home to me during counseling sessions in which I was struggling to develop a relationship with a truly nasty ten-year-old named Chris, who was able to resist my charm and training despite repeated serious attempts to get through to him. Finally, in desperation, I asked why he seemed so upset every time he came into the office. Without hesitation or embarrassment he shot back, "Because I should be home right now watching 'The Three Stooges' on television."

This little boy, angry to the core, was dead serious about what was bothering him. He *lived* for after-school television. Chris was a single-parent boy who had no contact with his father and whose mother worked until nearly six in the evening. Chris had learned to entertain himself through a vicarious relationship with the television screen, and in many ways he was being parented by the images on that screen.

As I worked with Chris and his mother, I was reminded on many occasions to consider who was really raising this child. Certainly it was not his absent father who had moved away and did not maintain his child support obligations. His mother was the most influential person in his life, but on a typical weekday they spent less than two hours together.

We hear much about "quality time," and there is no doubt that this is important. Yet what most of us remember as important from our own childhood is not the special times so much as the everyday events of taking meals together, watching television *together* in the evening, or simply talking to one another. In the final analysis, quality time will not replace *quantity* time.

THE ABSENCE OF FAMILY TRADITIONS

Becoming civilized involves primarily the internalization of society's rules for conduct. Although children can learn to be civil by sitting in a classroom and experiencing rewards and punishments from society as they grow up, being socialized is much more complex and important. For a child to become a social being, that child must experience social interaction with a range of people inside as well as outside the family and from a variety of races, sexes, and age groups. Each of us is diminished to the extent that we were cut off from other people groups and religions as we were growing up.

The issue here is a sense of continuity and individuality. From our older relatives we acquire a sense of the continuity of the family, that we are but one link in a historical chain that reaches back centuries. It is from those outside our families that we gain an appreciation for our own uniqueness: the individuality that is stamped upon us by our culture, genetic heritage, geographic placement, and timing in history.

When children of today live away from their extended families, as many must, a sense of aloneness is inevitable. Certainly they have parents and siblings, and perhaps the grandparents they see a few times a year, but this generation is largely cut off from extended family and from the sense of continuity taken for granted by so many previous generations.

Fourth of July in my boyhood was a time of family reunion. As I think back to my youth, I remember those times as being especially significant in confirming who I was becoming. I knew my aunts, uncles, cousins, and grandparents, and I knew that we all looked somewhat alike. The adults all talked about the same kinds of things and seemed to know each other well in spite of seeing some of the others only this one time each year. I felt a sense of continuity and individuality in my family.

Today, families are less likely to attend family reunions, to get together on holidays (especially with extended family), and to attend one another's weddings and funerals. They have fewer traditions to give children the sense of continuity and individuality that made such an impact on me as a child. We are too busy and too far away from each other it seems, and convenience is the watchword in an overworked society.

Regardless of a person's stand on religion, there is little argument that religious traditions have also diminished more rapidly and profoundly than most other forms of tradition. Yet religious traditions are powerful in building the chain of heritage consistency discussed above. Raised Lutheran, I experienced my confirmation at age twelve and was accepted into the little neighborhood Lutheran church that my parents and grandparents attended (though my parents did more sending than attending when I was a child). I remember Christmas Eve services in the church when we would be given a box of hard candy and an orange as we left to go home.

These may be small memories, but along with birthdays and holidays, mealtime and bedtime, waiting for Dad to come home from work or Mom from the grocery store, I felt like I knew who I was because of the special memories my family handed down to me. The present generation, with stressed-out parents working more hours to make ends meet than the previous generation and experiencing single parenting at an all-time high, has left family traditions and special events behind, given over to the hard push of necessity and the comfort of convenience.

What will my children and yours remember about growing up? Will there be significant pleasant memories to think about during the difficult days of growing up? Will the next generation of children experience confirming events to help them learn who they are and what they are here for? What will they remember about church? Will they know any relatives other than immediate family and grandparents? In short, will today's children be able to develop a sense of the heritage consistency so important to earlier generations? Are we sensitive to the great loss in these areas when a family divorces?

THE VANISHING NEIGHBORHOOD

Despite the ease of modern transportation, the world of the child remains the home and neighborhood. Most children still have homes, but few know a neighborhood anything like that experienced by previous generations. Certainly there are many negatives about the "good old days." Nevertheless, in a typical neighborhood today, it is unlikely that 10 percent of the houses will have someone at home during the day. Most American families are headed by two parents, each of whom works full time, or by a single parent who also must work full time.

Children who are home often feel isolated, surrounded by empty houses for most of the day. Many lock themselves away inside their homes for security. There are more small children enrolled in day-care programs in many neighborhoods than are at home playing. In fact, the day-care environment will be remembered as the "neighborhood" for many of today's children. Schools all over America have seen the necessity of offering both before-school and after-school activities. Some children must be dropped off at school as early as 6:00 A.M. so the parent or parents can get to work. Other children whose parent(s) work a later shift, must stay at school until five or six in the evening.

Neighborhood has ceased to be important for the majority of today's children. In many instances, the neighborhood has taken on an unfriendly atmosphere because of the number of homes with no one at home. One of the benefits of growing up in a traditional neighborhood was knowing that in an emergency, we could knock on just about any door and there would be an adult there to help, usually someone's mom.

Many neighborhoods today are made up of empty homes, deserted streets, backyards absent of small children playing and mothers chatting across the fence. Some of these neighborhoods are dangerous places to be, even during daylight hours. It is important to recognize reality, but many of us confess to wishing that our children could have some portion of the reality that helped us grow up.

LOSS OF FAMILY SECURITY

As I remind participants in my parenting workshops, the best thing you can do for your children is to have a good marriage. Knowing that parents are going to stay together (through thick and thicker) is a tremendous advantage for children. I am aware that my parents probably had problems, but I can attest to the feeling of knowing that my mom and dad were never going to get a divorce. (And with my parents in their seventies and still married to one another, I would assume that my childhood sense was accurate.)

Experiencing the loss of a parent for any reason including death, divorce, even chronic illness or incapacitation is the most traumatic event in anyone's life. With divorce, children face the added burden of the parental absence being voluntary, as compared to the involuntary separation of death, illness, or military service. The damage done to children of divorce hinges on their ability to understand that one parent left the home because he or she did not want to live there anymore. Consider the following interview excerpts.

Interview Number One

The first interview is between a three-year-old boy and a counselor. Following the divorce of his parents and the departure of his father from the home, the boy had been experiencing nightmares, difficulty with separation, and a fear of monsters at bedtime.

C: Can I tell you a story about a mommy and a daddy?
BOY: Yeah.
C: This mommy was sad, and so she moved to a different house and this . . .
BOY: I know a different story.
C: Will you tell me your story?
BOY: Somebody stole the daddy.
C: Somebody stole the daddy?
BOY: Yeah, someone took him away.
C: Why did they do that?
BOY: So the little boy would feel bad. The daddy doesn't love the little boy.
C: Why doesn't the daddy love the little boy?
BOY: Cause he went away.[9]

This illustrates why incomplete explanations or those that fail to take into consideration the child's ability to understand can be harmful. Most divorcing parents, experts tell us, incorrectly assume the child cannot understand, and so they do not explain what is happening.

Interview Number Two

As is typical with younger children, this five-year-old girl assumed that she had done something that precipitated her parents' arguments and eventual divorce.

C: So you think that their arguments were the reason that made them get a divorce?
GIRL: No, because you know what? I think that I can remember more than my dad and my mom and my brother. But they think that's not true. But it is.
C: What do you remember that they don't?

GIRL: When I fell off the slide and bumped my
       head. My mom thinks that I really got hurt
       badly, and my dad says that I'm just cranky.
       And then they got a divorce after they ar-
       gued it out. And it's true![10]

Interview Number Three

The following interchange took place with a ten-year-old
boy whose parents had recently divorced.

C: Do you know why your parents decided to
       get a divorce?
BOY: Well, they said they've changed, and so it'd
       be better if they weren't together anymore.
C: Do you understand what they mean by that?
BOY: Sort of.
C: Can you explain it to me?
BOY: Yeah. It's like if somebody is in a club, and
       they decide that they didn't belong in that
       kind of club anymore, and so they wanted to
       not go anymore.[11]

This boy was reflecting what he had been told, but it was
obvious to the interviewer that he was not sure if he should
believe this. Children, who tend to love their parents unques-
tionably, have a hard time understanding how such a feeling
can change so quickly in adults.

Interview Number Four

This interview with a nine-year-old girl of divorced parents
illustrates the difficulty many children have in understanding
why parents could not resolve their difficulties and stay together.

C: Do you know why your mom and dad de-
       cided to get a divorce?
GIRL: Not really. They said that they didn't love
       each other anymore.
C: Do you know what they mean by that?

GIRL: Not really.

C: What do you think it might mean?

GIRL: That they just lost interest in each other.

C: Do you think they could have prevented it?

GIRL: Yeah, if they really wanted to.[12]

Interview Number Five

Adolescents have an increased ability to understand why people sometimes do the things they do as well as an increased tendency to place responsibility for a family breakup on one or the other parent. A thirteen-year-old boy described his father in the following interchange.

C: How do you think he feels about it?

BOY: Well, he acts like it's worse when he's by himself. He'll say it's bad one minute, and the next minute he'll be out having a good time and all that. He doesn't care.

C: So he acts as if he cares about you, but you think he doesn't.

BOY: Yeah.

C: Do you know why he's like that?

BOY: Yeah, he's a mixed up person.[13]

What do all these children have in common? They are being forced to deal with a sense of desertion and abandonment that would frighten anyone at any age, and they are just children. These children, and Sue Craig's children, will not have what we know to be the best for them. They will not have both parents to help raise them and give them love. They will not have access to all the relatives they once had, especially when Mom or Dad remarry. These children will have some of their family traditions and memories taken away or negatively changed. They may have to move and change school and neighborhood. They will have less of both quality and quantity time with Mom and Dad. Finally, in time these children will be burdened with worry over their own future marriages. This is heavy baggage to ask a child to carry.

KEYS TO MARITAL SUCCESS

What do Christians think about how to prevent marital failure? In the research done by Richard Stellway, mentioned earlier, Christian parents were asked what it takes to sustain a marriage. Those couples who responded had a combined total of 1,498 years of marital experience. Counselors and other helpers can benefit from these perceptions about marital success when dealing with clients or friends who are not doing well in their marriages.[14]

COMMUNICATE REGULARLY AND OPENLY

At the top of the list was communication. Respondents expressed concern for open, easy access to one another not only for the critical periods in the life of a relationship, but for the more mundane, everyday interchanges that give a marriage texture and substance. Conversation about the work of that day, important news stories, the comings and goings of the children and their friends, even gossip is included among the elements needed for building a relationship and a family.

Healthy communication is not only open, but reciprocal and relevant to the lives of both marriage partners. *Reciprocal* implies two-way communication with ease of access roughly equal for husband and wife. *Relevance* is important in that each partner is willing to be involved in conversations felt to be important to the other spouse, regardless of whether the topic is actually important to the listener. True love, one balladeer wrote, is always ready to listen.

STAY CLOSE TO GOD AND LIVE YOUR FAITH

Marriage for Christians is supposed to take the form of an inverted pyramid with husband and wife at the top corners and God at the bottom supporting the marriage and the relationship. Reading the words of God through Moses reminds us of the foundation God has ordained for the family:

> Then the LORD God made a woman from the rib
> he had taken out of the man, and he brought her to
> the man. The man said, "This is now bone of my
> bones and flesh of my flesh; she shall be called

'woman,' for she was taken out of man." For this reason a man will leave his father and mother and be united to his wife, and they will become one flesh.

(Gen. 2:22–24)

Clearly, those participating in the survey identified the need of married couples not only to build their marriages on the foundation of deity but to incorporate God's wisdom into their decisions and relationships with one another.

BUILD TRUST THROUGH DEVELOPING HONESTY AND INTEGRITY

Those responding to the Stellway survey emphasized not only trust itself but the components that work together to make trust possible. Trust must be built on mutuality, a sense of equality and freedom that can lead to the best of all marital relationships—a husband and wife who remain together for one reason alone, that they *choose* to.

It is impossible to conceptualize a marital relationship that is healthy but involuntary, where the husband or wife stays in the relationship not because he or she wants to but out of a sense of responsibility, duty, loyalty, even fear. Any experienced family counselor can attest to the reality that many Christian marriages are holding together with nothing more than the frayed cords of duty or fear of public embarrassment should they separate.

Trust in a relationship is always earned. Nothing else is remotely possible, even though many have foolishly persuaded themselves that they are pleasing God by sacrificing themselves to a dead relationship rather than committing their energies to reviving that relationship and restoring it to health. Trust in a marriage cannot be forced, purchased, bribed, or threatened into reality. Trust is built on the foundation of godly values and exemplified in years and years of proving love for one another through ordinary everyday care and consideration.

We were several years into our marriage when Linda became seriously ill with an ovarian cyst that could have become life-threatening. After medical treatment the cyst vanished, and Linda quickly regained her health. Once home from the hospital, my wife of only a few years confided in me that for the first time she was now sure that I would stay with her through dark times that might come. This was determined, she told me, on my actions in this first of many illnesses. Trust must be earned in a marriage.

PUT YOUR SPOUSE ABOVE YOURSELF

True love involves caring more for one's mate than for oneself. Psychologists call this altruism or allocentrism and treat it as something special that accounts for such acts as risking one's life to save another. Christians in this survey identified "commitment to the happiness of the other" and "willingness to give more than to get" as critical attitudes in a healthy marriage.

This again exemplifies the error in believing a healthy Christian marriage can be based on commitment alone. Commitment is important, but its companion must be the care and concern that allows a human being to experience joy from the good experiences of a husband or wife or sadness and pain from the difficult experiences of another. When we care more about the happiness of the person we are married to than about our own happiness, we are on our way to knowing a peak marriage experience.

DEVELOP A SENSE OF HUMOR

A sense of humor can be cultivated and strengthened through frequent use and by observation of others. I believe the strongest marriages have an underpinning of lightheartedness and the sense that there is something wrong with taking oneself too seriously. I have seen many couples pull through dark days by finding that tiny glimmer of humor that sparkles in most situations. Humor breaks the tension common to marriages. A sense of humor is the oil that lubricates the marriage machine.

As challenged parents, Linda and I know firsthand how helpful a sense of humor can be. We did not know until a few years after her birth that our first child was hyperactive. And if being hyperactive was not enough of a challenge, she was *bright* as well!

At the time we were new parents, we were also new Christians deeply involved in the ministry of our young marrieds Sunday school class. One evening Linda and I had invited another young couple over for a time of fellowship. We had carefully prepared our small home to receive the guests, Linda had arranged refreshments, and we thought we were ready for company. But we had forgotten about our three-and-a-half-year-old hyperactive daughter who *never* wanted to go to sleep on time.

Our guests arrived and sure enough, there was Laurie in her pajamas, peeking around the corner. After several unsuccessful, frustrating, and embarrassing attempts to get her to stay in her room, Linda asked Laurie what she wanted before she went to bed.

Some potato chips and dip was Laurie's price for going to bed. This seemed to be a reasonable request, so we agreed but specified that she could have only one chip and one scoop of dip. This agreed, Laurie came shuffling into the family room to meet our guests and get one chip and one scoop of dip.

To our surprise, Laurie chose a very small potato chip. We thought that she would try to find the biggest chip in the bowl. We were even more surprised when she placed the small chip carefully in the palm of her hand and closed her tiny fingers around it, making a fist. Then, in full view of everyone, she plunged her pudgy little fist into the dip bowl up to her wrist, pulled her dip-covered fist out of the bowl, said goodnight to the company, and shuffled down the hallway to her bedroom.

We roared with laughter! Our guests roared with laughter! We laughed until we were all in tears. As a result, the evening was a huge success. Linda and I felt more at ease with each other and with our guests. Three decades later, that story is still told when we get together with those old friends. Humor is so important in smoothing out the rough spots in a marriage.

The ability to laugh with, and sometimes at, one another not only breaks the tension but illustrates an ease of relationship that indicates comfort with one another, a lack of fear, an absence of judgmentalism, and mutual humility. Humor shows that we are not taking ourselves too seriously, and the lack of humor just as surely shows that we are!

FULL CIRCLE

Christians, in most cases, seem to know how to build a strong marriage, yet our marriages are failing at a rate just slightly lower than the secular world in general. What is wrong?

This question begs for an answer that is only slowly emerging. Perhaps Christians are more similar than different when compared to secular people. This similarity was becoming important to Sue Craig now that her own marriage had ended. Perhaps we do not trust God to lead us in choosing the "right" marriage partner. Or we may simply be falling victim to the sin nature that plagues us all. Other possibilities exist and bear investigation, but at least one thing is sure. The church of Jesus Christ in the next years must become as much a hospital as a sanctuary and must be prepared for an onslaught of marital failures unlike anything we have ever seen. Paul warned Timothy two millennia ago that "evil men and impostors will go from bad to worse, deceiving and being deceived" (2 Tim. 3:13), and people today have no reason to think that the trend toward marital failure will turn around. But in the same book, Paul encourages Timothy to fight the good fight and finish the course (see 2 Tim. 4:7). The emphasis is on acknowledging the temptations of sin while holding onto the security offered by God.

In the modern church, single parents are a fact of life. There is no escaping the reality of a failed marriage and the children and parents who must now cope with a challenge that grows day by day. Single parents and stepparents ask to be ministered to, and they deserve a positive response. Counselors, pastors, and others in the church who attempt to meet the psychological and spiritual needs of single parents and their children have assumed an awesome task that becomes possible only through God's strength. Both for the single parent and the counselor, the words of Paul to young Timothy ring as true today as years ago. "For God did not give us a spirit of timidity, but a spirit of power, of love and of self-discipline" (2 Tim. 1:7). Counselors and other helpers need to encourage single parents to own the promises of God.

Imagine that Sue Craig is sitting in your living room, church office, or counseling room. Imagine that she is asking you to help her and her children. In the chapters to follow, we will address issues and provide information that is vital to meet the needs of single parents like Sue and their children in a God-pleasing manner.

NOTES

1. D. Popenoe, *Disturbing the Nest* (New York: Aldine De Gruyter, 1988), 284.
2. R. J. Stellway, *Christiantown USA* (New York: The Haworth Press, 1990), 34.
3. Popenoe, *Disturbing the Nest*, 8.
4. T. Z. Andersen and G. D. White, "An Empirical Investigation of Interaction and Relationship Patterns in Functional and Dysfunctional Nuclear Families and Stepfamilies," *Family Process* (1986): 407–22.
5. G. A. Rekers, *Counseling Families* (Waco, Tex.: Word, 1988), 19.
6. N. D. Glenn, "The Recent Trend in Marital Success in The United States," *Journal of Marriage and The Family* 53 (1991): 261–70.
7. Andersen and White, "An Empirical Investigation."
8. Rekers, *Counseling Families*, 23.
9. L. A. Kurdek, ed., *Children and Divorce* (San Francisco: Jossey-Bass, 1983), 7–12.
10. Ibid.
11. Ibid.
12. Ibid.
13. Ibid.
14. Stellway, *Christiantown USA*, 136–38.

Chapter 2

The Trauma of Divorce:
Disturbing the Nest

"Sing to God. . . . A father of the fatherless, a defender of
widows, is God in his holy dwelling. God
sets the lonely in families. . . ."
Psalm 68:4–6

T HE CHALLENGE TO THE FAMILY IS TO RESIST the pressure that disturbs the nest, to fight the forces that seek to rearrange the family and give it new priorities. This challenge is not diminished by divorce. The family continues to be primarily responsible for the care of children, meeting the needs of both young and old family members, and meeting God's requirements in the process. The competent family counselor must be at ease in opening the Bible to suitable passages and presenting God's plan to single parents as to any other parent, because neither the challenge nor God's expectations of parents is diminished by divorce. It is important that we consider the trauma of divorce and search for answers that will help us minister to this growing population.

SHORT-TERM AND TEMPORARY IMPACT OF DIVORCE

Children of divorce experience intense emotions when they see a parent leave the home. Chief among these emotions are anger and fear about the future.[1] Children of divorce will always experience anger to some degree and will direct that anger most often at the custodial parent in the early weeks and months following the divorce. Then, depending on how that custodial parent deals with his or her own feelings and those of the children, the child may later redirect the anger to the noncustodial parent, in most cases the father. Only older children will grasp the reality and practicality of such reassuring passages as, "In God I trust; I will not be afraid. What can man do to me?" (Ps. 56:11) and "Peace I leave with you; my peace I give you. I do not give to you as the world gives. Do not let your hearts be troubled and do not be afraid" (John 14:27). While not totally lost on younger children who have recently gone through the divorce of their parents, such truths as these need to be presented with great patience, understanding, and most importantly, caution.

Other short-term effects for children include diminished physical health. A study of 341 children from divorced homes and 358 children from intact homes found that single-parent children are at greater risk for physical illness and that the occurrence of such illness was controlled by environmental stress impacting the family. Specifically, stress that was of greater magnitude, intensity, duration, and higher ambiguity produced greater negative health problems.[2] Another study, completed in 1990, demonstrated that children who have experienced divorce or separation are at greater risk for reporting health problems compared to children from intact families. Researchers concluded that the health concerns were real rather than imagined and that children of divorce experience approximately 10 percent more illnesses per year after divorce than before.[3]

Depression and withdrawal are also short-term reactions typical in children following parental divorce. A 1981 study of fourteen hundred children between twelve and sixteen years of age found that depression and withdrawal were more common after marital disruptions particularly when the pre-divorce family was characterized by high levels of parental conflict. This was more profound among girls than boys, with boys tending to show their feelings more as anger than depression. The study concluded that the effects of parental divorce are more negative and powerful when the child becomes alienated from both parents, is not able to maintain regular contact with both parents, and experiences the continued antagonism of parents toward one another.[4]

Social competence is compromised by family disruption and tends to show up in increased school absences, low popularity ratings by peers, lower scores on IQ and achievement tests, lower grades in reading, spelling, and math, and behavioral problems at home and at school.[5] Other social competence problems include alcohol and drug use and experimentation and increased rates of teenage sexual intercourse.[6]

LONG-TERM NEGATIVE EFFECTS

While some studies demonstrate some positive long-term effects in maturity and self-confidence for children whose parents have divorced,[7] most research on divorce impact shows effects that are negative.

Educational performance is an area profoundly impacted by parental divorce. When compared with children from intact families, children of divorce experience lower levels of terminal educational attainment,[8] lower academic self-concepts, especially when there is father absence and pre-separation marital conflict,[9] lower test scores,[10] and poorer grades.[11] On twenty-five of twenty-nine measures of school behavior ranging from tardiness to expulsion for alcohol use, children from one-parent families adhere less well to school expectations.[12]

To further illustrate the dilemma facing counselors and educators working with single-parent children, a study involving eighteen thousand elementary and secondary school children was carried out by the National Association of Elementary School Principals (NAESP) and the Institute for Development of Educational Activities (IDEA). They looked at single-parent versus two-parent families and found that at the primary level, 38 percent of the one-parent elementary school children were low achievers as compared to only 24 percent of two-parent children. At the secondary level, of the one-parent children, 34 percent were classified as low achievers versus 23 percent for those children from two-parent families.[13]

Additionally, children of divorce worry about their own future marriages, and apparently with good reason. A 1986 study published in the journal *Family Relations* concluded that children raised in single-parent homes have an increased likelihood that their own marriages will fail. This and other research also found that children of divorce experience an increased risk of unwed pregnancy, first pregnancy at a younger age, and lower educational, occupational, and economic attainment compared with their counterparts raised in intact families.[14]

Perceptions of one's family of origin moves in a negative direction following family dissolution,[15] and we find higher rates and more frequent occurrences of depression in grown children of divorce. The depression rates are even greater if the pre-divorce family was torn by conflict.[16] Adolescent and adult children of divorce reported lower levels of life satisfaction[17] and experienced problematic intimate relationships as adults.[18]

When considering both short- and long-term effects of divorce, the trauma to children is obvious and significant. With rare exceptions,[19] the research clearly indicates that divorce is bad for children *and* parents. With the exception of situations where the children may be placed at risk by the continued presence of both parents in the home, separation and divorce have a strongly negative impact on children and their parents.

DISTURBING THE NEST

The interviews in the first chapter show that children of varying ages and levels of understanding will experience widely different perceptions of their parents' divorce. Those reasons most commonly offered will be discussed from the perspective of the child or teenager witnessing their parents' behavior.[20]

WHY MARRIAGES FAIL AND WHAT IT MEANS TO THOSE INVOLVED

People who divorce give various reasons for dissolving their marriages. These perceived causations have an impact on the ability of each spouse to cope in his or her post-marriage life and control to a varying degree the ability of children to adjust to their new lives with divorced parents. More than creating problems for adults in the family, children and teens become stressed out when they see their parents failing to save their marriage.[21]

Infidelity is often identified by husbands and wives as the reason they terminated their marriage. Failure to honor the marriage commitment is reported to occur in 52 percent of divorce decrees. For children and teens, the failure is more than simply a sexual one—it involves either being exceedingly foolish and willing to place adult needs above the children's needs or being dishonest as a husband or wife and failing to keep the marriage vow. Children of different ages will approach this differently, but there is not much doubt that the parent's image is permanently tarnished.

Many couples (38 percent) say that the reason they are divorcing is that they no longer love each other. A youngster will respond to this by asking, "Why not?", to which parents typically have no answer. Children and teens know or suspect that their parent is really saying that he or she has simply chosen someone else to love and has placed this need above the desire to have an intact family. Divorcing parents who try to convince themselves that the divorce is actually for the betterment of the children will one day hear what the children truly think.

Others claim emotional problems or incompatibility as the reason for ending their marriages. In about 38 percent of divorces, this is the stated reason. Except in cases of child or spouse abuse, or when alcohol or drugs are involved, this reason means very little to children and teens. Youngsters tend to believe that people choose to feel certain ways and wonder why Mom or Dad cannot just decide to change the way they feel and act.

Financial trouble is offered as a reason for divorce in 28 percent of the cases studied. Although they may be serious, financial disagreements or stressors like unemployment will typically not be understood by children and teens as sufficient reason for ending the marriage and tearing apart the family. Especially in retrospect, grown children of divorce report even more negative feelings toward their divorced parents when finances are given as the reason for disrupting their young lives.

Twenty-three percent of couples surveyed stated sexual incompatibility as the reason for divorce. Specifics were not provided as to the nature of the incompatibility, whether it was homosexuality, deviance, impotence or any of a variety of others. As with finances, except in the most obvious and unavoidable cases such as a parent being arrested for some criminal act, children do not understand the need to end a marriage and change their family because of a problem. Children expect parents to be able to solve problems and are confused and disappointed when parents fail to live up to their expectations.

Regardless of the reason for divorce (and there are many more we did not discuss), children are usually negatively impacted. A parent may struggle with alcohol or drug abuse, develop a physical condition that limits employment, or experience any of a multitude of other stressors on a marriage. Children only ask, "What will this do to me?" Children and teens are egocentric and unable to avoid relating adult decisions such as divorce solely to what it does to them.

Most Christians would agree that each one of the problems listed above results from sin. But counselors are likely to find that clients going through a divorce are not helped by the application of such a truth. The client might correctly ask, "How does this information on the sin nature of human beings help me deal with my family problems?"

THE DIVORCE EXPERIENCE

Bohannan divided the divorce process into six overlapping experiences.[22] Each experience is distinct but may occur simultaneously or overlap only slightly with others. Each type will have a different kind of impact on individual family members.

THE EMOTIONAL DIVORCE

Just as a relationship begins when one person makes emotional contact with another, so an existing relationship begins to dissolve when that contact weakens and eventually breaks.

In this divorce stage the partners move away from each other emotionally, experience a decrease in the concern that each feels for the other, and no longer are able or willing to put the needs of the other above their own.

Divorces are typically loaded with negative emotions. When feelings surface, the common intent is to hurt, to get revenge, to show superiority, and to stake a claim as being the correct spouse. Sex, money, religion, even the children can be used as weapons in the early stage of divorce.

During this phase or within this continuing type of divorce, the needs and personalities of the parents will largely control their actions. Children, however, react more like than unlike one another. Even allowing for differences in personalities and coping styles among children, the typical reaction of children is one of great fear and emotional upset as they witness what threatens to be the worst event in their lives.

Children will typically enter a stage of profound denial, controlled only by the reality they face each day. Children and teenagers commonly will do all they can to keep family problems from their friends, school personnel, even church workers. They are frightened yet unsure how to get the help they need because the actual separation or divorce may only be threatened at this point. How does a youngster ask for help with something that *may* happen?

At this point the husband and wife are sleeping separately, not going to church together anymore, not taking meals as a family, and are beginning to build their individual financial support systems. As this stage evolves, each partner will begin the process of grieving for the dying marriage and either have found or are seeking another person to help take the pain away. Husband and wife may be feeling the initial sting of social ostracism from family and friends and will resist any attempt by concerned people to help. It should be noted that the emotional reactions and behaviors will not be felt or demonstrated equally by each partner.

THE LEGAL DIVORCE

This phase includes the judicial aspect of a marriage that has already gone through the emotional turmoil of ending a relationship. Most states have some form of uncontested divorce, and this form seems to be preferred by most.

The impact of this overlapping stage of divorce on children is the unavoidable realization that Mom and Dad are no longer married to each other. Divorce represents closing the grave over the dead marriage and family. It may be that parents have separated years ago and have only now finalized their emotional divorce with legal action. It is not at all unusual for children who had once worked their way through the early phase of dealing with parents who did not want to live together any longer to experience a new and unexpected eruption of problem behavior. Children may experience emotional turmoil, nightmares and other sleep disturbances, and any number of other reactions. This confirmation that the marriage is dead tells the child or teenager that there is no longer anything to hope for, that no matter how much they wish and pray, Mom and Dad are *never* going to get back together. Most counselors have learned to expect an upsurge of problem behavior at various stages of the dissolution of the original family, and we are not surprised.

For some parents, divorce signals a new period of freedom. For others, it means financial bondage. Still others will feel emotionally abused, unwanted, or unloved. Just as Sue Craig struggled with the finality of the end of her marriage to Ron, legal divorce says that there is no turning back; life is changed forever.

THE ECONOMIC DIVORCE

There is substantial evidence that families of divorce are adversely affected economically. Recent government statistics indicate that the single-parent family is the most significant new factor contributing to an increase in poverty in America.[23] Most single-parent families are headed by women, and women earn fifty-nine cents for every dollar earned by men. Seventy-five percent of poor Americans are women and children. Following divorce, a woman's income drops by 73 percent while the man's increases by 42 percent, largely because only 19 percent of divorced fathers continue to pay child support three years after the divorce.[24]

Translated into practical terms, all members of the divorced family have to say good-bye to important parts of themselves. For some the family home has to be sold and a much smaller apartment found for mom and the kids. A house full of furniture will not fit into an apartment and will have to be disposed of in some way. The children may have to relinquish a room of their own, or go without a Christmas present that was expected. For teenagers, clothes will probably become an issue as the single parent tries to conserve limited finances by buying cheaper, off-brand clothing instead of the trendy clothing the children were used to. The family car that remained after the divorce will have to last longer, and both parents may have to forget about vacations for a while.

Often these financial penalties, paid primarily by the mother and children, will be accompanied by guilt. The single parent will have to say "no" to requests for new things and explain why field trips and uniforms for activities cannot be afforded this year. The absent parent is less likely to have to say "no" or to answer the difficult questions, but he or she is still very likely to feel guilty for the financial hardship brought about by the divorce.

Dad may be paying alimony (a word derived from Latin that means sustenance or nourishment), and he may be in that 19 percent paying child support, but if so, he is likely to feel financial hardship for doing his duty. We will see in later chapters that most divorced people remarry within three years of their divorce, and this second marriage is one prime reason child support and, less frequently, alimony are discontinued.

An economic divorce means much more than dividing the bank account and choosing who gets what piece of furniture. The financial hardship caused by divorce is a primary reason so many divorced parents suffer psychological breakdown, become alcoholic, and are more at risk for suicide. There is no escaping the guilt over putting one's family under financial hardship.

THE COPARENTAL DIVORCE

Bohannon uses the term *coparental divorce* to emphasize the perspective that parents can divorce each other without divorcing the children.[25] From the perspective of a working family counselor, however, it often seems that parents do in fact divorce their children when they terminate their marriage. And research by Furstenberg and several colleagues that appeared in the *American Sociological Review* argued that there is child abandonment by most absent fathers.[26] The cogent point for this discussion is that in their sample of children of divorce, only 49.3 percent of boys and 48.8 percent of girls had seen their absent father at least once during the previous twelve months. The truth is clear: For most American children, a parental divorce includes the divorce of the children by the noncustodial parent.

But Bohannon's point is still valid. Psychologically and emotionally, parents remain parents after the divorce even if they fail to live up to their responsibilities. Recently, there has been some movement in the direction of joint custody, but with more than 90 percent of custody settlements placing children in the mother's care, we who work with single parents must emphasize the single mother as parent.

THE COMMUNITY DIVORCE

Becoming divorced changes one's relationship with the community in a profound way. In American culture, and particularly in Middle America, divorce is a stigma that continues to have great effect on a life.

Letters from school continue to come home with "Mr. & Mrs." on the envelope. Telemarketers, who always seem to call at just the wrong time, continue to ask for "the man of the house." Classroom teachers too often assume that their students have two parents and may ask a student to have his father call, insensitive to the large number of students who do not live with a father.

The situation is not much better, and some believe it is worse, in the church community. Single parents complain that they no longer feel at home in their church congregations, that they feel like second-class Christians after their divorce even though many are well-known to be the victim of someone else's sin. Children may be socially ostracized for the sinful behavior of a parent, even by adult Sunday school teachers and church workers.

Ferri examined the school situation and asked teachers to rate parental interest in children.[27] Teachers rated single parents as less interested in their children's performance, particularly for the divorced mother. In spite of this attitude, the frequency of school visits did not differ for single mothers as opposed to two-parent families. In a study on preschool children in Boulder, Colorado, preschool teachers predicted that the single-parent families would represent the most disturbed children, and yet their own ratings did not agree with that judgment.[28]

The divorced person has difficulty coping with the return to single status, and the presence of children complicates matters. Often the divorced parent feels he or she is in a state of social limbo that may remain for several years.

THE PSYCHIC DIVORCE

Bohannon suggests that this may be the most difficult of the six aspects of divorce and may continue for a lifetime. In most cases, psychic divorce involves splitting oneself from a partner of some years. Sue Craig clearly had difficulty with this part of her new reality. She struggled for many months to come to grips with the fact that she was no longer one member of a pair—a part of a team. With Ron definitively out of the picture, Sue felt as if she *was* the team.

Months or years of dating, beginning a life together, gaining an education, buying homes as the family grew, facing middle age, and expecting to grow old as a couple together all came to an abrupt halt. Sue related that she felt as if a part of her had died, and she was partially right. Her marriage had suffered a terminal illness and had passed away. Sue was grieving for that recently deceased marriage, and her mind was not adjusting very well.

Sue had the challenge of dealing with forgiveness for herself (for choosing Ron in the first place and for being so blind) and forgiveness for Ron, for whom she retained extremely deep, if confusing, love. She knew that she had to accomplish this break with her past if she was going to be able to raise her four children properly, but the battle was not going to be easy.

THOUGHTS AND FEELINGS OF CHILDREN OF DIVORCE

What do youngsters think when parents divorce? How do they feel? Based on my own counseling experience and research, let me suggest a list of their most typical thoughts and feelings. If there is any doubt about the trauma of divorce, this should put that uncertainty to rest.

ANGER

Without question, anger tops the list of most common feelings in children of divorce. Anger at self is common, but so is anger at one or both parents. It is common to find children and teens angry at *both* parents *and* themselves all at the same time. This anger may be direct or displaced. Direct anger is targeted at the true source of the child's pain—the adulterous father, for instance. Displaced anger is seen when youngsters act out against teachers or the custodial parent who may not be in any way responsible for their feelings.

Nine-year-old Kevin Craig had been sent to the school counselor for picking fights at school in the weeks immediately following his father's departure from home. This was not typical of Kevin and was understood to be an expression of his anger at his father for which he had no available outlet. Kevin received help and support by agreeing to participate in an after-school group for children living in single-parent and stepparent homes. Key to Kevin's ability to deal with his anger was his mother's mature handling of her own emotions, at least in the presence of the children. Sue did not model angry outbursts for the children as happens in so many families experiencing this kind of turmoil. As a child, Sue had memorized a verse of Scripture that comforted her in the face of her anger and that of her children. Paul wrote to the church at Ephesus, "In your anger do not sin. Do not let the sun go down while you are still angry. Get rid of all bitterness, rage and anger, brawling and slander, along with every form of malice" (Eph. 4:26, 31). Small comfort, some would say to Sue, but these words learned in her youth seemed to make a difference. Sue knew that God would honor his word because she had experienced such provision many times in her life, though she had not been tested like this before.

ABANDONMENT

Child experts and watchful parents have long known that children fear abandonment more than death. Death is not well comprehended until early adolescence in most, but the fear of being left alone is primal and universal from the earliest days.

It is the rare child who has not already known the fear and panic of realizing that mother is no longer in view in the department store. I am acquainted with a person who was severely traumatized by being left standing in a beach parking lot when the family, thinking the child was in the other car, drove off for home and was gone nearly an hour before realizing what had happened. This person, now an adult, still shudders when she tells this story and remembers it as the single greatest trauma she experienced as a child.

Alicia, Kevin, Scott, and Emily Craig were abandoned by their father. Surely Ron would not agree to such a characterization of his behavior, but the children are correct in knowing how they felt when he left. They had been abandoned just as much as that little girl left standing in the parking lot. They felt as hurt as any other child experiencing more traumatic life experiences.

Fourteen-year-old Scott had an especially difficult time dealing with his feelings after the separation. It is not acceptable in this culture for a teenage boy to admit to feeling afraid and abandoned, so while the younger children could express their feelings through their tears, Scott became more and more depressed and angry. A sensitive youth pastor at their church was the first to get Scott to express how he really felt, and after some embarrassed tears, the depression became less of a problem.

All children who lose a parent for any reason feel abandoned, but children who know that a parent has left them voluntarily struggle even more. Being left accidentally in a parking lot is one thing. Being left at home when a parent walks away *intentionally* is quite something else. Adults may rationalize this process all they wish, but a few moments listening to the pain in a child who has been left behind will convince even the greatest skeptic that the sense of abandonment is real and nearly universal in children of divorce.

Loss

Elizabeth Kubler-Ross hypothesized a predictable pattern of reactions for those suffering the death of a loved one.[29] I believe it is appropriate to apply this paradigm to children of divorce as well. Though the missing parent has not died, there is still much to be mourned.

Kubler-Ross suggested an overlapping five-stage process of coping with a major life loss such as the death of a close loved one, the destruction of the family home, or one's own impending death. She suggested the acronym "DABDA" as a way of formulating and understanding this process as it applies to children of divorce.

Denial. The first stage survivors experience is denial of the reality of what is happening to them. Children are known to continue speaking of their parents as if they were still together, even months or years after the marriage has ended. Denial is based on an instinctual resistance to hearing bad news. Once the bad news cannot be avoided, as when a parent moves out of the home, a child can continue to pretend that that parent is still living in the family. Some children will defend this position in the face of the most undeniable evidence; the pain is just too much to bear.

Anger. When the reality can no longer be denied, anger appears. Anger at God is common. The child wonders, for example, "Why would the God who is supposed to love me let this terrible thing happen to me and my family?" Anger at *both* parents is also common. The absent parent is focused on because of his or her leave-taking, but the present parent also experiences some expressions of childish anger. Mothers who are now on their own with the children will sometimes experience angry outbursts such as, "Why did you let Daddy move out?" or, "Wasn't there *anything* you could have done to get Daddy to stay at home?"

Bargaining. After the trauma of divorce has subsided, after the children have adapted to their new life and family, after the emotions have quieted, then we hear of the bargains attempted with God. Asking God to bring a mother or father back in return for good behavior in the future is common.

But nothing works to return that parent to the home, and it is easy for the child to feel discouraged and unhappy with God and to be confused about his or her feelings. Caregivers need to be very careful here. A promise of God's love and reassurances about his sovereignty may be followed with, "Then why did God let my daddy leave us?" Counselors and other helpers need to be careful to avoid raising questions for which there are no ready answers.

Depression. When the bargaining has failed and the child realizes nothing is going to alter the unhappy situation, childhood depression can be expected. Usually not of clinical severity, the depression is nonetheless likely to be serious and worthy of professional attention. Again, counselors and other helpers want to be careful to avoid suggesting Bible verses that may do more to remind the child of God's failure to help them in the first place than of his unremitting love and care.

If the depression advances to the point where clinical symptoms are exhibited, there is a need for intervention. Symptoms could include loss of appetite, anhedonia (failure to play), sleep disturbances, weight loss, self-mutilation, voluntary self-isolation, or frequent unexplained school absences.

Acceptance. Eventually, the child traumatized by divorce and grieving over the death of the original family progresses to the point of acceptance. Not happy with the present situation, but resigned, the child accepts this new reality as something to be dealt with rather than feared or avoided. Acceptance means the child of divorce can call on resources that may be newly discovered.

Denial, anger, bargaining, depression, and acceptance are stages of grief reaction common to both parent and child when the comfortable previous family situation is replaced by a new kind of family headed by one rather than two parents. Each of the stages discussed above are as likely to be experienced by parents as children, though symptoms will differ. These manifestations should be expected and accepted when they appear. They should not be smothered or avoided but allowed to run their course and manifest the varying symptoms unique to each family member. Counselors are facilitators of this process more than healers, witnesses to growth as well as initiators.

SELF-BLAME/GUILT

Though not common, children can find ways to assume responsibility for the breakup of their parents' marriage. Wallerstein and Kelly suggest two major reasons why children would want to take the blame for what has happened to their family.[30] First, because of the egocentrism common to children and teens, it is easy for a child to conclude that parental quarrels must be over his or her grades, social behavior, disobedience, etc. Second, recognizing the common feelings of experiencing circumstances beyond their control, a child or teen may assume responsibility as a means of gaining control over the situation. Not only does this reduce some of the uncertainty connected with family breakup, but it also provides a measure of hope that good behavior in the future may cause Mom and Dad to get back together. In either case, the youngster is better off if parents insist that he or she was not the cause of the breakup and that there is nothing a child can do to reverse the situation.

MATURITY VARIANCES

I have seen children only ten years of age assuming the role of parent and partner to their single-parent mother, and I have seen teenagers regress nearly to infancy following a divorce. Either hypermaturity or extreme immaturity can be an expected response to the trauma of parental divorce.

Hypermaturity, sometimes called "parentification," is more likely to be seen in the oldest child in a family with younger children. This child, with the tacit permission of the single parent, assumes control and responsibility for the care of siblings, household chores, even supervision of the parent's social life. This child has in effect become a second parent, a substitute parent who is of great help to the overburdened single parent but who will expect adult privileges later on as payback for all the hard work he or she has invested.

Immaturity is more likely to be experienced by children other than the oldest, and seems to be based primarily on intense fear and insecurity following the family dissolution. Immaturity may be manifested in a return to the symbols of earlier years. It may be the five-year-old who demands a bottle to go to sleep. Others may return to thumb-sucking or blanket-dragging in an attempt to remind themselves of the good feelings of earlier times when Mom and Dad were still together. Still others may cry or talk to themselves after they have gone to bed.

In summary, research findings indicate clearly that children will find a way to cope with parental divorce. The particular manifestation such coping will take varies from situation to situation and personality to personality, but some evidence of adaptation, even if destructive, will surely surface. The counselor dealing with a child of divorce needs to be ready to employ a variety of strategies based on the need presented and be just as ready to adopt a new procedure should the situation warrant.

IMPACT ON PARENTS

Sue Craig wondered aloud if the divorce that had been inflicted on her and the children was the beginning of the end or the end of the beginning. Perspectives will differ of course, but for Sue and the children, it was the end of the beginning.

But the beginning of what?

A new life?

New relationships?

Or just new problems and crises to deal with?

Sue had never experienced such stress before and never wanted to again. Sue could see that she was in the process of experiencing marital separation, divorce, sexual difficulties, a change in financial status, trouble with in-laws, a change in living conditions, a change in residence, a change in social activities, and a change in the number of family gatherings. Taken together, these stressors are far above that needed to put a person at risk for depression, accidents, and other forms of psychological breakdown.

The danger of a reduced level of life satisfaction can be illustrated by the research done by Bloom and colleagues.[31] Summarizing a large number of studies that document the overwhelming negative impact of divorce on adults, they found:

- The suicide rate for divorced men is three times higher than for married men.

- Risk of death by homicide is far higher for divorced men and women.

- Car accidents average three times higher for the divorced than for the married. These rates double between the six months prior to and the six months following the divorce.

- Death rate by disease is much higher for divorced people.

- The widowed and divorced have higher age-adjusted death rates for all causes of death combined than for married people of equivalent age, sex, and race.

Other studies have focused on suicide among the divorced. Trovato found that the rate of suicide in Canada varied directly with the rate of family breakup.[32] Wasserman concluded that the divorce rate in the United States explains variations in the suicide rate.[33] Stack found that divorce rates and suicide rates matched in both the United States and Sweden.[34]

Is anyone spared the impact of divorce? It would appear not!

Children, adolescents, adults in all phases of the life cycle, extended family, and even friends experience the painful ripples of a family breakup. There are survivors and overcomers, but very few are not touched at all by divorce. The nest is disturbed, and there is every indication that it will remain disturbed. Christians believe that evil will grow until God judges and Jesus returns. But in the meantime, there are those whom God has allowed to be in special places of opportunity for helping.

A child who was experiencing the divorce of her parents described her feelings as like "having a hole in your heart." She would have some good days and happy experiences, but as soon as she took them in, they drained away through the hole in her life caused by her parents' divorce, and she would feel bad again. What do we say to a child like this? Is there a counseling strategy for use with such children? Or is our love and concern more important than counseling techniques and strategies? Does a divorced woman enter the category of a widow in distress described in James 1:27?

The church is not the cause of the family nest being disturbed, but the church holds primary responsibility for the care of believers who have become single parents and of the children of single parents. Our responsibility as church leaders or professional counselors is to the disturbed nest that is now a major part of our mission field. Our responsibility extends to providing professional counseling services often within the context of the local church. The emphasis on training will become clear in chapters to follow.

So here we are, trying to help Sue Craig and her four children adjust to the departure of their father from the home. They are there, all five of them, sitting in *your* office or *your* living room asking *you* for help. Sue feels like a total failure as a wife, mother, and Christian. Sixteen-year-old Emily holds her mother's hand and weeps too, but the anger at her father is palpable. Scott, fourteen, stands at the window and sullenly stares into the darkness, unwilling to talk to anyone right now. Kevin, nine, absent-mindedly stares at the television set in the corner, and five-year-old Alicia sleeps on the couch next to her mother.

And there you are. Counselor, pastor, friend, perhaps all three, trying to feel God's leading as to how you can help this family. Chapter three begins the long process of recovery.

NOTES

1. S. E. Bonkowski, S. J. Boomhower, and S. Q. Bequette, "What You Don't Know Can Hurt You: Unexpressed Fears and Feelings of Children from Divorcing Families," *Journal of Divorce* 91 (1985): 33–45.

2. J. Guidubaldi and H. Clemenshaw, "Divorce, Family Health, and Child Adjustment," *Family Relations* 34 (1985): 35–41.

3. J. Mauldon, "The Effect of Marital Disruption on Children's Health," *Demography* 27, no. 3 (1990): 431–46.

4. J. L. Peterson and N. Zill, "Marital Disruption, Parent-Child Relationships, and Behavior Problems in Children," *Journal of Marriage and the Family* 48 (1986): 295–307.

5. E. Devall, Z. Stoneman, and G. Brody, "The Impact of Divorce and Maternal Employment on Pre-Adolescent Children," *Family Relations* 35 (1986): 153–59; and T. E. Smith, "Parental Separation and the Academic Self-Concepts of Adolescents," *Journal of Marriage and the Family* 52 (1990): 107–18.

6. R. L. Flewelling and K. E. Bauman, "Family Structure and Initial Sub-

stance Use in Early Adolescence," *Journal of Marriage and the Family* 52 (1990): 171–82.

7. J. Guidubaldi and J. D. Perry, "Divorce and Mental Health Sequelae for Children: A Two-Year Follow-up of a National Sample," *Journal of the American Academy of Child Psychiatry* 24 (1985): 531–37; and N. Kalter et al., "Locus of Control on Children of Divorce," *Journal of Personality Assessment* 48 (1984): 410–14.

8. V. M. Keith and B. Finlay, "The Impact of Parental Divorce on Children's Educational Attainment, Marital Timing, and Likelihood of Divorce," *Journal of Marriage and the Family* 50 (1988): 797–809.

9. Smith, "Parental Separation."

10. J. W. Santrock, "Relation of Type and Onset of Father Absence to Cognitive Development," *Child Development* 43 (1972): 455–69.

11. Y. Peres and R. Pasternak, "To What Extent Can the School Reduce the Gaps Between Children Raised by Divorced and Intact Families?" *Journal of Divorce and Remarriage* 15 (March/April 1991): 143–58.

12. A. Evans and J. Neel, "School Behaviors of Children from One-Parent and Two-Parent Homes," *Principal* 60, no. 1 (1980): 38–39.

13. National Association of Elementary School Principals Report, "One-Parent Families and Their Children," *Principal* 60, no. 1 (1980): 31–37.

14. D. P. Mueller and P. W. Cooper, "Children of Single-Parent Families: How They Fare as Young Adults," *Family Relations* 35 (1986): 169–76; and N. D. Glenn and K. B. Kramer, "The Marriages and Divorces of the Children of Divorce," *Journal of Marriage and the Family* 49 (1987): 811–25.

15. P. R. Amato, "Parental Divorce and Attitudes toward Marriage and Family Life," *Journal of Marriage and the Family*, 48 (1988): 453–61.

16. D. Mechanic and S. Hansel, "Divorce, Family Conflict, and Adolescents' Well-Being," *Journal of Health and Social Behavior* 30 (1989): 105–16.

17. L. J. Albers, J. A. Doane and J. Mintz, "Social Competence and Family Environment: 15-Year Follow-up of Disturbed Adolescents," *Family Process* 25 (1986): 379–89.

18. A. C. Acock and K. J. Kiecolt, "Is It Family Structure or Socioeconomic Status? Family Structure during Adolescence and Adult Adjustment," *Social Forces* 68 (1989): 553–71.

19. A. Goetting, "Divorce Outcome Research: Issues and Perspectives," *Journal of Family Issues* 2 (1981): 350–78; and M. J. Bane, "Marital Disruption and the Lives of Children," *Journal of Social Issues* 52, no. 1 (1976): 103–17; and P. R. Amato and A. Booth, "Consequences of Parental Divorce and Marital Unhappiness for Adult Well-Being," *Social Forces* 69, no. 3 (1991): 895–914.

20. S. A. Grunlan, *Marriage and the Family: A Christian Perspective*, (Grand Rapids: Academic Books, 1984), 322.

21. G. A. Rekers, *Counseling Families* (Waco, Tex.: Word, 1988), 19–20.

22. P. Bohannon, *Divorce and After* (Garden City, N.Y.: Doubleday, 1970).

23. T. Flynn, "Single Parenthood," *The Sunday Denver Post*, 25 March 1984.

24. Bane, "Marital Disruption."

25. Bohannon, "Divorce and After."

26. F. F. Furstenberg et al., "The Life Course of Children of Divorce: Marital Disruption and Parental Contact," *American Sociological Review* 48 (1983): 656–68.

27. E. Feri, *Growing Up in a One-Parent Family: A Long-Term Study of Child Development* (Windsor, England: NFER Publishing, 1976).

28. W. F. Hodges, R. C. Wechsler, and C. Ballantine, "Divorce and the Preschool Child," *Journal of Divorce* 3 (1979): 55–69.

29. E. Kubler-Ross, *On Death and Dying* (New York: Macmillan, 1969).

30. J. S. Wallerstein and J. B. Kelly, "The Effects of Parental Divorce: Experiences of the Preschool Child," *Journal of the American Academy of Child Psychiatry* 14 (1975): 600–616.

31. B. L. Bloom, S. J. Asher, and S. W. White, "Marital Disruption as a Stressor: A Review and Analysis," *Psychological Bulletin* 85 (1978): 867–99.

32. F. Trovato, "A Longitudinal Analysis of Divorce and Suicide in Canada," *Journal of Marriage and the Family* 49 (1987): 193–203.

33. I. M. Wasserman, "A Longitudinal Analysis of the Linkage between Suicide, Unemployment, and Marital Dissolution," *Journal of Marriage and the Family* 46, no. 4 (1984): 853–59.

34. S. Stack, "New Micro-Level Data on the Impact of Divorce on Suicide, 1959-1980: A Test of Two Theories," *Journal of Marriage and the Family* 52 (1990): 119–27.

Chapter 3

Children of Divorce: The Broken Bough

Rock-a-bye baby in the tree top,
when the wind blows the cradle will rock,
when the bough breaks, the cradle will fall,
and down will come baby, cradle and all.
Traditional nursery rhyme

And whoever welcomes a little child like this in my name
welcomes me. But if anyone causes one of these little ones
who believe in me to sin, it would be better for him to have
a large millstone hung about his neck and to be drowned
in the depths of the sea.
Matthew 18:5–6

GOD AND MAN ACKNOWLEDGE THE HELPLESSNESS of children and their need for protection, provision, and love. God and man are repulsed by the behavior of those who hurt children, and both reserve their harshest words and punishment for those who exploit little ones.

In the months after their father had moved out of the family home, nine-year-old Kevin Craig had experienced frequent nightmares, was once again having problems with bedwetting (which had been under control since he was six), and had gotten into trouble at school for fighting (also a behavior that was uncharacteristic of the pre-divorce Kevin). Alicia, Kevin's five-year-old sister, also suffered from the post-divorce turmoil. Alicia clearly missed her father but seemed to be most upset because her mother was so often emotionally troubled and crying, especially in the weeks immediately following Ron's departure. Alicia was having bad dreams regularly, and most of them related to a theme involving desertion, abandonment, or the death of her mother.

While it may appear harsh and judgmental, there is little doubt that Kevin and Alicia, as well as their older brother and sister, had been "offended" in the sense that Jesus used the term. Typical of children going through a parental divorce, Kevin and Alicia greatly needed reassurance from their mother and other important adults that everything was going to be okay. This is a difficult thing to ask of parents who are unsure themselves of how things are going to turn out, but it is critical for children like Alicia and Kevin who had experienced the breakup of their family, their own personal "broken bough."

The following interchange, which took place between Sue and me in one of our sessions soon after the separation and just prior to the divorce papers being served, illustrates the level of emotion commonly experienced by custodial parents charged with raising children mostly on their own.

DAVE: Tell me how you're feeling these days, Sue.

SUE: Confused and angry most of the time, I guess. I know I don't understand what just happened to my family, and maybe I never will. I just get so angry at Ron for doing such an awful thing that I have a hard time keeping my emotions under control in front of the kids.

DAVE: I can see that you are concerned about how your reactions may be impacting the children. Are you seeing differences in the way the children are trying to deal with this?

SUE: They are all so different. I guess it is more their age than anything, but part of the reason I'm so stressed out right now is from trying to figure out how I should try to help two teenagers and two children who are each reacting in their own ways. It just seems so overwhelming.

DAVE: What can you tell me about how they react in their own ways?

SUE: Well, take Alicia for example. Just a sweet, pleasant little girl who has never given me a moment's trouble in her life. Easy to get along with, happy to help, a typical baby of the family I suppose. The bad dreams she has been having recently are really bothering me. To have a child her age so upset about something that was not of her doing seems so unfair.

DAVE: This divorce thing really has pounded your family.

SUE: Oh, more than that. I really worry if the kids and I will ever recover ourselves. It seems that some big part of each one of us has been lost, and there is little hope of recovery. At least that's how it feels right now.

DAVE: Have there been some developments following the divorce that have turned out better than you had hoped?

SUE: Yes. The kids are showing strengths I never knew they had. Especially the older kids—Emily and Scott have really been a help to me. I guess I don't know what to ask of them yet, but each of the kids seems more than willing to help if they can.

DAVE: What about spiritually?

SUE: What do you mean?

DAVE: I guess I'm just wondering if, during all these traumatic events, you have found strengths within yourself that were a surprise?

SUE: I see what you mean. I think the answer is "yes." I'm not sure, but I seem to be more angry and depressed, and that anger seems to motivate me to make sure that my family survives and overcomes what their father has done. In some strange way, I feel as if God wants me to be angry right now. I'm not sure, but I think I trust both myself and God more now than before the breakup. Does that sound weird?

DAVE: Sounds realistic to me.

SUE: And the kids have been praying more than before, at least as far as I can tell. I think we may be growing spiritually through this, but I also think it's too soon too tell for sure.

DAVE: Sue, do you think that God will enable you to continue to raise your children even in the face of Ron's failure?

SUE: I wouldn't have thought so a few months ago, but I
         think you may be right. All of us seem to have re-
         sources within us that we had not been required to call
         upon previously, but there's no doubt that those re-
         sources are there. Thank God for that!

As I worked through the post-divorce concerns with Sue,
her felt need for recognizing and dealing with her children's
reactions to the divorce grew. We can look at Alicia and Kevin
in the following pages and get a sense of what was on their
minds. Young children have unique ways of dealing with unpleasant realities. Very young children, for example, will
simply close their eyes tightly believing that what they cannot
see has gone away. Those a little older will try to wish bad
things away, or promise to be good if their wish comes true.
The older two children, Scott and Emily, have also developed
coping skills and will be discussed in the next chapter.

ALICIA

Five-year-old Alicia was experiencing nightmares of abandonment. She had these three or four times a week in the first
three months following the departure of her dad from the family home. She had become more irritable since the breakup and
had even started a fight with her older brother, something that
had been unheard of previously. Kevin was not impressed
with his sister's fighting ability.

More worrisome to Sue were the regressions she had been
observing in her daughter. Alicia had returned to toileting accidents since the divorce, and while apparently embarrassed
by this, she did not seem able to take the normal precaution of
visiting the bathroom before going out to play or other activities. More than this, when Alicia did have an accident, she
would cry and ask her mother to help her change her clothing.
Again, a return to a behavior pattern more typical of three- or
four-year-olds.

Sue reported that she had found candy and gum wrappers
under Alicia's bed and was beginning to worry that she was
hoarding food to eat late at night or when she was able to be

alone. Crumbs in Alicia's room presented Sue with more than a cleanliness concern. Sue decided to carefully inventory the refrigerator and other food sources before going to bed in order to see if Alicia was actually hoarding food in her room, and she soon found that her concerns were justified.

One of the major problems Sue and Alicia had involved sleeping arrangements. While not unusual after a separation or divorce, allowing a child to sleep in the parental bed is not a good idea.[1] Sue had occasionally allowed and even encouraged this with her daughter, in part to help Alicia sleep better and in part to help herself feel less lonely at night. I had cautioned Sue about using the children to lessen her pain, and she had agreed to be careful, but Sue viewed allowing Alicia to sleep with her as something that Alicia wanted and possibly needed. After further discussion and reflection on Sue's part, she suggested it would be best to wean Alicia back into her own bed.

Sue's concern for Alicia's well-being at night was somewhat resolved by setting aside a special time of story reading just before bedtime followed by bedside prayers and tucking in. Alicia was firmly told that special circumstances would mean that she could sleep with Mom if she wished, but *only* under those circumstances. These included storms, illness, and bad dreams. Bad dreams would allow Alicia to get into bed with her mother, but Sue would then put Alicia back into her own bed once she had fallen asleep. Alicia had also agreed to knock on her mother's door before entering as a way of helping her to understand that this room was for parents to sleep and children to *visit*.

Alicia had also begun to throw tantrums when her requests were turned down. This was not related to sleeping arrangements but to daytime or evening hours when the family was together (without Dad, of course).

Throwing tantrums is common to children and is usually not complicated to deal with. Apparently, Alicia thought that because she felt so bad about her dad leaving and making her mom cry, she deserved to get what she wanted without argument. When her requests to stay up a little later or eat something too close to dinner time were turned down, she would drop to her knees with a dejected look on her face, fall forward with her hands at her side, and cry and scream.

Tantrum behavior was not typical of this five-year-old and only surfaced following Ron's departure. In the early days of the breakup Sue would routinely give in, not only to Alicia's tantrums, but to almost any request or demand by any of the children. This, too, is common behavior for a custodial parent struggling to adjust to a new and usually unwanted lifestyle. After all, Sue reasoned, maybe I *should* be more giving and lenient with the children considering all they have been through. Parental guilt such as Sue experienced is common, but despite her grief Sue eventually dealt with Alicia's tantrums by isolating her from all attention until her tantrums ceased. As with most children, this "extinction" process did not take more than a few attempts to accomplish.

We continued to attend to Alicia's other less serious reactions to her family problems while working on some of her out-of-home reactions. Chief among Alicia's negative reactions was separation anxiety coupled with increased dependency of the type that had led to her need to sleep with her mother.

Researchers have found a pattern of reactions not unlike Alicia's when studying children from many different backgrounds who were also experiencing the loss of a parent.[2] Alicia, who had been raised in a church family and who had gone to Sunday school and church from earliest infancy, suddenly began to resist any attempts to drop her off at her Sunday school class or anywhere else. She was able to verbalize her fears early in treatment, and it was clear that she was extending her unrealistic nightmare-type fears to her waking hours. She was able to keep her fear under control until faced with a requirement to be separated from her mother, at which point her defenses crumbled and she became like a much younger child afraid of leaving mother.

While separation anxiety was Alicia's most troublesome reaction, it was not her only reaction. She had become aggressive with her dolls and had torn limbs and heads from a few. She was noticeably more restless and exhibited moodiness and whining behavior that had not been part of her pre-divorce makeup. Alicia was cranky and irritable and would break into tears at the slightest confrontation. The hoarding of food mentioned earlier put her at risk for more serious eating disorders later on, and her fears warned of the possible development of phobias—all this in a five-year-old girl who had not exhibited the slightest sign of developmental or adjustment disorders prior to losing her father.

Eventually, Alicia was able to make significant progress, based more on her mother's growing ability to handle her own difficult situation than any counseling. At one point, Alicia shared with me that a major part of her fear was based on her worry that she was unlovable, the proof for which was found in her father's departure from the home. Thinking egocentrically as most five-year-olds do, Alicia naturally thought her father did not love her anymore and maybe never did! This was irrational but typical in a divorcing family with young children.

One final point regarding Alicia. As mentioned above, Sue's recovery from the divorce greatly influenced the progress her five-year-old daughter was able to make. We know that the mother-daughter bond is typically very close. In the early days following Ron's departure when Sue felt worthless, unattractive, unlovable, and stupid, Alicia identified with her mother's negative self-image and developed the same feelings about herself. However, as Sue found her way out of her depression and low self-concept, so did Alicia, though somewhat later.[3]

KEVIN

Nine-year-old Kevin struggled to understand what had happened to his family. His overriding emotional expression was anger. When his mother said that his dad would never live with the family again, Kevin, unlike Alicia, was burdened with the cognitive ability to understand what that meant. He was experiencing his own broken bough and reacted in expected if unwelcome ways.

Kevin loved his father, but more than that, he *liked* him too. Ron had always taken the boys with him on fishing trips and, while not an avid outdoorsman himself, thought it important to teach his boys many of the traditional outdoor skills he had learned from his father as a boy. Because of their close father-son relationship, it did not come as a surprise when this nine-year-old began to manifest his confusion through his behavior at home.

Very quickly, Kevin's schoolwork began to suffer, and he dropped from a *B/B-* average to a steady *C-* average in the course of one semester, the part of the school year when his ·dad officially left the family home. Consistent with current research, Kevin demonstrated every one of the troublesome behaviors identified by Hetherington and colleagues in a 1977 study of the impact of divorce on children Kevin's age.[4]

DEPENDENCE

Both Kevin and Alicia showed strong dependency needs in their own ways. Alicia, as we have discussed, wanted to sleep in her mother's bed, became frightened when left with a babysitter, and was apprehensive and anxious when it was time to be dropped off at her Sunday school classroom.

Kevin's dependence took a different form. While unwilling to admit discomfort when his mom was not around, he showed his fear by pretending to take charge when she was gone and making phone calls to see if she arrived safely. When Sue returned home, Kevin would take it upon himself to ask her questions about where she had been (even though he knew where his mother had gone) and would present a generally disapproving and somewhat parental attitude as if this inquiry was part of his duty now that his dad was not living at home anymore.

DISOBEDIENCE

Preadolescent boys are more likely to exhibit disobedience under any circumstances, but when the child's security is threatened or disrupted, disobedience quickly becomes more typical and more apparent. This nine-year-old second son knew that he could not get away with the walking-out-the-door behavior that his older brother exhibited when he became upset at home. But what he could do was manifest his feelings by being noncompliant and generally disagreeable. Though this was not typical of Kevin in the days when his family was still intact, it was becoming much more prevalent and troubling now. His mother was reassured that such behavior was common in the year or so after a divorce but was also expected to diminish and the situation return to normal not too long after that.

AGGRESSIVENESS

Because of the age gap between Kevin and his older brother and sister, Alicia was the only person upon whom he could take out his feelings. Kevin was sports- and competition-minded, much to his father's pleasure, and it did not take long for him to become competitive and something of a bully with his younger sister. Sue expressed to me how mystified she was that this little boy who had never been known to strike anyone in the family or use nasty words was now showing these behaviors regularly. He was more destructive with his toys, played rougher games with his neighborhood friends, got into more frequent fights at school and in the neighborhood, and generally made a nuisance of himself.

We talked at length about the ways boys and girls of elementary school-age manifest sexual differences, and I assured Sue that with time and firmness on her part, Kevin's bullying behavior should diminish and disappear. But it would take time.

DEMANDING

Sue described Kevin as being terribly impatient since Ron left. But what Sue described was not so much impatience as a need for reassurance through having demands satisfied upon request. Not unlike an infant who cries in the night but who does not need to be changed or fed, Kevin needed to be reassured that his needs would continue to be met in his new family situation. Again, the process of counseling with Sue Craig focused on helping her understand that many of the new behaviors and attitudes she was seeing in all her children represented their own ways of coping with the trauma of the divorce and that once they were reassured, the need to prove it to themselves by making demands or otherwise acting out would slowly diminish.

WITHDRAWAL OF AFFECTION

In stepfamily situations, it is called the "burnt child syndrome." In Kevin's case, all he knew was that his mom and dad had let him down, and he was not going to trust either parent again for a long time, especially when it came to expressing emotions. Kevin never was comfortable expressing positive emotions. He did not care much for hugs and kisses, and now that he had been burned by his parents, he was angry and determined to remain cool and detached. He was not going to risk being hurt again.

In the beginning it was difficult for Sue to understand that Kevin, in directing his detachment toward her, was not singling her out as the guilty parent but as the present parent, the only parent around on most days. I was reasonably sure that Kevin was behaving typically for someone in his situation given his history of a good pre-divorce situation.[5]

Kevin's situation was compounded by his strong loyalty to his father in the face of Ron's leaving the family. His resultant confusion was difficult to resolve. Kevin did not understand the reasons for his father's departure and could not grasp what was happening. We speculated that the confusion he was experiencing left him with only detachment and anger as acceptable solutions for his troubled emotions. Counseling would help, but it would be a tough year or two for Kevin.

SUMMARIZING THE IMPACT ON YOUNG CHILDREN

Parents who must parent alone should be aware of several common aspects of their challenging situation.[6] In a majority of cases, marital disruption effectively destroys the ongoing relationship between children and the biological parent living outside the home. In spite of Ron's promises that he would not only support the children financially but emotionally with regular visits, holidays, and summer vacations, Sue knew that the burden for childrearing was primarily on her shoulders and would remain there. Ron had become a weekend father, with all the expected reluctance to discipline, to ask about schoolwork, or do any of the other hundred-and-one things that weighed Sue down on a day-to-day basis.

The fear that lay behind Alicia's nightmares and Kevin's aggressiveness was a reflection of a reality that afflicts most divorced families with well-intentioned fathers. They feared that their dad would stop caring about them one day. The growing awareness that something had changed about their dad only strengthened their secret fear that Dad was moving away from them in more ways than he would admit. Ron's relationship with each of the children was now primarily social rather than functional, and even though they enjoyed the nonconfrontational time they had with their father, each was troubled by the realization that Dad had become friend more than parent.

It is significant to note that children of divorce do not always complain about this changed relationship. It is, after all, fun to go to movies and play miniature golf with Dad every weekend, and no one is going to complain about the extra nice gifts from Dad at Christmas and birthdays. Again, the fear that eventually surfaces builds slowly with the realization that Dad is no longer really Dad.

Research on the behavior and adaptive abilities of preschool children[7] led to the conclusion that the cumulative effect of divorce-related stress on preschool-age children was significant and followed four pathways:

1. *Antisocial behavior.* Experiencing parental divorce may lead directly to aggression, acting out, and distractibility primarily through the impact of father absence. Preexisting family conflicts that may continue after the separation also work to increase the young child's stress levels.

2. *Economic stress.* Divorce may create stress for young children through the increased likelihood of economic problems, geographic mobility, and similar adjustments in the year or two following the divorce.

3. *Parent reactions.* Stressors being experienced by parents may produce an additive effect to the stress of divorce on the child.

4. *General home conditions.* The findings of seven major studies conducted by the National Institute of Mental health concluded that children who were under six years of age when their parents divorced were three times more likely to need psychological

help than older children. It is noted in the research that divorce per se does not automatically put a child at risk for maladjustment. What emerges, say the researchers, is the importance of the overall psychological climate at home and the central role played by economic conditions.[8]

Runyon explains this impact on young children in three ways:[9]

1. *Abandonment.* The young child, aware of the absence of one parent, fears abandonment by the remaining parent. Children at this stage of thinking reason that if one parent can leave me, why should I believe that *both* parents would not leave me?

2. *Rejection.* The young child may experience considerable fear over the possibility of being unloved and unlovable. Again the cause and effect sequence becomes important to preschool-age children in attempting to explain to themselves in their own terms what their parents have been trying to explain to them in adult terms. Children at this age do not understand the ability to stop loving someone, which is probably the most common explanation given by parents.

3. *Problematic sex-role identification.* For boys, masculine aggression and other male sex-typed behaviors may be interpreted as unacceptable and the reason Dad had to leave the home in the first place. This perception may be strengthened by Mother's male-negative comments following the breakup that the young boy overhears.

THE IMPACT ON SCHOOL-AGE CHILDREN

A child of elementary-school-age who experiences parental divorce struggles with the dual issues of wanting to develop peer relationships and the need to keep family problems a secret. Given that the primary peer relationships tend to be school-based, it should not be a surprise to find that school performance is affected. Divorce disrupts the process of being able to learn and places the child in a category that often leads to negative expectations by teachers and other school personnel. In a study of 341 children from divorced homes and 358 from intact homes, Guidubaldi and colleagues found that children from intact homes were better on fourteen of sixteen classroom behavior ratings, were absent less often, had higher peer popularity, higher internal locus of control, and higher IQ scores.[10] Researchers Gelbich and Hare found that even in a gifted school population, there was a negative relationship between school achievement and single parenthood.[11]

Data from the National Health Interview Survey of Child Health representing a sample of 17,110 children under eighteen years of age found that children living with single mothers or with mothers and stepfathers were more likely than those living with both biological parents to repeat a grade in school, to have been expelled, to have been treated for emotional or behavioral problems in the previous year, to have elevated scores for behavioral problems and health vulnerability, and to be at greater risk for accidental injury and asthma.[12]

Research has taught us several things about children of divorce. A study of the relationship between crisis events and school mental health found that children from divorced single-parent homes were more likely to have school adjustment problems than those whose mothers had never married and therefore did not have a father. Acting out behavior was more common. However, if the father left the family through death rather than divorce, the child's reaction was more likely to be one of moody withdrawal and self-destructiveness than acting-out against others.[13] Other divorce researchers concluded that the single-parent/only-child family displayed a greater degree of disturbance than other family types and number of children.[14] Others studying the same divorce-based problem strongly recommended early intervention by teachers and school counselors and commented that elementary-age children tended to be ashamed of the divorce and blamed their parents[15] and could benefit from both individual and family counseling.

A summary of the impact of divorce on elementary-age children includes the following findings:

1. Divorce disrupts the process of being able to learn. Though divorce adjustment is usually a time-limited process, the damage that can result from repeating a failed grade as well as gaining a reputation as a troubled

student can become a permanent aspect of the growing child's self-perception and may continue to be a negative life force long after the initial trauma is resolved.

2. For most children, behavior fluctuates between noncompliance and excessive fear-based obedience. Single parents in counseling regularly comment on the unpredictable emotional state of the children, which in many cases is described as nearly schizophrenic.

3. Blame for the divorce is always assigned by the children in the family and is usually directed at the custodial parent. This blaming is usually irrational and tied to the child's developmental level and can be expected to resolve itself depending on how parents adjust.

4. Children, depending on age and level of maturity, tend to question their parents' values and challenge whether they are behaving morally. Accusations of immorality and irresponsibility are common and need to be understood as one aspect of the stressed child trying to find a way to deal with emotional trauma.

5. One reason for the need of school personnel to become proactive when dealing with divorce-related issues is the child's often intense sense of shame and embarrassment over what the parents have done. So many divorces involve sexual immorality and infidelity that it can be virtually impossible for the child who still loves his or her parents to tell a stranger what is troubling him or her.

6. Children of divorce need to be reassured that there are adults in their lives, including their parents, who will continue to take care of them. Children need to feel safe and protected, especially during times of crisis such as divorce.

7. The child's adjustment is strongly related to parenting skills possessed by the primary caregiver. Uncertainty in parenting will surely be perceived by the children as incompetence when there is only one custodial parent to provide care. Perceived incompetence, even in the presence of love, will frighten a child and lead to increased negative coping strategies.[16]

MINIMIZING THE IMPACT OF DIVORCE ON CHILDREN

Research clearly demonstrates that the age of a child at the time of a parental divorce is of prime importance in predicting and controlling negative reactions. One group conducted a long-term follow-up study of the impact of divorce on children and found that those children whose parents divorced before they were eleven years old had parent-child relationships characterized by greater distance, poorer communication, less affection and warmth, and less positive feelings in general about their parents. Young people from divorced families rated their relationships with their parents as average while those from intact families rated theirs as above average. It was also found that parents who were able to cope efficiently with the divorce had better relationships with their children.[17]

Specific factors that encouraged good post-divorce adjustment included a positive pre-divorce family life, higher quality pre-divorce father-child relationships, parents who maintained more frequent post-divorce contact with each other, and an adequate income.

Other researchers have reached similar conclusions. Tschann and colleagues supported the conclusion that more frequent and more intense marital conflict leads to deterioration in parent-child relationships.[18] Such deterioration will tend to produce in the children poorer ability to cope, lowered self-esteem, more intense anger, and depression. However, the researchers also concluded that damage can be moderated if one or both parents can remain reasonably warm and empathetic with the child without showing rejection, can avoid involving the child in conflicts, can resist using the child for emotional support, and can have age-appropriate expectations of the child.

WHAT PARENTS SHOULD AND SHOULD NOT DO

Provide predictability for the children. They should be informed (appropriate to their age and ability to understand) what will probably happen next, where the family will live if the residence must change, what the visitation arrangements will be for the noncustodial parent, and who will care for them in emergencies such as mother's illness or injury. It is significant that up to 80 percent of custodial parents fail to tell their children that they will continue to be cared for under any circumstances.

Tell the children what is going to happen, but avoid burdening them with details. We need to remember that children need *both* parents to remain heroes in their lives. It may be appropriate to share the whole truth with adult helpers and friends, but it is *not* appropriate to share this information with children. There is *no* age at which the details should be revealed unless it cannot be avoided. For instance, if a child may learn through schoolyard gossip what his father or mother did to encourage the family breakup, then the child should hear that information first from a parent. We find this to be particularly important when the divorce was related to sexual immorality or criminal behavior. Parents who move quickly to tell children how badly they were mistreated by the absent parent are often surprised to hear that same child rising to the slandered parent's defense. Children will tend to defend the absent parent in the face of the most convincing (to adults) evidence of wrongdoing.

Tell the child that a separation or divorce is pending, but share the information at the proper time and in the proper manner. There is little if anything to be gained from a premature warning of what may be happening to the family. Parents often feel compelled to warn their children that something bad looms on the family horizon because they, as adults, would want to know to make plans, garner emotional support, etc.

Children are different, however, and should be protected as long as possible. Their security should be kept in place for as many days as is reasonable so that they can store up strength for the future. Every day that the child can feel protected, cared for, and loved builds strength for the day when he or she will not be so certain of these things. Parents often provide excessive information prematurely because they fail to consider the child's perspective as being different from their own, and in doing so, they make a serious mistake.

Parents can tell the children a week or two before the decision to separate or divorce is to be implemented, but only if there is no doubt that the separation will occur. Surely it is cruel to scare a child with impending bad news that fails to materialize because parents have reconciled. The child's sense of security will never be the same again if this happens.

Tell the child's teacher and school counselor about the change in the family. Parents often fail to consider the help that is available through the professionals at their child's school. Frequently, teachers and school counselors have participated in in-service and seminar training specifically targeting special problems of elementary school children, particularly separation/divorce adjustment.

Professionals can also be helpful in recommending books on divorce for children at different ages. Public libraries often have filmstrips or videos that can be checked out and used for discussion at home. Other services available through schools and libraries include group counseling opportunities. Though single parents typically feel alone in their post-divorce struggles with the children, there are often excellent and underutilized resources available.

Do not allow children to become messengers between parents. Divorce is an adult thing. Children should not be expected to ask questions of either parent on behalf of the other one. We remind parents that children will quietly resent being messengers, in part because they correctly understand that the messages are nothing more than a continuation of the battles and personality conflicts that led to the dissolution of their family in the first place.

Make promises carefully, and then keep them. Given the threatened security typical of children of divorce, broken promises carry extra heavy psychological baggage. One of my earliest and most vivid memories as a counselor is of a client, a man in his late thirties, who could not sustain a marital relationship. He related to me his intense depression when, as a ten-year-old, he waited for his noncustodial father to pick him up on a Saturday morning to spend the day. His father never arrived. Excuses aside, this grown man had apparently never recovered from that early experience.

Do not berate the ex-spouse in front of the children. As with carrying messages, continued assassination of the absent parent simply reminds the child witnessing such comments that Mom and Dad still hate each other. Even though they say one of them will always be there to care for them, the children may not be so sure. Counselors need to remind the accusing parent that children will rise to the defense of an accused parent even if the accusations are correct. Making verbal attacks in front of the children is a lose-lose situation for any single parent.

Avoid discussing or arguing about money in front of the children. The child's world is threatened by divorce, and arguing or complaining about money, even though justified in many cases, only further frightens the child. Financial matters are exclusive territory of adults, and even though a parent may have to say "no" to a request that cannot be afforded right now, the reason for the negative response should not be shared except in the most general terms.

Do not allow guilt over the separation and divorce to interfere with parenting responsibilities. While it is typical and expected that the custodial parent will feel some degree of guilt following a family breakup, personal emotional needs must be balanced with the children's need for strength and structure from a parent. Children will often challenge rules and become untypically noncompliant for no other reason than that of seeing if the custodial parent is strong enough to take care of them. This is not so much a conscious, thought-out plan as an emotional reaction to the fear of abandonment that accompanies every divorce involving children.

Protect the attachments of the child as much as possible. Within reasonable limits, custodial parents should strive to retain as much of the child's pre-divorce environment as possible. This serves to minimize emotional reactions such as sadness and crying. Parents should attempt to retain the same school, neighborhood, friends, and residence if at all possible. One of my clients duplicated the wallpaper that had been in her daughter's bedroom in their previous home in their new apartment. She was sure that this simple tactic helped her seven-year-old daughter adjust to the new living arrangements.

Attachments also applies to grandparents. One of the more serious and long-term tragedies of a marital dissolution is that children may be cut off from one set of grandparents. This normally is done to meet the needs of one of the parents involved and as such is the wrong thing to do. It harms the child's sense of continuity in the family and further threatens his or her already fragile sense of security.

Remind the child that there is nothing he or she can do to change the situation. Children often will try to find ways to get Mom and Dad back together. This is termed "reconciliation preoccupation" and should be seen by parents and professionals as a normal and expected aspect of trying to restore their lives to the former, and better, state. Constant but gentle reminders are called for to assure the children that they did not cause the divorce of their parents and that there is nothing they can do to fix the situation.

Encourage the children to talk about their feelings and ask questions. Open lines of communication are never more important than during times of crisis. If a parent is in a state of emotional upset and does not feel comfortable dealing with such issues and questions, perhaps there is another trusted adult who could become something of a listening ear for the child. A member of the pastoral staff, the pastor's wife, youth pastor, or Sunday school teacher could step in temporarily and assist the child in his or her struggle to adapt to the new situation.

CONCLUSION

Children are a blessing from God. They are described as an inheritance in Psalm 127, a passage that conveys the idea of children as an heirloom—something that is not so much possessed as stewarded by one generation of a family so that it may be passed on to the next generation. Children do not belong to their parents; they neither begin nor have their end in their parents. Children belong to God.

The Bible teaches that parents have primary responsibility for raising their children in a way that would please the heavenly Father (see Gen. 33:5; Ps. 78:1–8; Prov. 17:6; Eph. 6:1–4). Every parent is his or her child's image of God. When one parent walks away from a marriage and leaves both the spouse and the children behind, it matters little if that absent parent brings special gifts on Christmas and remembers birthdays. The image is in place, and people of all ages can testify to the difficulty they experience in trusting God when they have had their trust in a parent violated.

When we work with parents who have been forced to deal with their own divorce, counselors and other helpers must keep the children in the family a top priority, even if the children are not identified clients in the counseling office. What we do as Christian counselors reflects not only our concern for doing good counseling but also for obeying God's command to protect his little ones.

NOTES

1. W. F. Hodges, *Interventions for Children of Divorce* (New York: Wiley, 1986), 16.

2. J. S. Wallerstein and J. B. Kelly, "The Effects of Parental Divorce: Experiences of the Pre-School Child," *Journal of the American Academy of Child Psychiatry* 14 (1975): 600–616.

3. C. M. Kaseman, "The Single-Parent Family," *Perspectives in Psychiatric Care* 12 (1974): 113–18.

4. E. M. Hetherington, M. Cox, and R. Cox, "The Aftermath of Divorce," in *Mother-Child, Father-Child Relations*, ed. J. H. Stevens, Jr. and M. Matthews (Washington, D. C.: National Association for the Education of Young Children, 1977).

5. A. P. Copeland, "Individual Differences in Children's Reactions to Divorce," *Journal of Clinical Child Psychology* 14, no. 1 (1985): 11–19.

6. W. F. Hodges, C. W. Tierney, and H. K. Buschbaum, "The Cumulative Effect of Stress on Preschool Children of Divorced and Intact Families," *Journal of Marriage and the Family* 46 (August 1984): 611–17.

7. Hodges, Tierney, and Buschbaum, "Effect of Stress," 351.

8. M. Adams, "Kids and Divorce: No Long-Term Harm," *USA Today*, 20 December 1984.

9. N. Runyon and P. L. Jackson, "Divorce: Its Impact on Children," *Perspectives in Psychiatric Care* 3, no. 4 (1988): 101–5.

10. J. Guidubaldi et al., "The Impact of Parental Divorce on Children: Report of the Nationwide NASP Study," *School Psychology Review* 12 (1983): 300-323.

11. J. A. Gelbich and E. K. Hare, "The Effects of Single Parenthood on School Achievement in a Gifted Population," *Gifted Child Quarterly* 53, no. 3 (1989): 115–17.

12. D. A. Dawson, "Family Structure and Children's Health and Well-Being: Data from the National Health Interview Survey of Child Health," *Journal of Marriage and the Family* (1991): 573–84.

13. R. D. Felner, A. Stolberg, and E. L. Cowen, "Crisis Events and School Mental Health Referral Patterns of Young Children," *Journal of Consulting and Clinical Psychology* 43 (1975): 305–10.

14. S. Bayrakal and T. M. Kope, "Dysfunction in the Single Parent and Only Child Family," *Adolescence* 97 (1990): 1–7.

15. J. S. Wallerstein and J. B. Kelly, "The Effects of Parental Divorce," *American Journal of Orthopsychiatry* 46, no. 2 (1976): 255–69.

16. F. F. Furstenberg and C. W. Nord, "Parenting Apart: Patterns of Childrearing after Marital Disruption," *Journal of Marriage and the Family* (November 1985): 893–906.

17. M. A. Fine, J. R. Moreland, and A. I. Schwebel, "Long-Term Effects of Divorce on Parent-Child Relationships," *Developmental Psychology* 19, no. 5 (1983): 703–13.

18. J. M. Tschann et al, "Family Process and Children's Functioning during Divorce," *Journal of Marriage and the Family* 51 (May 1989): 431–44.

Chapter 4

Adolescents and Parental Divorce: A Twisted Chain

Emily Craig had just turned sixteen when she was told of the separation and upcoming divorce of her parents. As the oldest child, Emily keenly felt a burden to try and help her parents recover their lost marriage. Typical of adolescents forced to share in a family trauma as severe as divorce, Emily's sense that her life was undergoing permanent and unwanted change grew heavier as the news began to sink in. What could she have done, she wondered, that might have prevented this awful thing? What might she be able to do now to recover the sense of security and family identity that was slipping away?

Questions without answers soon gave way to depression for Emily, and depression slowly became anorexia nervosa, the self-induced starvation syndrome growing more common among stressed-out and media-influenced American adolescent females. Emily was subconsciously trying to prove to herself that there were some aspects of her life that *she* was in charge of, no matter what her parents or others might do.

Fourteen-year-old Scott had always been his dad's buddy, and until his little brother came along, Scott was convinced that his dad liked him more than the others. Scott was only beginning to become aware of what relationships mean to people and what had happened to cause the divorce of his mom and dad.

Scott did not know what to do when he was told about the divorce. He was so angry at what his dad had done to his mother that he sometimes thought he would kill him if he got the chance. But at other times, he was fiercely loyal to his father and would react with extreme anger if anyone mentioned that the divorce might be his father's fault. It was as if Scott had become two persons: one who still loved and wanted to be with his dad, and the other who hoped that he never would see him again. Sometimes Scott wished that God would find a way to get even with his dad for what he had done to his mom.

Scott was growing more and more emotional following the separation and divorce of his parents. His depression turned outward, manifesting itself in fighting at school and in constant problems because of his need to be in control. As Emily had turned her anger inward and had virtually stopped eating, Scott had turned his anger outward against others.

For Emily and Scott, adolescence was becoming much more complicated and harder to understand compared to most of their friends. They were being asked to adjust to a negative family transition at the very time when each of them was trying to focus all of his or her energy on simply growing up. Any family crisis is likely to disrupt the process of development, and divorce can be expected to be more traumatic, in most cases, than even the death of a parent. Death, after all, is usually not voluntary, and no matter what adults told the Craig children, they each knew in their own way that their dad had *chosen* to end his marriage to their mother. Rejection hurts, no matter how young or old a person is.

THE NATURE OF ADOLESCENCE

In my sessions with Sue that focused on her two teenagers, I found it helpful to explain the biblical position on adolescence. What I was able to offer was not exactly what Sue had in mind.

I reminded Sue that the Bible does not seem to acknowledge the teen years as a separate stage of life as we do today. I suggested that most people on earth will not experience anything like what we call the adolescent stage of life. In rural and developing areas around the world, human beings move directly from being older children into young adults with adult responsibilities. Of course, most people live in rural and underdeveloped parts of the world, so this absence of anything in the Bible relating to our views of adolescence is significant for our understanding.

When we look to the Bible for insight on adolescence, we find only silence. Certainly the Bible does teach from silence at times, but in the case of adolescence, we believe the silence reflects an absence of the concept rather than an intent to teach. In Scripture, we read instead about only two broad groups: children and adults.

For example, the Apostle John talked about children, young men, and fathers (1 John 2:12–14). A closer examination will reveal that these young men were not adolescents but full adults in the prime of their lives, probably in their twenties and thirties rather than teens. Paul addressed this subject in his letter to the Corinthian church: "When I was a child, I talked like a child, I thought like a child, I reasoned like a child. When I became a man, I put childish ways behind me" (1 Cor. 13:11). Paul did not mention what it was like to be an adolescent because he never was an adolescent. In Exodus 2:10–11 we find Moses described as a child in verse ten and as a grown-up in verse eleven. There is no mention of any teenage years. Luke 2:52 tells us that the young Jesus "grew in wisdom and stature," but then we hear nothing more until Jesus is in his thirties.

In my own counseling practice I sometimes find myself dealing with a parent, usually a father, who is experiencing family turmoil because he insists on spanking an adolescent "child." Parents who think this way will usually refer to passages in Proverbs recommending the use of a rod to discipline. The argument continues that if spanking with a rod was acceptable in the Old Testament, we should follow those teachings today. In the Bible, however, physical discipline in the family was limited to children only, and people stopped being children in

Bible culture when they were approximately twelve or thirteen years old.

So I worked intensely with Sue to help her understand that just because the Bible says very little about the age bracket of her two oldest children, we were not left out in the cold as to what to do. The requirement is to treat adolescents as the young adults they really are rather than the "old children" we so often assume them to be.

In this regard, we should be aware that biblical principles match scientific findings that adolescence is a developmental process. We will find differences between teenagers of different ages and maturity levels as they move through the process of becoming young adults.

Sue and I were able to reach an agreement on this issue that allowed us to continue to talk about ways she could help her two teenagers adjust to the divorce. We spent a great deal of time discussing egocentrism, separation, absolutism, sexuality, self-esteem, and school performance.

EGOCENTRISM

Jean Piaget, the famous European child psychologist, described the world from the perspective of an infant: "The world to the infant is a thing to be sucked." With this proclamation, Piaget founded the concept of developmental egocentrism.

Egocentrism, however, does not vanish with baby bottles and diapers; it remains an important part of the psychological makeup of every person. This was the case with Emily and Scott Craig as well. American and Canadian adolescents (among others) are not allowed, except in extreme cases, to experience the independence common to their agemates around the world. For those other people of their same age, egocentrism tends to be smothered in adult responsibilities related to family needs, caring for younger children, working to bring in family income, and so on. But in countries like the United States, egocentrism continues to be a life force because our culture does not allow the same level of independence experienced in some other countries.

Characteristic of egocentrism among American adolescents is "universal audience," a term coined to explain the psychosocial processes leading American teens to behave in anti-adult and often bizarre ways. Each relatively normally functioning teenager in our culture believes emotionally (if not cognitively) that he or she is being watched constantly and that the slightest awkward or stupid move will be instantly noticed by all the other adolescents in his or her environment.

An unzipped fly or surprise pimple will cause psychological havoc to the afflicted teenager who believes that (1) *everyone*, absolutely *everyone*, noticed it and told *all* their friends who will (2) undoubtedly remember the embarrassment *forever*!

American teenagers behave, dress, talk, and generally conduct their lives in accordance with the cardinal belief that everyone (among their agemates only) will notice the slightest departure from what is "accepted" at the moment. Thus we see the spread of various fads among adolescents. Hair styles, music, clothing, to notch or not to notch one's eyebrows, or, to have a hole pierced for jewelry in some part of one's body all are included among the areas where teenagers are influenced when faced with peer pressure through the universal audience phenomenon.

It is the universal audience process that accounts for the extreme embarrassment felt by many teens going through the divorce of their parents. Talk to one of these teenagers, and you will hear references only to the self. "How could they do that to *me*?" comes the complaint, oblivious to the pain being experienced by others in the family. "What will *my* friends think?" asks the fifteen-year-old, unmindful of the feelings of a parent or sibling.

Egocentrism is instinctive in human beings, diminishes with age, but is easily revived by stress. No stress is greater for the adolescent than parental divorce, and as a result, egocentrism resurfaces from the once-buried childhood emotions and again controls the reactions of adolescents in the family going through a divorce. Egocentrism replaces empathy, the ability to feel *with* rather than *for* a person. Empathy implies some ability to sense the true feelings of another, to identify with those feelings, and then to react appropriately. Here most adolescents face a difficult obstacle. The more egocentrism fights for control the less able the adolescent will be to feel empathy for anyone else. Teens facing family turmoil such as divorce will typically just walk away to be alone or with their friends, but rarely will a teen stay and try to help.

Sue Craig struggled with the information I shared with her on this subject. She certainly wanted the support of her two older children, and while she was getting a degree of help from Emily, Scott would have none of it. Only slowly did Sue come to grips with the truth that Scott's negative feelings and behavior were not directed at her but at the situation that was forced upon him. He could care little for his mother right now because he cared so much for himself. Scott wanted so badly to have his father back and the family return to normal that he could only become angry when faced with the reality that this was not going to happen.

SEPARATION/INDIVIDUATION

It is the nature of adolescents in the United States to break away from the family. The peer relationships and ever increasing amounts of time spent with friends rather than family illustrate the typical American adolescent's need to move out of the family. Customarily smooth yet exciting, this transition experienced by adolescents presents no great problems to most families.

But consider the plight of Emily and Scott. Just at the time when they were in the process of preparing to exit the family, their father cut ahead of them in line, and *he* left the family first. Both Emily and Scott, in their own way, expressed resentment that their dad had preempted their movement toward independence by his decision to leave the family.

Both Emily and Scott behaved as predicted by withdrawing from the family, albeit each in their distinct way.[1] This withdrawal was probably not conscious but rather served as a defense mechanism for their fragile and threatened self-concepts. A study of a group of twenty-one adolescents experiencing parental divorce indicated that each one tried to withdraw from the family. The greater difficulty experienced by fourteen-year-old Scott is consistent with research on that age group.[2]

ABSOLUTISM

Adolescents tend to see everything in black or white, with no shades of gray. This is the case with loyalty to parents as well. Scott, the younger of the Craig teenagers, felt very strong loyalty to his father in spite of being confused regarding the obvious responsibility his father bore for the family breakup. It was important to help Scott understand that the feelings he was experiencing were completely natural and expected and would probably resolve themselves in a few years. The slightest opportunity to take the side of one parent over the other will not be missed by adolescents in a divorce situation. It is almost as if an expression of anger or hostility is cathartic, a part of the psychological and spiritual healing process that must eventually take place.

Counselors and other helpers can facilitate the healing process by assuring the adolescent that his or her ambivalence and uncertainty are natural. It is important that the teenager sees people as complicated beings possessing both good and bad qualities. Some researchers have found anger and hostility directed toward the custodial parent,[3] while others have found those negative emotions directed at the absent parent.[4] Reduction in negative emotions can be helped along by parents who are able to avoid exposing adolescents to the negative aspects of the marriage and divorce. Not an easy task, I admit, but one that must be accomplished if youngsters are to be protected.

I also expected Scott to turn on his father at some point. Heroes are the quickest to fall, and with Scott, disillusionment with his father was becoming apparent even in the earliest days. In spite of his strong protests of loyalty and belief in his father, Scott was having doubts. I knew that one of the major counseling concerns with Scott would be his confused feelings about his dad.

Fortunately for all the children, Sue and Ron did a good job of keeping their disputes and disagreements relatively quiet. Though all four children knew something was wrong, they were not exposed to any violence (there was none) or loud arguments at home. In the long run, this was to prove extremely important to the children's ability to adjust. Researchers studying a group of 648 young people ranging in age from ten to eighteen found that the youths' evaluations of their parents varied significantly as a function of family status.[5] Fathers *and* mothers from divorced families were rated significantly more negatively than those from intact families.[6] No surprise, perhaps, but grist for the counseling mill nonetheless.

Such negativism may be explained, in part, by the child holding parents responsible for the trauma of their post-divorce family environment.[7] The reality of financial hardship, geographic mobility, and an unwanted stepparent can cause youngsters to blame their parents for such intrusions into their lives.[8]

SEXUALITY

Researchers have concluded that because teenagers have difficulty with parents' sexuality, pre- or post-divorce, parents should control and probably minimize exposure to parental sexuality. This recommendation appears to be particularly important in the first months following a divorce.[9] Knowledge of or exposure to parental sexuality can be a roadblock in the adolescent's progress to adulthood and a potential source for psychological trauma. Others have expressed concern that mere knowledge of parental dating forces teenagers in the family to confront not only their own sexual concerns but issues related to loyalty as well.[10]

The case study literature supplies ample evidence that some divorced parents may be prone to revert to the adolescent role themselves, thereby further traumatizing the teenagers in the family struggling to establish independence. Divorced parents have been known to ask their teenage children for advice on dating protocol, suggestions about where to have dinner, and what time is appropriate to come home. The competitive nature of this concurrent dating should be obvious. Imagine the consternation of a sixteen-year-old daughter asked by her divorced and newly dating mother if it is still okay to refuse to kiss on the first date!

Beyond the dating behavior of parents, the issue of proper parental control over family dating rules for teenagers remains important. It is not uncommon to learn that divorced parents with custody of teenagers have virtually surrendered their power to influence the dating life of their teens. Certainly guilt tops the list of reasons for this, but this explanation does little to heal the hurt that often comes from such parental powerlessness.

When teenagers are allowed to begin dating without parental limitations, disaster is the expected outcome. Parents need to be reminded that teens often ask us to tell them they cannot do something because they do not have the strength to resist it themselves.

Our son, Doug, was about fifteen when a friend called and asked if he could go out on the night before an exam. We liked most of Doug's friends, so we were not particularly worried about his going out that evening. But I was concerned about the exam.

A few minutes into the conversation Doug said to his friend, "Just a second," placed his hand over the phone and said to me, "Dad, I can't go out tonight, can I?" Sensing what he was really asking, I replied with a smile, "No!" Doug turned back to the phone and said to his friend, "No, I can't make it. My dad won't let me go out tonight."

Now imagine a different scenario. Suppose I was a recently divorced parent with custody of teenage children. Suppose also that I was feeling guilty for inflicting family turmoil on the children, and also suppose that I was asked the same question that Doug asked me but in this new scenario. Can we see how easy it would be for that divorced parent to say, "Well, son, I am pretty busy right now. Why don't you just do what you think is best?"

Divorced parents need to resist the temptation to become overly permissive out of guilt. Teenagers and children of all ages need *more* structure, not less following any kind of family upset. Parents need to be aware that challenges to rules and complaints about being too controlled are often requests for parents to demonstrate their strength. Very often children and adolescents in divorced families are asking for help in managing their lives, but they must ask for this help without being too obvious, because this would not be "cool."

Unique challenges confront daughters in divorced families. Researchers have widely discussed the psychological process that a girl usually goes through when her father leaves the home. The girl will experience father absence as sexual rejection regardless of the actual circumstances of the breakup.[11] She is then at risk for premature sexual experiences due to her need to prove to herself that she is attractive to males.

Risk is increased because girls in separated families tend to begin dating earlier than girls from intact families[12] and to move to more intense levels of intimacy once dating begins.[13] Others have discussed the role of family acrimony in encouraging early dating in both boys and girls as a means of getting out of the house as often as possible.[14] A pattern of teenagers in the family running out to be with their friends rather than listen to Mom and Dad fight is an old problem and one that does not stop when the combatants decide to end the war and divorce. Patterns of dating will *not* be reversed in a family; once the standard has been established, there will be no going back to more healthy rules.

SELF-ESTEEM

Adolescents live and die by self-esteem. The perception teenagers have of themselves controls virtually every aspect of their development. One group of researchers proposed a set of categories of self-esteem and identified them as *popular, controversial, neglected,* and *rejected* adolescents. Each category was essentially a statement of how an adolescent viewed the self in relation to peers and significant others.[15] Others suggest that it is the experience of negatively perceived events that is a primary contributor to lowered self-esteem among adolescents.[16] One study of adolescents concluded that self-esteem rises until age twelve and then drops until eighteen years of age, whereupon it gradually begins to rise again.[17] Self-esteem losses are strongly influenced by parent absence and do not appear to be so impacted by the reason for the parent's removal from the child's life.[18]

Another aspect of self-esteem following divorce is accelerated or decelerated entry into adulthood. According to Wallerstein and colleagues, some youngsters may hold on tenaciously to symbols of their childhood that remind them of happier and more secure days while others will attempt to move out of the family and into the peer group as quickly as possible.[19] Studies of both boys and girls who experienced parental divorce during their teenage years demonstrated that they were more likely to be involved in substance abuse and to suffer more negative consequences of such abuse compared to those from intact families.[20]

SCHOOL PERFORMANCE

Research on the academic performance of adolescents from divorced families clearly indicates that lowered performance at all levels should be expected.[21] While exceptions will certainly occur, parents, counselors, and other concerned adults should be vigilant for signs of developing problems. Problem indicators include unexplained failures and low grades, excessive and unexplained tardiness and absence from school, poorer on-task performance when in class, more frequent conflicts with authority figures at all levels from the lunchroom employees to the principal, and reorientation to a different group of friends in a short period of time.

While some have concluded that the impact of family problems on school performance may not be uniform due to differences between families,[22] others have found more consistent results when family factors are accurately figured into the equation.[23] Acting out behaviors in school appear to spring from feelings of anxiety, depression, and hostility stemming from family conflict. Some have also found that physical separation from home does not always reduce the negative impact of a stressful home environment.[24] There seems little doubt that when the home environment experiences a negative change at the magnitude of a divorce, academic performance will suffer.

TYPICAL MISTAKEN GOALS OF
ADOLESCENTS FROM DIVORCED HOMES

Researchers interested in the thought processes of adolescents proposed that adolescents are likely to be limited and negatively impacted because they tend to work toward goals that are unproductive, error-filled, and mistaken.[25] Stressed-out families usually experience more of a negative impact when teenagers find themselves on the wrong track in life. Single-parent families often find themselves in just such a stressed-out environment. Others have described the struggle for identity as the major developmental task of the adolescent. In this struggle for identity, personal independence from parents becomes a major issue. Even the most trivial problems become a source of family conflict.[26]

Typical reactions seen in adolescents whose parents have divorced can be understood, at least in part, by considering the conflicting needs of the teenagers. Adolescents in divorcing or divorced families are trying to establish personal independence while experiencing the most threatening of all family problems, the loss of one's parent. At the time when the adolescent is attempting to break free of the family, so is one of the teen's parents. The conflict is inevitable and profound and may be understood by considering the goals adolescents set for themselves and how these goals are impacted by parental divorce.

GOAL 1: SUPERIORITY

Adolescents struggle with intense feelings of inferiority, a convincing sense that they are not worth as much as adults or are not as smart, strong, experienced, or liked as much as adults. Some have said that there is nothing wrong with having an inferiority complex as long as one is actually inferior. This certainly seemed to be true of both Emily and Scott Craig following the divorce. Coupled with their typical adolescent inferiority was the sense that now their family, too, was inferior. Statistics indicate that nearly half of all Americans will experience what Emily and Scott were going through, but the feeling of being placed into an unwanted and unpleasant category by their parents' divorce would not leave either teenager.

So Emily decided to work even harder on getting straight As, and Scott devoted his psychological and emotional energies into being as "old" as he could be. This explained his need to show that he could not be pushed around like a kid. The result was frequent fights over trivial conflicts in school and the beginning of a reputation for being a hothead.

Both Emily and Scott received initial approval from parents, teachers, and friends for their efforts at taking more control in their young lives. As is typical in such cases, most of the important adults in their lives did not pay enough attention to the underlying motivations pushing these two teenagers to be the best at what they did. Those adults who were able to help did so by avoiding blanket approval of their perfectionism while promoting the strength to accept the fact that they were going to remain different from many of their friends. Emily and Scott have only begun to understand what has been pushing each of them to try for superiority, but as understanding increases, so should the acceptance of their perceived faults and shortcomings—even those imposed on them by their father.

Goal 2: Popularity

Adolescents under stress often turn to externals for proof of acceptance. Both Emily and Scott became more peer oriented following their parents' divorce and showed a growing desire to be out of the home as much as possible. Even though the "rejection of home/acceptance of peers" process is common to adolescents, when youngsters under stress use this tactic, they tend to be less able to balance peer and family responsibilities. Remember that friends become the family for many teenagers and that adolescents tend to measure their self-worth by the number of friends they possess.

Adolescents usually make no distinction between friends and acquaintances, believing on an emotional level that everyone they know who is not an enemy must be their friend. Rarely will we hear teens describing a peer as anything other than a friend or someone they do not know at all. Friendships are the building blocks for adolescent self-concept, and when self-concept is threatened by family problems, friends can grow in importance and influence with teens.

Dealing with the popularity-seeking adolescent is usually best accomplished through careful adult feedback and encouragement for peer-group activities. Sometimes adults may give the impression that they agree with their teen that one can never have too many friends and that it is alright with them if they choose to orient themselves in that direction. Unfortunately, many single parents fail to realize that teenagers often need help in controlling a difficult part of their lives that has been exacerbated by the parents' divorce.

Goal 3: Conformity

Both of the Craig teenagers showed an unusual desire to conform to the expectations of adults following the divorce. Scott, in spite of the anger and aggressive behavior that was getting him into so much trouble at school, was talking about becoming either a preacher or a career military officer and was showing clear indications that he was prepared to offer up his developing individuality in exchange for the security of acceptance earned through conformity. Normal independence-dependence development had backfired on Scott, and this fourteen-year-old was struggling to find something to replace his family as a primary reference unit.

Emily, at sixteen, was somewhat more independent at the time of the divorce, but her eating disorder was a clear indication that she was trying to conform to a standard that no longer existed for her family. The depression that was becoming a part of her life was felt most sharply when Emily believed she was not conforming to the expectations of her teachers and her mother. In spite of repeated reassurances, Emily resisted being persuaded that she really was okay and did not need to prove her dedication by conforming to an artificial concept of the perfect woman, or perfect teenager. This desire to be perfect was leading her down the path to anorexia nervosa.

Extreme conformity in adolescents following any kind of family tragedy should be seen as a fear-based reaction to intense insecurity and dealt with from that perspective. Compassionate help will be characterized by careful reinforcement of activities and attitudes that show movement toward independence rather than conformity. Youngsters showing extreme conformity need reassurance that they are accepted as they are and do not need to change themselves to earn acceptance.

GOAL 4: INDEPENDENCE

Adolescents typically experience a strong felt need to establish their independence from parents, family, school, and any other authority figure or system. Teenagers express their developing autonomy in a manner consistent with their personalities and environments. American adolescent males tend to express their independence by acting out, sexual bravado, risk-taking, and being noncompliant to requests from parents and teachers. Females will typically express their independence needs by attempting to move into the peer group and away from the family in quieter ways, through dating, school

and peer group activities, and in extreme cases, by withdrawing into depression, eating disorders, running away, and
sexual acting out. Both boys and girls may express their independence through work.

Independence through defiance. Both boys and girls may become defiant to parents and other authority figures, but males
are more likely to express these feelings openly. There will be
arguments over clothing, hair styles, choosing the right friends,
dating regulations, curfew, schoolwork, and countless others.
Counselors can encourage family health by helping parents
understand that what they are observing in their adolescents is in
all likelihood a good sign. These issues may be difficult to deal with
and feel unpleasant and upsetting, but they are a clear sign that the
young adults in this family are making progress in their attempts
to break free of their family of origin and begin to establish their
own identity and eventually their own family system.

Parents and authority figures become annoyed, irritated,
and angry in response to defiant behavior. It is easy for parents to feel that they have failed in their attempt to raise their
children properly. But friends of the adolescent react differently. Peers not only accept defiant behavior by agemates, they
celebrate it! Counselor and parents may need to be reminded
that the behavior that is so upsetting at home and in other
structured environments may be strongly reinforced by peers.
"Why does he keep acting so rebellious?" parents ask, unaware
that the very actions that are plaguing their home are a badge
of courage to their teenager's friends.

Quick, firm action taken by parents can stem the tide of rebellion *if* parents are determined. The "tough love" concept
works well in many families by demanding strict accountabil-
ity when young people break home rules. Determination is the
key for parents. In the parenting workshops I have conducted
all over the United States, the one element that seems to be
missing in Christian families struggling with child or adolescent misbehavior is determination. Parents need to feel sure
that what they are doing is the right thing for all concerned
and that they will not be deterred by criticism from anyone.

Independence through aggression. Serious aggression is not
common in families where rules and limits have always been in

place and consistently enforced. However, even the best families will see an occasional episode of aggressive behavior such as fighting, as was observed with Scott Craig. Vandalism and other forms of serious illegal behavior may occur and come under the heading of delinquency.

Typically, this form of acting out following family turmoil is a warning flag that must not be overlooked or rationalized away. When a teenager becomes destructive to self, others, or property, he or she is in trouble and in need of intervention *now*! This type of unacceptable behavior may be the first step in a long slide into an adolescent subculture of drugs, sex, gang activity, and violence. Adults are typically blown away when this happens and tend to have difficulty remaining balanced in their response. Counselors can work to help parents understand possible reasons why this is happening and can encourage bold action by parents to let the teenager know in very certain terms that this behavior is not acceptable and will not be tolerated.

Independence through withdrawal. More typical of girls than boys, withdrawal can show itself through running away, suicide gestures, substance abuse, and eating disorders. Withdrawing to become more independent may seem contradictory, but youngsters in authoritarian, strict, over-controlled homes may not have opportunities to express their sense of independence as their defiant or aggressive peers have done. Withdrawal may be the only option.

Because of their vulnerability to independence substitutes, teenagers from authoritarian homes are in more long-term danger than are their defiant or aggressive peers. It is important to note, however, that adolescents will show varying degrees of withdrawal, ranging from barely noticeable to disabling. Those who are less severely withdrawn may show their feelings through dark clothing, spending long hours alone in their room, refusing to spend time with family or peers, writing dark and morbid poetry and stories, or daydreaming about unrealistic opportunities for the future, all built around a theme of independence. Those who are more disabled will show an all-consuming interest in death, suicide, self-destruction, or other forms of negative thinking. In no case should these expressions be taken lightly or written off as just a phase of adolescence.

Independence through work. Adolescent boys and girls work outside the home for various reasons. Many teenage boys work to buy and then maintain a car. A quick look at just about any high school parking lot will convince anyone of the growing need of high school youngsters to have their own car. Girls, too, may work to buy a car, but they will also be concerned with clothing and other appearance items essential to being accepted at school. Some work to help the family through difficult times, and others work because it makes them feel more grown up.

Independence through work can lead to a form of teenage workaholism. Careful parents of adolescents need to focus on schoolwork and activities while accepting the reality that this generation *will* work because their needs often cannot be met by allowances and occasional odd jobs. A balance should be sought and enforced. Teenagers need parental input into how much money to pay for a car (and insurance) and how much may have to be sacrificed to obtain this status symbol. Adolescent workaholics will see schoolwork and social activities suffer, and parents have the responsibility to prevent this from happening.

GOAL 5: SEXUAL ACCEPTANCE AND PERFORMANCE

Virtually every adult knows what it is like to be absorbed with sex as a teenager. For adolescents, sexual activity is almost always a substitute for something missing from their lives. Acceptance, popularity, significance, attractiveness, and maturity can all be affirmed in the mind of a teen through sex. As we discussed earlier, the absence of a father can motivate an adolescent girl to prove to herself that she can attract the love of another male. If sex is seen as the only way this can be accomplished, then sex it will be!

Counselors and parents should be reminded that religious participation does not inoculate an adolescent against sexual impulses. Several researchers have demonstrated that religious participation does help restrain the onset of active sexuality in adolescents, but there is no guarantee of continued sexual responsibility.[27] It is important to have open lines of communication between parents and teenagers and for parents to model sexual values and behavior that are consistent with healthy sexuality.

GOAL 6: SOCIAL POWER THROUGH CHARM

"If you can't beat 'em, join 'em" goes the old refrain, and some adolescents have found that this old adage works for them. Teenagers have relatively little power in the adult world and are unlikely to acquire much influence in the near future. But a form of power can be obtained through manipulating adults with charm, cooperation, agreeability, and generally pleasant behavior. Most adults can recall at least one or two high school peers who used this method to get what they wanted, sometimes using compliments that were insincere or syrupy.

Peers often react with disgust when they see this happening—until they realize how adults respond. Some adults become annoyed and even confront the teen to get real and quit trying to con everybody. But if this charm method produces even limited successes, the teen's power needs will have been reinforced and similar con-artist traits may persist into adulthood.

Other adolescents will become super compliant and pleasing because of fear rather than a need for power. These kids are more afraid of being criticized and rejected than of needing to feel powerful. The young teen who continually asks the Sunday school teacher if there is anything he or she can do to help should arouse suspicion in an aware youth leader or teacher. Rarely criticized for being so helpful, this supercompliant teen could be heading for just about as much trouble as his or her rebellious counterpart.

GOAL 7: PHYSICAL ATTRACTIVENESS, STRENGTH, AND BEAUTY

Many adolescents believe they are what they look like. Often teenagers accept without question that their appearance not only influences but controls their peer relationships, popularity, group acceptance, and level of self-esteem.

We should not be surprised then to find adolescent males down in the recreation room pumping iron with their buddies and then comparing biceps and triceps in front of a full-length mirror. Nor would we expect anything but countless dollars spent at the cosmetic counter, hair dresser, and clothing boutique, and endless hours in front of the bathroom mirror on the part of adolescent girls. It is the nature of the adolescent "beast" to be absorbed, overwhelmed, and totally involved in improving appearance.

Adults should not criticize this behavior but should be on the alert for evidence of steroid use by boys and eating disorders in girls. The need to prove oneself physically is so powerful for nearly all adolescents that the slightest imperfection can take on immense importance even to the point of using illegal substances like steroids or self-starvation to improve one's appearance.

I participated in an interview with a football player who had confessed to using steroids heavily but had the sense to know when he was in over his head. His reply about the danger of steroids really shook me. "Yes" he said, "I knew I could die from as many pills and shots as I was taking, but at that point in my life, all I could think about was how 'big' I would look in the casket."

GOAL 8: BEING INTELLECTUAL

Good grades, perfect attendance, and teachers who love you must be a good sign. Right? Maybe.

Surely there are bright and well-motivated teenagers who will excel academically and who will be intellectual superiors to their peers. One does not choose to be bright anymore than one chooses to be slow. But we do find numbers of adolescents who are driven by a need to perform academically not for the sense of accomplishment such achievement provides, but to please parents and other adults.

For counselors and parents, it is difficult to detect which high-achievers are doing well because they want to and are gratified by their performance and which are achieving out of fear of failure, impossible ego ideals of perfection, or attempts to earn the love of parents through school performance. The challenge to do something falls to those with opportunities to compare adolescents with their peer group, who may know something about the teenager's family background, and who know how to intervene appropriately.

Generally, we can come close to identifying which high-achievers might be in trouble by assessing their out-of-school activities. A bright high-achiever who goes to athletic events and social activities and who seems to relate reasonably well with peers is probably not heading for trouble. On the other hand, a high-achieving teen who has no social life, spends long hours alone, expresses no interest in dating or sports, and who is described as moody or depressed is cause for concern.

GOAL 9: RELIGIOUS INVOLVEMENT

The inquisitive mind of teenagers draws them to all forms of spiritual, supernatural, and mystical ideas. There are board games that worry many parents because of the mystical or occult themes of the games. Cult recruiters know that the most vulnerable convert is an older adolescent who is away from home for the first time and who expresses an interest in higher ideals.

Many of the young people in our churches are in trouble because of imbalance in their spiritual concerns. They seek saint-like perfection but are stressed by their developing sexuality and need for peer approval. In conservative churches especially, we find adolescents from good families who are active in their youth groups and leaders among the other kids, but who are quickly diverted from the traditional church message into more extreme or even cultic religions because of their curiosity and need to experience new things.

Parents and youth leaders need to pay attention to the super serious Christian teenager who is well liked and universally respected but who does not seem to have much fun. These kids may be at risk for suicide because of their perceived failure to measure up, or later on in their twenties or thirties be at risk for a relapse into the adolescence they never had, which can destroy marriages and hurt children. Parents and youth leaders must insist that responsibilities be shared by youngsters in the youth groups and maintain a watchful eye for signs of too-intense involvement in spiritual matters, inappropriate for a young person of a given age.

Finally, we want to acknowledge that goals for our adolescents, especially long-term goals, are important and need to be encouraged. But we adults, parents, counselors, teachers, and church leaders must be vigilant for signs of imbalance. All good goals can become negative if extreme and unbalanced. We want to encourage goals for our teenagers, but only reasonable goals that are positively motivated rather than fear based.

<h2 style="text-align:center">CONCLUSION</h2>

Divorce represents a loss of a tangible part of life for a teenager. What is lost is not only one parent but a life the teen once had. Losses may include the family home, a comfortable school with good friends, financial sufficiency leading to the right clothing and a car at the sixteenth birthday, and the feeling of being normal. This is a lot to lose, and a reaction should be expected.

When working with adolescent children of divorce, it is helpful to conceptualize the process as one of grieving, just as one would grieve the death of someone close and cared for. What has died is a normal family to grow up in, future expectations of marital success, a feeling of being good replaced by a feeling of being guilty, and a general sense of being normal. We would expect an adolescent to grieve for the death of a family member, but here it is the family itself that has died.

Several researchers have independently identified emotional reactions common to adolescents experiencing a loss.[28] These include:

Denial:	"This can't be true. You can't be getting a divorce!"
Anger:	"How could you do this to me? You have ruined my life. Don't I matter to you two at all?"
Bargaining:	"Please reconsider. I promise to do better in school. I won't *ever* give you problems again. Honest. Just stay together and I'll be perfect."
Depression:	"My life is ruined. I'll never get over this. There's no hope at all now. I don't know what I'll do."
Panic:	"If they go through with this, I won't make it. What will I do? I don't want this to happen."

Guilt: "Yes, I hear what you are saying. All I am sure about though is that I *know* this is partially my fault. There *must* have been something I could have done to prevent this."

Worry: "I am *not* going to let myself get hurt this badly again. If this means staying single, then I'll be single. I will *not* do this to my children."

Adolescent egocentrism is evident in these examples, and that should be expected. We adults err in assuming that young adults and adolescents who look grown up think like adults too. That a teenager assumes he or she is responsible for their parents' decision to divorce is both pitiable and typical. Counselors, parents, teachers, and youth leaders can do no better than understand where the teenager's head is and react appropriately to his or her developmental needs. The responsibility to help and understand is ours, not theirs.

NOTES

1. J. S. Wallerstein and J. B. Kelly, "Responses of the Preschool Child to Divorce: Those Who Cope," in *Child Psychiatry: Treatment and Research*, ed. M. F. McMillan and S. Henao (New York: Brunner/Mazel, 1974).

2. Ibid; and A. D. Sorosky, "The Psychological Effect of Divorce on Adolescents," *Adolescence* 12 (1977): 123–36.

3. J. S. Wallerstein, "Children of Divorce: Preliminary Report of a Ten-Year Follow-up of Young Children," *American Journal of Orthopsychiatry* 54, no. 3 (1984): 444–58.

4. D. McLoughlin and R. Whitfield, "Adolescents and Their Experiences of Parental Divorce," *Journal of Adolescence* 7 (1984): 155–70.

5. T. S. Parish, "Ratings of Self and Parents by Youth: Are They Affected by Family Status, Gender, and Birth Order?" *Adolescence* 26, no. 101 (1991): 105–12.

6. R. Forehand et al., "Interparental Conflict and Paternal Visitation Following Divorce: The Interactive Effect on Adolescent Competence," *Child Study Journal* 20, no. 3 (1990): 193–202.

7. F. Heider, *The Psychology of Interpersonal Relations* (New York: Wiley, 1958).

8. T. S. Parish and S. E. Wigle, "A Longitudinal Study of the Impact of Parental Divorce on Adolescents' Evaluations of Self and Parents," *Adolescence* 20, no. 77 (1985): 239–44.

9. Wallerstein and Kelly, "Preschool Child."

10. Ibid.; Sorosky, "Psychological Effect," 123–36; and M. L. Bundy and P. N. White, "Parents as Sexuality Educators: A Parent Training Program," *Journal of Counseling and Development* 68 (January/February 1990): 321–23.

11. A. E. Craddock, "Family Structure and Sex-Role Orientation," *The American Journal of Family Therapy* 18, no. 4 (1990): 355–62.

12. K. L. Kinnaird and M. Gerrard, "Premarital Sexual Behavior and Attitudes toward Marriage and Divorce among Young Women as a Function of Their Mother's Marital Status," *Journal of Marriage and the Family* 48 (November 1986): 757–65.

13. J. Hepworth, R. S. Ryder, and A. S. Dreyer, "The Effects of Parental Loss on the Formation of Intimate Relationships," *Journal of Marriage and the Family* 10, no. 1 (1984): 73–82.

14. A. Booth and J. N. Edwards, "Age at Marriage and Marital Stability," *Journal of Marriage and the Family* (February 1985): 67–75.

15. C. Frentz, F. M. Gresham, and S. N. Elliott, "Popular, Controversial, Neglected, and Rejected Adolescents: Contrasts of Social Competence and Achievement Differences," *Journal of School Psychology* 29 (1991): 109–20.

16. G. A. Youngs, Jr. et al., "Adolescent Stress and Self-Esteem," *Adolescence* 25, no. 98 (1990): 333–41.

17. R. C. Simmons, F. Rosenberg, and M. Rosenberg, "Disturbance in the Self-Image of Adolescence," *American Sociological Review* 38 (1973): 553–68.

18. B. Raphael et al., "The Impact of Parental Loss on Adolescents' Psychological Characteristics," *Adolescence* 24, no. 99 (1990): 689–700.

19. Wallerstein and Kelly, "Preschool Child."

20. R. H. Needle, S. S. Su, and W. J. Doherty, "Divorce, Remarriage, and Adolescent Substance Use: A Prospective Longitudinal Study," *Journal of Marriage and the Family* 52 (1990): 157–69.

21. T. Kempton et al., "Presence of a Sibling as a Potential Buffer Following Parental Divorce: An Examination of Young Adolescents," *Journal of Clinical Child Psychology* 20, no. 4 (1991): 434–38; and A. McCombs and R. Forehand, "Adolescent School Performance Following Parental Divorce: Are There Family Factors That Can Enhance Success?" *Adolescence* 24, no. 96 (1989): 871–79.

22. Ibid.

23. Kempton et al., "Presence of a Sibling."

24. S. S. Farber, R. D. Felner, and J. Primavera, "Parental Separation/Divorce and Adolescents: An Examination of Factors Mediating Adaptation," *American Journal of Community Psychology* 13, no. 2 (1985): 171–84.

25. E. W. Kelly and T. J. Sweeney, "Typical Faulty Goals of Adolescents: A Base for Counseling," *The School Counselor* 29 (March 1979): 236–46.

26. Ibid.

27. A. Thornton and D. Camburn, "Religious Participation and Adolescent Sexual Behavior and Attitudes," *Journal of Marriage and the Family* 51 (1989): 641–53; A. E. Craddock, "Family Structure and Sex-Role Orientation," *The American Journal of Family Therapy* 18, no. 4 (1990): 355–62; and J. R. Udry,

"Biological Predispositions and Social Control in Adolescent Sexual Behavior," *American Sociological Review* 53 (1988): 709–22.

28. J. Bowlby, *Attachment and Loss: Separation* (New York: Basic Books, 1973); A. Freese, *Help for Your Grief* (New York: Schoken, 1977); R. Kavanaugh, *Facing Death* (Baltimore: Penguin Books, 1974); E. Kubler-Ross, *On Death and Dying* (New York: MacMillan, 1969); and G. Westberg, *Good Grief* (Philadelphia: Fortress Press, 1962).

Chapter 5

The Single Parent: Forever Changed

Divorce is like experiencing a death in the family and having to keep the corpse in your living room." So said a divorced mother of three struggling to cope as a single parent for almost four years. "It gets better, but it never goes away," she lamented, anxious for the dawn of a new life optimistically assured by friends and family.

Virginia Satir, well-known family therapist, reflected the feelings of this young mother in these words:

> Divorce is a metaphorical surgery which affects all areas of life of the individual. . . . For many people, divorce is a broken experience, and before they can go on with their lives, they need to be able to pick up the pieces. This period often includes deep emotional feelings of despair, disappointment, revenge, retaliation, hopelessness and helplessness.[1]

Just as people are expected to experience the denial-anger-bargaining-depression-acceptance process following the death of a loved one,[2] Sue and Ron Craig were experiencing their own process following the death of their marriage. Depression following any significant family trauma should be expected, and sociological studies have verified this expectation.[3] Four or five years after their divorce, people have been found to be significantly more depressed than never-married and still-married people. This continued depression may result from increased economic pressure, the feeling that one's standard of living has declined, and the loneliness associated with living without a partner after years of having had someone close.

Depression is particularly a problem when the divorce has violated one's personal value system. Sue Craig not only felt the sting of being a divorced woman, but of being a divorced *Christian* woman. Using *divorced* and *Christian* in the same description remains an impossible combination for many people.

Ron Craig was also beginning to experience his version of a divorce reaction. Where Sue felt injured and abused by her husband's decision to end their marriage, Ron, still a professing Christian, was experiencing guilt in ever greater amounts. Ron had begun to drink a little, only when alone, but he was finding alcohol an effective short-term solution to feeling guilty.

WHY DIVORCE ADJUSTMENT IS OFTEN DIFFICULT

There was no saving the Craig marriage. In anyone's mind the divorce was, in fact, final. For Ron, Sue, and their children, it was time to adapt to their new lifestyle and to get on with living. But there are obstacles in the road to recovery.

The society is two-parent oriented. Schools and other child-focused organizations do not seem to recognize that in many communities *most* children are living in single-parent families. Mail from school or day care comes addressed to "Mr. & Mrs.," often in spite of repeated requests by single parents to make the simple change on the envelope. Churches tend to think in terms of two-parent, father-headed homes regardless of the actual demographics of the neighborhood. One single parent told me that he felt as if the authorities believed that pretending single-parent families were rare might make them so.

Single parenting reduces the amount of emotional support available to both parents. Researchers have discovered clear evidence that separation and divorce increase one's likelihood of developing both psychological and physical problems.[4] The most accepted explanation for this increased risk is found in the reduction of emotional support available to people experiencing divorce. Emotional support means that the nondivorced segment of the population does not like to be around divorced people, is not comfortable allowing children to play together, and generally rejects attempts at socializing by separated or divorced people.

It is not unusual to hear from single parents in the church that they were surprised to be cut off by old same-sex friends after the divorce. Even pastors have only recently begun to acknowledge divorced people and single parents as a group in the church body meriting special attention. Though growing in acceptance, single-parent Sunday school classes and other special services are still considered to be experimental by church leadership. Rejection of the single-parent segment appears to be most prevalent in conservative churches.

I have had opportunity to conduct workshops for single parents in churches around the country. When I ask married people how they feel about welcoming single parents into the church, the strongest negative reaction comes from married women. Discussion reveals a not-too-hidden fear on the part of these wives and mothers that divorced women represent a threat to their own marriages. Unrealistic and emotional as such fears may be, they are common.

Parenting alone limits family wisdom. Whoever said "two heads are better than one" was not kidding. God ordained the two-parent family for many reasons. Some reasons are known and others are only suspected. One obvious reason for the two-parent family is that two adults should be able to make better decisions than one stressed-out single parent.[5] For example, parents need wisdom regarding school-based problems experienced by most children. There are decisions to be made about after-school and club activities, athletic team participation, and social activities for teens. Perhaps the most common and troubling decision facing parents has to do with their young person choosing the right kind of friends, and in this area, a two-parent united front is *much* more powerful than one parent standing alone.

Beyond wisdom, a two-parent family allows extremes to be controlled more effectively. Parental wisdom influences important decisions such as discipline (which may be too harsh or too lenient), rules and regulations for children of different ages, and acceptance of temporary failures and setbacks in childrearing.

Children in the one-parent family will have a reduced opportunity to see their parents work out disagreements, solve everyday problems, and still get along. Being raised by a single parent means that, to a greater or lesser degree, children are deprived of the chance to see wisdom in action.

Sex-role development may be hampered. Sex-role is understood by child development experts to be acquired between the ages of three and six, approximately. If a same-sex parent is unavailable during these critical years, the subtle refinements that lead to polarized and secure sex-role identity may be limited. Sex-role includes obvious aspects such as how one walks, talks, carries books, asks questions, flirts, shows aggression and submissiveness, as well as less obvious aspects such as mind-set and sexual orientation.

Having a father absent from the home deprives male children of an adult male role model but also often deprives female children of a normal female role model in that mother may be so stressed out and emotionally overburdened that girls in the family grow up never learning how a woman is expected to behave under reasonably normal conditions. Added to this is the possibility that mother may be too overtaxed to be available to her children as needed.

The custodial parent may experience an emotional reaction. Single mothers and single fathers in the counseling office have expressed to me how emotionally draining it is to go through even a friendly divorce. Parents report feeling lonely, rejected, odd, socially ostracized, hopeless, and forever and unalterably changed.

The custodial parent may experience the common reaction of being cut off from friends and family members of the former spouse. The law courts may have instituted no-fault divorce, but the orientation of not blaming anyone for an obvious marital failure is missing in many post-divorce families. There seems to be a real need to reject the idea that something as traumatic as a divorce could just happen. In many this leads to a felt need to point the finger of blame at someone—preferably someone from the *other* family.

The custodial parent may worry excessively about the impact of children being raised in a single-parent home. Parents, single or married, run the gamut of poor to excellent, and this range does not change after a divorce. Parents who were neglectful and careless while married will continue to be neglectful and careless after a divorce. Of course, the opposite is also true. Parents who are conscientious and careful will, though stressed and challenged as never before, usually continue to be conscientious and careful as single parents.

What changes is the way parents *feel* about their parenting. Both custodial and absent parents will experience a time of questioning regarding their ability to continue to be competent in their parenting activities. This self-doubt leads parents to shift from the normal range of parenting behaviors to one or the other extreme of parenting. Fear and worry will tend to push a parent who has been at the midpoint of the parenting continuum to one side or the other, to extreme leniency or excessive harshness. "Pushover or drill sergeant" was the way one therapist described this reaction in her single-parent clients.

As parents move to an extreme, so do children and teenagers. Children of all ages will adapt to what they see in their parents if at all possible. Thus, youngsters who have been more or less normal prior to a family breakup may react with extremes of behavior once the breakup occurs. Reactions happen because of the psychological need in child or teen to adapt, regardless of the consequences of the reaction. While counselors recognize that it is only with difficulty that parents can be brought to the point of maintaining pre-divorce parenting styles in the post-divorce family, this is precisely what is needed.

Researchers on the family have discovered that the attitudes about self and parenting held by single parents are powerful in controlling the actions of the single parent at home. Counselors are encouraged to pay attention to the mind-set and level of self-esteem manifested in the single parent.[6] Single parents need to be alerted to the power their attitudes have on their children. Both single parents with custody *and* noncustodial parents need to be counseled to be alert for signs of how they may be having an adverse influence on their children.[7]

THE SINGLE MOTHER WITH CUSTODY

Single-parent mothers have been found to be more rigid on several parenting variables compared to mothers with husbands present. Single mothers were especially concerned about expressions of aggression by the children as well as worrying about undue outside influences on the family. Single mothers appeared to be less secure in knowing whom to trust and in whom to place their confidence.[8]

Sexual information was a worry as well. With no male present to deal with boys in the family and an unwillingness to ask a former husband to assume this responsibility, single mothers are left with uncertainty in knowing how to teach their sons about sex. Economic hardship was another concern that was typically assigned to the former husband and absent father. Single mothers reported feeling worried about their general status in the community and felt that status reduced by post-divorce financial pressure. Single mothers correctly believed that raising children alone would place their children at increased risk for acting out, general maladjustment, and for more problems in raising boys.[9]

THE WORKING CUSTODIAL MOTHER

Several factors determine the work status of custodial mothers following divorce. While the need to work is a complex and multifaceted issue, some generalizations can be made based on recent research. Those factors that appear to control maternal employment are:

1. The number of preschool children in the home. Where there are fewer children, employment is more likely.

2. The child's age. Older children are more likely than younger children to have working mothers.

3. Level of education. Mothers with higher levels of education are more likely to be employed.

4. Maternal age. Older mothers are more likely to be employed than younger mothers.[10]

THE NONCUSTODIAL FATHER

We will examine the life of the father with custody later in this chapter. However, given the reduced likelihood of a father being granted custody (estimated to be less than 5 percent of custody arrangements), it may be more effective to focus first on noncustodial fathers.

Absent fathers tend to experience guilt and depression in about equal proportion to their felt responsibility in the divorce and the visitation that they maintain with their children. Ron Craig was certainly experiencing such feelings and was doing what so many noncustodial fathers do to make themselves feel better. He resorted to alcohol as a pain killer. Ron is typical in this regard to many other absent fathers, and his behavior brings to mind a former client who was also an absent father. Though extreme, his story illustrates the power of guilt in leading absent fathers to maintain contact with their children.

My first contact with the Drumbaugh family was through the mother of the wife seeking a divorce. The Drumbaughs were a church family as were both sets of grandparents, and it was Betty Drumbaugh's mother who spoke to me at church and asked if I would be able to see her daughter and son-in-law if they were willing to see a counselor. This grandmother warned me that the situation was quietly becoming desperate and if something was not done quickly, separation and divorce appeared to be unavoidable.

The first appointment was made and then canceled, as was the second. I knew that the dissolution of this family had probably begun in spite of the best efforts of the pastor and others. Some time after the divorce, Betty Drumbaugh made an appointment to see me with her son and only child, ten-year-old Scott. A reason for the appointment was not offered.

Betty came into the counseling office and left Scott out in the waiting room. She wanted to share with me that Scott had been diagnosed with a rare bone disease that was beginning to disfigure him and would eventually, without the discovery of a cure, take his life. The doctors said that Scott would probably not live past twenty and would spend his last year or two of life bedridden and probably hospitalized. A severe blow without doubt, but I was to learn that this was not the reason they had come for a counseling session. What had prompted the appointment was that Scott's father, since learning the news about his son's condition, had drastically reduced his visits, and Scott was reacting very negatively.

Betty explained that Scott's condition was hereditary on his father's side of the family, and while her husband did not have the condition himself, he was a carrier and had passed it on to his son. I found through other sources that Scott's father was being driven away by shame and guilt over what he believed to be his fault—his responsibility for the disease that would kill his only son.

Scott's father could not face his son because of his guilt. While different in degree from other divorced fathers, this father was similar to others in felt responsibility for post-divorce problems. Whether real or imagined, the majority of non-custodial fathers seem to blame themselves for the breakup of their family and all the negative results that typically follow. So many divorces, even among Christian families, result from stress created by an adulterous relationship on the part of the husband, physical or emotional abuse, or financial hardship. Stress that results in separation and divorce often causes guilt for both parents but in the extreme for the absent father. Scott Drumbaugh's father provides a sad but common example of the feelings experienced by so many divorced and absent fathers.

There are four broad sets of circumstances that lead to reduced father-child contact after a divorce.

1. *The battle rages on.* Many fathers report that due to the continuing conflict with their former spouses, they find it nearly

impossible to make reasonable arrangements to spend time with their children. The children's mother may make arrangements that intentionally interfere with what she knows to be court-mandated and controlled visitation privileges. Often the activities that are used as an excuse for not allowing the children to spend time with their father are fun activities such as movies and amusement parks. Mothers know that even if the children would like to see their father, which is typical, choosing between a day with Dad or a day at the amusement park usually results in a day without Father. This is a form of psychological bribery perpetrated on children but one that is difficult for the court authorities to deal with if the absent father complains. When the children are expressing a wish to go ahead and do the fun activity, Father knows that by the time he makes an interference complaint to the court, the time for visitation will be long past. Of course, children do not realize that they are being manipulated by an angry and hurt mother. All they know is that for some unknown reason, they are not seeing their father as much as they expected.

2. *Roadblocks and obstacles.* Both parents experience significant life changes, but the noncustodial father's experiences are in many ways unique. Sometimes, for example, Father may have to take a job that requires lengthy commuting every day. Since he arrives home late and leaves early, he is unavailable for the children except on weekends. Or perhaps he is remarried and has assumed new financial responsibilities making additional work hours necessary.

Still others might experience personal problems stemming from divorce-based guilt, leading to alcohol or drug abuse. In time, such fathers might be in required drug or alcohol rehabilitation programs that could interfere even more with regular visitation. A few fathers might be in jail or prison. Some will be in the military and gone for various lengths of time ranging from one weekend a month to several months or even years overseas. Perhaps the absent father is experiencing unusually severe psychological and emotional reactions after the divorce and is limited in what he feels up to doing.

3. *Distance is too great.* It is common for a divorcing couple to experience an intense desire *not* to see one another for a while.

Unless Father has relatives in the area, he may choose employment elsewhere to escape the stigma of others knowing he is a divorced father with children and therefore, in the eyes of some, of no character or value. We know that income declines for both husband and wife after a divorce, more for the wife than the husband. This is somewhat misleading in that pure income statistics do not take into account the expenses involved in moving, settling into a new job, or finding a place to live.

4. *Children are getting older.* Parents in intact families know how difficult it can be to schedule any kind of activity or event and assure that all family members will be there. As children become teenagers and move away from the family sphere and into the peer group, visitation with the absent parent becomes less valued and more of an interference with the normal process of adolescent living. Even though Father does not live at home any longer, he is still "just" a parent, and in comparison to the fun of spending time with friends, going to miniature golf or a movie with Dad can become a duty rather than the pleasure it once was.

It is the nature of the adolescent to complain about parents to friends. A scheduled time with Father can be both an opportunity to complain to friends about how difficult life has become *and* a chance to express rebellion and independence. Noncustodial fathers regularly report a decline in visitation as children reach adolescence but note that it is the teenager who wants to limit contact, not Dad.

Beyond these four most common problem areas, absent fathers identify several other factors that also discourage regular contact.[11] These are:

Reason	Percent of Fathers
1. Adversarial divorce or custody proceedings	39%
2. Required to return to court at a later time, thus interfering with work	36%
3. Considerable conflict at separation	72%
4. More conflict immediately after the divorce	19%

5. Ex-wife uncooperative with visits at the time of
   the divorce   36%
6. Ex-wife uncooperative with visits now   32%
7. Father desired considerably more visitation time
   at the time of the divorce   18%
8. Father desires considerably more visitation time now   35%

Ron Craig had been experiencing several of these factors and was struggling, as he put it, to maintain sanity while producing income for two families. In my extensive sessions with Sue Craig and infrequent conversations with her former husband, Ron, I had the distinct feeling that both were expressing some degree of "If I had known it was going to be this difficult after the divorce, I would have tried harder to work it out." This was nothing more than speculation on my part, but I believe I have seen evidence of this in the intervening months.

My counseling with Ron will be discussed in detail in a later chapter, but it may be appropriate to introduce now some of the concerns faced by fathers in Ron's position. I want to emphasize that Ron Craig did not experience all of these problems.

For example, divorced fathers often have intense anger toward their ex-spouse, and whether these feelings are justified or not, they need to be resolved before additional divorce adjustment can occur. Most fathers are naive about court proceedings, and many are blown away by the aggressive stance of a wife's attorney. Fathers report feeling overwhelmed upon the realization that an outside authority now has major control over the family. Income, expenditures, visitation, even the freedom to move away may now be controlled in whole or in part by court-appointed authorities. Some divorced fathers feeling this pressure have sought help in advocacy organizations for divorced fathers without custody.

There will be fathers whose sexual orientation, once known, may cause the divorce judge to place constraints upon visitation. Some fathers will have alcohol or drug problems, pre- or post-divorce, that may cause a judge to limit the father's freedom to see his children. Those fathers who have moved away will need help dealing with guilt over the decision to leave and the resulting less frequent contacts with the children.[12]

We will focus on counseling strategies later, but for now we can emphasize the human tragedy that commonly surrounds divorce. Who suffers? In most cases, the answer is "everyone!" Exceptions exist, of course, but it remains true that very few people are truly better off after a divorce than before.

FATHERS WITH CUSTODY

The most important single factor controlling the ability of the father with custody to do a competent job of parenting was found to be whether or not he had chosen to be the custodial parent.[13] Those who desired custody tended to possess strong, positive beliefs about being a parent and had been highly involved in child care from the beginning. These fathers had demonstrated an early desire to be involved in the lives of their children, and this desire had continued after the divorce. It is important for family therapists and divorce counselors to note that motivation for seeking custody is all-important. Fathers *and* mothers who are seeking custody as a form of revenge or out of a need to prove something to themselves will very likely eventually have difficulty with their single-parent role.[14]

Particular stressors on the single father with custody include:[15]

Finances. We have known for some time that income level and standard of living decline more for custodial mothers than noncustodial fathers. It is now known that custodial fathers experience a similar, though less extreme, decline in income and living standard.

Childcare. Father is more likely to have been employed prior to the divorce and is also more likely to try to continue normal full-time employment after the divorce. Whereas many mothers with custody will not work outside the home or will work only part-time and so need childcare less frequently, fathers with custody will almost universally need to find full-time childcare to enable them to continue working. Both the expense and the logistics of the childcare can quickly become a significant burden to the working single father with custody.

Social life. A feeling of social isolation commonly afflicts divorced parents, but there seems to be more social ostracism and less social support for single fathers with custody. There are a variety of social support groups for single parents, but in recent years the emphasis has appeared to shift from parenting support to providing an avenue for making social contacts. More than a few divorced parents have complained that what they believed to be a support group was in reality a dating club.

Homemaking. Previous research on the adjustment of single fathers with custody revealed that fathers can be expected to do well if (1) there is anticipatory socialization allowing the custodial father to plan ahead for social activities and recreation, (2) prior experience in childrearing, (3) education in child development, (4) previous participation in household responsibilities, (5) prior participation in child discipline, and (6) prior experience in nurturing the children. Some would sarcastically ask why a husband who has been doing all these things would be involved in a divorce in the first place.[16]

Personal problems. Divorce is generally accepted to be one of the primary stressors of modern life and naturally carries with it guilt, physical and psychological exhaustion, social isolation, social castigation, and anxiety. Add to these adjustment challenges the normal problems of childrearing while employed, and it should be easy to recognize that any custodial parent, male or female, is going to be significantly stressed-out for a year or two following the divorce.

Lack of community support for single fathers with custody. This problem afflicts the custodial father in about equal proportion to mothers with custody. As we have seen, schools, churches, government agencies, and businesses routinely assume that if there is a father at home, there must be a mother there too. Custodial fathers commonly express frustration at how often they feel called upon to explain their situation, sometimes to near strangers.

WHY FATHERS GET CUSTODY

Research conducted during the last decade reveals the following reasons for divorce and eventual child custody by the father. Through information supplied by divorced husbands and fathers, researchers have verified these conclusions.[17]

Divorces That Lead to Child Custody by the Father

REASONS FOR THE DIVORCE:

1. Shared reasons—both partners felt about equally responsible for the divorce.   30%

2. Infidelity—the wife had been sexually unfaithful.   25%

3. Wife left the marriage—for varied and often unspecified reasons, the wife and mother decided to leave husband *and* children.   19%

4. Wife had a serious problem—the wife was alcoholic, abusive, mentally ill, etc.   12%

REASONS FOR THE FATHER BEING GRANTED CHILD CUSTODY:

1. Mutual agreement.   36.6%

2. Children chose to live with father.   26.3%

3. Father could provide better living conditions.   21.6%

4. Wife could no longer handle the children.   19.6%

5. Father won the custody battle.   19.4%

6. Wife deserted the family.   19.2%

7. Father and mother agreed that father was a better parent.   13.9%

8. Wife wanted to avoid a court battle.   10.7%

Other specialists in divorce adjustment have concluded that there are clear and rational reasons for a mother surrendering custody of the children to their father. For example, 72 percent of noncustodial mothers believed that things had worked out better because the father was granted child custody. For some mothers the decision was based on the belief that surrendering the children was the only way to escape further emotional and physical abuse by the husband. Researchers also found that younger mothers tended to have less contact with the children over time and that visitation by noncustodial mothers of any age tended to follow a U-shaped curve, frequent visitation right after the divorce with a gradual decline as the children become older, and then increasing again as the children reach adulthood.[18]

Single Parent Lifestyle Types

We know that children raised in single-parent homes tend to be more resilient and responsible than their counterparts raised in intact homes. While obvious negatives also exist, we can be reminded that single parenting is not automatically traumatic or failure-bound. Many experts in the field hold that single-parent families possess strengths that intact families are missing. Families in which one parent is trying to fulfill all parental roles and responsibilities should be encouraged to consider a more reasonable expectation for themselves. While there are special considerations for Christian parents in these circumstances, such considerations relate more to therapy than actual life. Counselors will find that emotions such as anger, rejection, or depression will appear with equal frequency regardless of a person's religious belief system. Competent counselors of any religious orientation will need to factor in the religious belief structure of a divorced client and use that religious faith as a support for therapy. Balance is the key when working with a client with strong religious beliefs.

Sole Executive

This is the single parent who has assumed total control and responsibility for the family. This single parent has been described as a tyrannized parent who feels compelled to meet all the children's needs alone. Responsibility for nurturing, meeting basic physical needs such as food, clothing, and shelter, educating, and socializing the children are felt to rest at this parent's weary feet. If we remember that more than 90 percent of custodial parents are mothers, we can begin to understand the high stress levels experienced by parents who find themselves in this category.

The sole executive single parent will need help in finding a role that is less stress-producing while still guilt-reducing. This is not an easy task. As the challenge continually goes unmet, as is surely going to happen in this type family, the overwhelmed single parent will feel shame and a sense of failure for being imperfect. Stress will continue to build, accompanied by more guilt, fatigue, anger, and an ever-growing sense of failure.

Counseling strategies with stressed-out single parents often involve groups. Other single parents who are at different levels of adjustment can be helpful in suggesting ways to reduce stress levels while dealing more realistically with parental responsibility. Groups can also be helpful in providing social support.

Some single parents will have found a way to function as sole executive and still maintain their sanity. The term *coordinating expert* fits this category. This is the parent who has been able to become the only adult on board while still being able to delegate responsibility. When this happens, exhaustion and stress are reduced. In explaining why some parents are able to utilize this strategy while others remain overwhelmed, it is thought that the parenting experienced in the family of origin must have been both competent and clear, leading to well-learned lessons that have now surfaced in the single parent's own family.

AUXILIARY PARENT

The auxiliary parent is the noncustodial parent who does not live with the children and who does not bear primary responsibility for their upbringing. The primary parent retains control of the basic life circumstances of the children including discipline, socialization, the residence, education, and decision making while the auxiliary parent visits, supports emotionally and financially, and generally functions more as a visiting relative than a parent.

It seems obvious that conflict between parents would control to a great degree the role of the auxiliary parent and the resulting impact on the children. The more conflict children experience, the less willing they will be to accept the auxiliary parent as a parent.

UNRELATED OR RELATED SUBSTITUTES

Divorced parents with sufficient financial resources may seek to provide a mother surrogate. This can be accomplished by hiring a live-in mother substitute. These employees are sometimes called nannies and serve as combination cook, babysitter, and housekeeper for the family. Extended family members who find themselves at a point in life where moving in with another family is appropriate can also become parent substitutes. Depending on the age and developmental status of the children, the parent substitute can be a helpful adaptation.

Care must be exercised when choosing a substitute from a group of siblings. Role confusion often results when a sibling assumes parental responsibility for younger children. While this arrangement can work, it is filled with possible pitfalls for everyone involved. This is especially true when new responsibilities limit the socialization and development of the older sibling now in charge of the family.

TITULAR PARENT

This parent has abandoned, in part or in whole, his or her parenting role in the family. Essentially surrendering to the stress of being a single parent, this parent has, in effect, become one of the dependent children.[19]

When intergenerational boundaries are blurred to this extent, all family members are at risk. Strategies to prevent, correct, and discourage this problem include helping the single parent accept the responsibilities of being a parent, helping to find and apply better conflict-resolution strategies with children, learning stress-reduction methods, permitting the child to express feelings about family changes, and examining and modifying parent-child communication patterns.[20]

Parental abdication will be more or less a challenge to prevent depending on the life circumstances of the family and the custodial parent's willingness to resume an authoritative role with the children. Success is controlled to a large extent by the support available to the single parent and is directly related to problem behaviors that may be showing up in the children. How post-divorce stress affects the parent-child relationship and either encourages or discourages adjustment is summarized in the following comments:

• Single mothers reported more parenting stress and perceived the children as having significantly more behavior problems when compared to mothers in intact families.

There is a direct cause-and-effect problem involved in attempting to learn if poor parenting created misbehaving children or if the presence of misbehaving children might have diminished parental effectiveness. There is no disputing that the two factors are related.

- Single-parent children interacted with their mothers with more total deviance and noncompliance than children in intact families.

- Single mothers were observed to be more critical and authoritarian and used more spanking for child control than others.

- In contrast to the remarried or still-married mothers, single mothers were significantly more depressed, lonely, less satisfied with life, and more controlling and negative in their parenting.[21]

Those conducting this research conclude that there is an important need to develop multifaceted parent training programs that not only teach more positive parenting skills but also incorporate stress management and interpersonal relationship skills. Others have found that single parents have the least amount of time available to spend in chosen activities with overall single-parent time available being 1.8 hours per day compared to 6.0 hours for mothers in intact families. More specifically, if the single mother works, she will average .75 hours per day to spend with the children versus 1.4 hours per day for the employed married mother. In terms of recreational time available, single mothers who work averaged 2.4 hours of kick-back-and-relax time per day compared to 2.6 hours for working married mothers. This compares with 5.5 hours of free time for nonemployed single mothers and 4.8 hours for nonemployed married mothers.[22]

RAISING THE OVERBURDENED CHILD

Judith Wallerstein, a recognized authority on children in single-parent homes, has concluded that the average time needed for divorced women to reestablish a sense of continuity in their lives ranged between three and three-and-a-half years. For divorced men, the recovery time needed is two to two-and-a-half years.[23] There is no doubt that this adjustment period will have a profound impact on children and adolescents in the family. Specifically, children and adolescents most at risk are those who:

- take on primary responsibility for their own upbringing;

- are called upon to meet the psychological and emotional needs of regressed parents following a divorce;

- are the targets of continued disputes between divorced parents; and

- experience a subsequent parental divorce.

Though the emphasis in this chapter is on divorced parents who are forever changed by the experience, no one should doubt that the feelings experienced and understandings gained by young people in the family will have a powerful and long-term impact on the ability of single parents to adjust successfully.

Children themselves highlight the dilemma they face in a study involving forty fourteen-year-olds who had lived in a single-parent family an average of 4.7 years. These young people listed the advantages of living with just one parent as:

1. being closer to mother (in most cases, the custodial parent);

2. having more responsibility;

3. helping with household chores;

4. getting along better with siblings;

5. having more friends;

6. being trusted more by both parents;

7. being able to move to a new area and start over; and

8. being closer to father.

Disadvantages listed were:

1. not being close enough to father;

2. having to move into a different house or apartment;
3. being asked to help out more at home;
4. coming home after school to an empty house;
5. having more responsibility;
6. moving to a new area;
7. not getting along as well with siblings; and
8. having fewer friends.[24]

It does not take much analysis to see the conflicting attitudes possessed by this sample of single-parent youngsters. Good and bad elements are apparent, but the young person's way of understanding and dealing with those elements are problematic for some and not for others. Counselors and other helpers will need to be prepared to hear and validate feelings and attitudes that may not appear to be consistent or congruent. These often are specifically the reasons why children of divorce should be able to benefit from counseling.[25]

School was not mentioned in the survey cited above, but other research has revealed disturbing statistics about the impact of divorce on school-age children. A study conducted by the National Association of Elementary School Principals (NAESP) involved approximately eighteen thousand elementary and secondary school children in fourteen states and reached the following conclusions:

1. At the primary level, 38 percent of single-parent elementary school children were low achievers compared to 25 percent of children from intact, two-parent homes.

2. At the secondary level, 34 percent of the one-parent children were low achievers as compared to 23 percent of those from two-parent homes.

3. Three times as many single-parent secondary school-age children were expelled from school compared to their counterparts from intact families.

4. Single-parent children at both levels were more likely to

be late for school, truant, and receive some form of disciplinary action.[26]

There are no serious grounds for challenging the overall negative effects of divorce on children and the subsequent impact those children will have on their single parent. There is a great deal of cause and effect analysis needed when studying this issue and preparing to counsel with a divorced family. I have found one of the major challenges of my work with single-parent families is to determine if child or adolescent misbehavior is creating the stress being experienced by a single parent or if ineffective parenting techniques and attitudes are at the root of child and adolescent misbehavior.

We know that single parents are going to struggle with a wide variety of personal and family concerns. In our example, whether Sue and Ron Craig will be able to raise Kevin, Alicia, Emily, and Scott successfully following their failed marriage has not yet been decided and will not be decided for many years. Sue and Ron Craig face the challenge to reassemble their lives, and each will develop their own format for doing so. Ron is, in many ways, the typical absent father experiencing all the guilt, remorse, defensiveness, and so many other feelings we would expect from a father in his position. Sue has and will continue to have her own struggles with depression, guilt, and exhaustion. Factor in the growing and ever changing developmental needs of their four children and it quickly becomes apparent that there is a major puzzle being created. It may fall to counselors and other helpers to find ways to put the puzzle back together. The problem will be the realization that some pieces of the puzzle are permanently missing and may have to be replaced rather than found.

Underlying this "crazy quilt" of emotions is the knowledge in Ron and Sue that as Christians, they have additional responsibilities to raise their children in the nurture and admonition of the Lord. This is no easy task under the best of circumstances and Ron and Sue are light-years away from the best.

NOTES

1. B. Fisher, *Rebuilding: When Your Relationship Ends* (San Luis Obispo, Calif.: Impact Publishers, 1981), 1.
2. E. Kubler-Ross, *On Death and Dying* (New York: MacMillan, 1969).
3. E. G. Menaghan and M. A. Lieberman, "Changes in Depression Following Divorce: A Panel Study," *Journal of Marriage and the Family* 48 (1986): 319–28.
4. G. C. Kitson and L. A. Morgan, "The Multiple Consequences of Divorce," *Journal of Marriage and the Family* 52 (1990): 913–24.
5. E. A. Blechman and M. Manning, "A Reward-Cost Analysis of the Single-Parent Family," in *Behavior Modification and Families*, ed. E. J. Mash, L. A. Hamerlynck, and L. C. Handy (New York: Brunner/Mazel, 1976).
6. S. Machida and S. D. Holloway, "The Relationship between Divorced Mothers' Perceived Control over Child Rearing and Children's Post-Divorce Development," *Family Relations* 40 (1991): 272–78.
7. M. M. Brevino, "The 87 Percent Factor," *The Delta Kappa Gamma Bulletin* 54, no. 3 (1988): 9–16.
8. D. W. Phelps, "Parental Attitudes toward Family Life and Child Behavior of Mothers in Two-Parent and One-Parent Families," *Journal of School Health* 39 (1969): 43–46.
9. W. F. Hodges, R. C. Wechsler, and C. Ballantine, "Divorce and the Preschool Child," *Journal of Divorce* 3 (1979): 55–69.
10. D. J. Eggebeen, "Determinants of Maternal Employment: White Preschool Children: 1960–1980," *Journal of Marriage and the Family* (1988): 149–59.
11. J. R. Dudley, "Increasing Our Understanding of Divorced Fathers Who Have Infrequent Contact with Their Children," *Family Relations* 40 (1991): 279–85.
12. Ibid., 280.
13. H. A. Mendes, "Single Fatherhood," *Social Work* 21 (1976): 308–12.
14. B. J. Risman, "Can Men 'Mother'? Life as a Single Father," *Family Relations* 35 (1986): 95–102.
15. B. Schlesinger, "Children's Viewpoints of Living in a One-Parent Family," *Journal of Divorce* 5 (1982): 1–23.
16. R. M. Smith, "The Impact of Fathers on Delinquent Males," *Dissertation Abstracts International* 35, no. 10-A (1976): 6487–88.
17. G. L. Grief, "Single Fathers Rearing Children," *Journal of Marriage and the Family* (February 1985): 185–91.
18. G. L. Grief and F. Emad, "A Longitudinal Examination of Mothers without Custody: Implications for Treatment," *The American Journal of Family Therapy* 17, no. 2 (1989): 155–63.
19. B. H. Johnson, "Single Mothers Following Separation and Divorce: Making It on Your Own," *Family Relations* 36 (1986): 189–97.
20. D. S. Glenwick and J. D. Mowrey, "When Parent Becomes Peer: Loss of Intergenerational Boundaries in Single Parent Families," *Family Relations* 35 (1986): 57–62.

21. C. Webster-Stratton, "The Relationship of Marital Support, Conflict, and Divorce to Parent Perceptions, Behaviors, and Childhood Conduct Problems," *Journal of Marriage and the Family* 51 (1989): 417–30.

22. M. M. Sanik and T. Mauldin, "Single- Versus Two-Parent Families: A Comparison of Mothers' Time," *Family Relations* 35 (1986): 53–56.

23. J. S. Wallerstein, "The Overburdened Child: Some Long-Term Consequences of Divorce," *Social Work* (March/April 1985): 116–24.

24. Ibid., 117.

25. Schlesinger, "Children's Viewpoints," 14.

26. National Association of Elementary School Principals Report, "One-Parent Families and Their Children," *Principal* 60, no. 1 (1980): 31–37.

Chapter 6

The Remarriage Family

Ron Craig has married the woman he left Sue to be with. A few years younger than her new husband, the new Mrs. Ron Craig brings two young children to the marriage. Ron and Sue's four children from their first marriage experienced a mixture of anger, confusion, and depression upon learning that their father had remarried. Sue admitted to feeling both gratified and angry—gratified that some other woman would have to deal with Ron's apparent lack of reliability within a marriage, and anger when she thought of all that had been lost, now never to be regained under any circumstances.

Yet Sue also felt a strange kind of empathy for Ron's new wife, Rebecca—an empathy built on the knowledge that Sue also would probably marry again and would herself bring children into that second marriage. What would she do when faced with an opportunity to share her life with someone new? How would she feel with a different last name, different friends, different church perhaps? And what would the children think?

Sue was not yet at a point where remarriage was something she could let herself think about seriously. At the moment, she was absorbed with the children and all the struggles they were facing and could not imagine bringing a new husband into that mix. But Sue also admitted that she knew it would probably happen someday. She was beginning to feel lonely.

Sue had been able to rationalize her divorce from Ron because there really was no other option. Everyone who knew anything about the Craig family acknowledged that Ron's public behavior and his decision to be unfaithful made it virtually impossible for Sue to continue in the marriage. Sue did not want to divorce Ron, but his behavior forced the decision. But the possibility of a second marriage would be totally Sue's decision. If she continued to think remarriage was wrong, how would she deal with those feelings? Sue had become accustomed to the role of the suffering martyr, but if she decided to get married again, she could find herself in the role (at least in her own mind) of being the "other" woman.

PLANNING FOR THE SECOND MARRIAGE

We learn to be parents by being children, and we learn to be husbands and wives by being children. We are not surprised to find that marriage expectations come from the family we grew up in, and with second marriages no less than first, we base our hopes and dreams on the foundation of what we learned long ago.

Unlike the first marriage, the second often comes with children as standard equipment—ready-made and ready to go! Certainly there are second marriages that do not involve children, but they are in the minority. The rate for second marriages has been estimated to be extremely high. One study found that approximately 80 percent of divorced people remarried within three years.[1] A report from *American Demographics Magazine* cited statistics from the National Center for Health Statistics as follows:[2]

1. Second marriages involving one or both partners
    who are widowed.   11%

2. Second marriages involving one partner marrying
   for the first time. 50%
3. Second marriages involving both partners remarrying. 39%

Other researchers have surprised even themselves with the complexity of second marriages involving children. They suggest that in a nuclear family made up of two parents, two children, and four grandparents there are 28 possible pairings and 247 different possible combinations. If one parent remarries a person with three children, there are now 136 pairs and 131,054 possible combinations! It will come as no surprise to learn that the same researchers who did all this figuring propose that it will take approximately two years for a second marriage involving children to stabilize. [3]

A Christian Perspective

It would be presumptive for anyone to claim to have the final and authoritative word on a subject as controversial as second marriages among divorced Christians. Notice that the title of this section is "A Christian Perspective" rather than "The Christian Perspective." My position is that the Bible is inerrant and authoritative on all matters addressed. In reality, though, God has seen fit to provide us with a maximum of principles and a minimum of specificity on the subject of second marriages and single parenting. Bible scholars are often at odds over whether second marriages can, under certain circumstances, meet God's criteria for an approved marriage. Questions arise as to the spiritual component related to remaining married to a person who has turned his or her back on the Lord and is threatening to take the children along on a downward trek, or how much physical or mental abuse one should take before deciding that survival is more important than maintaining respectability by remaining married.

My position is that the appropriateness of second marriages is basically an open question, and beyond that, it may well be a moot point. In my conversations with church leadership as I travel the country doing single-parent workshops, I try to lovingly tell them that if they wish to minister to single parents in their churches, they will have to come to the point where they accept, if not support, second marriages.

The reality is, divorced people *will* remarry. The question of whether they should or not is answered by statistics that indicate they are going to do it regardless of what their religious leaders think about it. Shall we in the pastorate and the helping professions learn to deal with their decisions, accept them as people but consider them second-class Christians, or cast them out of the church altogether? Shall we accept them and their new family and let God sort them out, or should we try to do the sorting ourselves? Divorce and second marriages are a fact of Christian life in the last days of the current century, and there is no indication that we should expect a reversal of the trend.

Does God hate divorce? The answer is a resounding "yes" (see Mal. 2:16). Is divorce ever permissible? Again, the answer is "yes," and verification can be found in Ezra 10:44 (RSV), and Matthew 19:9.

Note, however, that divorce is not the major question in this discussion. Remarriage is the issue, and on that we have much less clear support for any one position. If we counselors cannot accept the truth that remarriage is a fact of Christian life today, we are going to miss a wonderful opportunity to help a large group of people on the fringes of our churches waiting for an invitation to come in out of the cold. Can we say they are not welcome? Do we believe that while it takes two to make a marriage, it takes but one to make a divorce?

Jesus may have given us a special insight into how God feels about second marriages. Consider the New Testament words of Jesus warning about child abuse in any of its several forms:

> But whoso shall offend one of these little ones which believe in me, it were better for him that a millstone were hanged about his neck, and that he were drowned in the depth of the sea. Woe unto the world because of offences! for it must need be that offences will come; but woe to that man by whom the offence cometh (Matt. 18:6–7 KJV).

Now considering the power and threat in these words, is it conceivable that this same Jesus would sacrifice the well-being of children in a second marriage to honor the letter of the law some believe exists against second marriages? I will not try to answer that question for anyone but myself. I cannot convince myself that it is better to let children suffer the deprivations of being raised in a single-parent home for the sake of legalistic purity. I cannot see that Jesus, whose every word about children is kind, protective, and compassionate would want them to pay the price for what their elders have done. Perhaps it is time to put the theological question in the hands of theologians and reaffirm our position of simply being helpers. Let every counselor become a Berean and search the Scriptures for his or her own answer to this dilemma.

THE NEW STEPFAMILY

Emily and John Visher, founders of the Stepfamily Association of America and acknowledged authorities on the stepfamily, have suggested that stepfamilies grow, develop, and change at different rates and in response to different sets of circumstances.[4] We can apply their insights to the Christian stepfamily.

STEPFAMILY CHARACTERISTICS

The new family has experienced many changes and losses. Remarriage usually occurs before the children have had an opportunity to adequately resolve their grief associated with the divorce and subsequent loss of their original family. The major determinant of whether a child will adjust well to the second marriage is whether the original divorce trauma is resolved.[5]

Ron Craig and his new wife and stepchildren were each experiencing their own grief processes. Each parent had gone through a divorce, Ron as the main protagonist of the divorce and his new wife, Rebecca, as a victim of her abusive husband. Rebecca's two sons had lost their biological father and had gained a new father in Ron. Everyone had changed residence at least once since their respective divorce and remarriage. Rebecca's boys had changed schools, churches, and friends.

The boys were struggling with the feeling that they would not see their paternal grandparents anymore, and even though this proved to be untrue, it still worried them for some time.

Rebecca had to go through the hassle and emotional turmoil of changing her name yet again on her driver's license, social security card, credit cards, and what seemed like a million more documents and papers. She had to explain to old friends met in the shopping mall or post office that she was married again and to whom. Of course, Ron had to do the same. Divorced people, whether remarried or not, frequently comment that these street-corner explanations of what is going on in their lives represent one of the greatest hassles of being divorced or remarried.

Family members experience incongruent individual, marital, and family life cycles. Ron was much older than Rebecca and at a more advanced stage of his career compared to Rebecca's first husband. It was a source of contention that Ron was not as willing to take days off when Rebecca wanted to take a brief family vacation or trip to visit relatives. Her first husband had not been so uptight about work, she told friends on more than one occasion.

In spite of the arguments and violence the boys had witnessed before their father was forced to leave their family, they missed his willingness to wrestle and play rough physical games. Ron was older and not as physically fit and was just not as interested in getting down on the floor and messing around as the boys would have liked.

Rebecca naturally had friends who were much closer to her age than Ron's. On those rare occasions when Ron would agree to socialize with Rebecca's friends and their husbands, he felt out of place. This, too, became a source of conflict in the early weeks and months of Ron and Rebecca's marriage. Church even became a problem. Ron and Rebecca were committed to going to church and trying to be as actively involved as they each had been before their marriages ended. As small an issue as it may seem to those who have not experienced it, choosing a Sunday school class was a major problem. Just as with their friends, Ron felt out of place in the adult Sunday school class appropriate for Rebecca's age group, and Rebecca felt just as uncomfortable with Ron's age group. They eventually compromised in a way that left neither feeling completely satisfied. Things would eventually settle down, but the road would be bumpy on all these issues for a few more years.

Children and adults all come with expectations from previous families. Ron had helped raise four children. Two of his children, Emily and Scott, had been raised nearly to adulthood. Ron thought he knew what to expect from Rebecca's boys until he realized how different they had been raised in their original family. Ron expressed to friends on more than one occasion his dismay at what Rebecca and her first husband believed was appropriate for children.

Rebecca and Ron had each lived several years with a former spouse and each learned coping mechanisms that worked in the previous marriage. Ron and Rebecca also realized that what had been learned in a previous relationship was not necessarily applicable to their present marriage. Stepparents customarily reflect concern about their ability to adapt to this new marriage partner and his or her family history, experiences, children, and in-laws. Ron was learning that he could not live up to the physical expectations of his active and energetic stepsons. Ron and Rebecca were together learning how difficult it can be to adjust to another spouse when old issues from their previous marriages had not been completely resolved. They each knew that this was not going to be easy.

In a remarriage such as Ron and Rebecca's, it is almost always the case that the new marriage partners have received their training to be parents in two different family settings, and the children have been partially socialized through the original system that evolved out of the birth parents. So while we would expect a normal amount of adjustment to be required of the adults in a stepfamily, stepchildren have the extra burden of being asked to accept a new parent and reject, in whole or in part, what they learned from their original family system. In fact, confusion over role assignments, relationships, and expectations is so common that it is almost universally predictable that transitional trauma of some degree will result.[6]

Parent-child relationships predate the new couple. There is usually not a real honeymoon for second marriages involving children. Children come as standard equipment to most second marriages, and the standard equipment needs regular maintenance of love, attention, discipline, understanding, and acceptance. Even if Mom and her new husband are able to get away for a few days after their wedding, the subject of their children is rarely forgotten.

Children in remarriage families struggle to deal with fears and anxieties that are often too difficult or embarrassing to talk about. One of the concerns reluctantly voiced by Ron's two stepsons was that they feared that their real dad's feelings would be hurt if they grew to like their stepfather. Children have limited ability to understand that feelings such as love and respect can be directed at two distinct people without detracting from the feelings for either. It has been suggested that a primary challenge facing remarriage families is to resolve the losses experienced in the dissolution of the first family without negating the positive impact of those earlier experiences. Such an adaptation is generally accepted to be a prerequisite to the creation of a functional new family system.

Another issue is that just because two adults have grown to love each other and have chosen to marry does not necessarily mean that the children have the same feelings. Some have labeled this expectation "the myth of instant love" or "the Brady-bunch phenomenon" after the television program of the sixties and seventies involving a remarried couple, the wife having three daughters and the husband with three sons, all of whom quickly learned to love and accept each other with the help of a housekeeper and a big, friendly dog. As unrealistic as such an expectation obviously is, it remains common.

Contrary to common thinking, research indicates that the greater the amount of contact between the absent parent and the child living in a stepfamily, the less disruption will occur in the relationship between the custodial parent and child and between the child and the new stepparent.[7] One of the more typical concerns voiced by people considering a second marriage involving children relates to what they have heard from well-meaning but misinformed relatives and friends.

A biological parent exists elsewhere in actuality or in memory. The need to continue a relationship with a parent who is more or less out of the daily lives of children is common. Children and younger adolescents can be expected to have some degree of unresolved mourning for the previous family, some of which may be due to the child's young age and consequent inability to fully understand what has taken place.[8]

The idea of a take-away myth helps explain a child's reluctance to accept the new parent. According to this hypothesis, the child fears that his or her love for the new parent will drain away the love they hold for the original parent. Children think in concrete terms and tend to imagine concepts such as love to be of finite quantity. They believe they can hold only so much love, and if they give their love to a new stepparent, they will automatically lose some of their love for the original parent.[9]

This characteristic will be of greater or lesser importance depending on how often the child sees the noncustodial parent. Under normal circumstances, more visits mean fewer problems. Children who have regular visits do not need to fantasize and create characteristics and qualities for the parent who no longer lives at their house. The process of "hero creation" can be a particular problem when the original parent is deceased or totally out of the child's life for some other reason. Providing the child with photographs and other memorabilia of the original parent who is no longer a part of his or her life can reduce rather than increase the child's need to fantasize.

The children are members of two households. Circumstances vary between only occasional or no visits to the home of the noncustodial parent, regular weekly visits, or joint custody where the child actually spends half a week, month, or even year with each parent and whatever new family that parent has found. There may be two sets of rules for the children to follow or two sets of emotional expectations (for example, if one family is emotionally expressive while the other more reserved). The child may have to develop two sets of playmates or, for teenagers, two peer groups. Sometimes the geographic distance between homes may be hundreds or thousands of miles, climate and scenery can be vastly different, and the list of potential adjustment challenges could go on and on.

Far from stimulating and energizing the child, an extreme degree of difference can threaten the child's sense of security and personhood leading to comments such as, "I don't feel like I live at either house," or "Sometimes I feel like I'm two people instead of one." Counselors who play a role in custody decisions must be cautious to consider the child's ultimate benefit in the living arrangements and resist the temptation to sacrifice the child's welfare for the emotional needs of arguing parents.

The research already discussed clearly demonstrates the benefit of continued contact with both parents after a divorce. Whether those arrangements include shared or joint custody or another variation, the final decision should rest on what is good for the child.

Legal relationships between stepparent and children can be ambiguous. Many stepparents adopt their stepchildren. This gives the children the advantage of having the same last name as their parents and any siblings that are born into the new marriage. Adoption also gives the child a sense of being wanted by the stepparent.

Unfortunately, few divorces are sufficiently amicable to allow this kind of consideration of the child's emotional needs. There is also the important consideration that the biological parent, usually the father, does not wish to be removed from the child's life to this extent, choosing instead to maintain the bond through the name if nothing else. Adoption tends to work best in situations where the biological and absent parent has died, has voluntarily surrendered all rights to the child, or has deserted the family. If contact with the noncustodial parent is not possible, adoption by the stepparent is usually a desirable choice.

Church involvement often becomes a major issue. Rarely are divorced people able to continue attending the same church. I have observed several families try to continue their membership after a divorce, and in each case these attempts have failed. Even in a church with several thousand in attendance, divorced couples do not seem to be able to avoid contact with each other, to face the looks and stares of friends and family from the other side, who wonder how they have the nerve to show up in church after what they have done, and to allow the children to be in Sunday school and other activities with kids who ask embarrassing questions or tease them.

Added to these obvious problems is a more subtle discrimination that church leaders tend to direct at both parties in a divorce. I have listened to dozens of stories from divorced people from all kinds of church backgrounds and circumstances who say they have experienced such discrimination. Even though the church seems willing to recognize its role as hospital as well as sanctuary, too often church leaders behave as though they are more interested in protecting church members from negative influences like divorce than they are in ministering to the needs of these often hurting people.

BECOMING OVERCOMERS AS SINGLE PARENTS

The adjustment challenges that await a stepfamily can appear formidable unless adequate preparation is undertaken prior to the remarriage. For all the reasons just outlined, parents in the new family system are going to be called on to take the lead for their children in making the needed adjustments. We cannot expect children or adolescents to do for themselves what parents have not been able to do themselves. Stepfamily tasks will include some or all of the following:

Deal as a family with losses and transitions. One of the primary losses experienced by all members of the stepfamily is that of feeling normal, that one is now forced to be in a category that the rest of society looks upon as second-class to the normal nuclear family. Despite the decreasing number of intact families, other lifestyles, including stepfamilies, are still regarded by the mainstream of American society as deviant or inferior substitutes for the real thing.[10] The feelings and attitudes of significant others are critical in influencing how the members of a stepfamily adjust to their new life, and the ability of counselors to educate extended family on this issue should facilitate adjustment of the new family unit.

Acknowledge different developmental needs. Though traumatic events such as divorce and remarriage can have a positive effect,[11] significant transitions may also place family members at risk for personality disorganization and regression. Adaptation to separation, divorce, and remarriage has long been viewed as possessing high likelihood for stress due to the interpersonal nature of the transitions being experienced. Divorce and remarriage are known to involve the potential for negatively impacting personality development through the power of the trauma to unbalance.[12] Failing to take the age and maturity levels of all family members into account is reported to be one of the chief causes for a 40 percent divorce rate among second marriages.[13] Concerns about discipline rank at the top when parents discuss the reasons for trouble in their second marriage.[14] Rarely is discipline of children or adolescents discussed prior to remarriage, and frequently it is only brought up after the first serious child or adolescent misbehavior meriting some form of discipline. Those cracks in the marital foundation common to second marriages are widened by discipline disagreements, and unless these issues are settled quickly, the second marriage can be swiftly moved into the category of a failed attempt.[15]

Establish new family traditions. Many elements work together to give family members a sense of belonging and continuity. As a first marriage develops relationship rules, expectations, and privileges, so a second marriage must take time to do the same. With children as well, time to develop patterns of interacting in the new family system must be allowed. This should be a time when rules may be suspended or handled with a good measure of parental grace so children and teens will have time to do some trial-and-error learning. Traditions within the family will take time to develop and mature, and if a parent is expecting too-rapid progress, disappointment can become frustration leading to stress in the marriage.

There are practical aspects of establishing new family traditions. New vacation spots should be considered, with a balanced emphasis on fun for the children and relaxation for parents. Both parents need to resist the temptation to return to favorite recreation places. The familiar surroundings will probably serve to remind the adult of what has been taken away, thus having the potential for creating arguments, emotional upsets, and general moodiness, often in spite of not knowing the reason for the negative feelings. "But we used to have such fun here," says the recently remarried mother unmindful that she and her children are being reminded of what they have lost.

New traditions can be established around Christmas and other family holidays with an emphasis not on rejecting the old but of establishing the new. A family that usually spent the holidays in Florida with grandparents might want to consider continuing to take a holiday trip, but to New England, a place to establish new family traditions. Parents in stepfamilies will want to work hard to establish new traditions to ease the transition of their children and themselves into the new family environment.

Build a solid marital relationship. Overcoming the pitfalls of a second marriage and becoming a stepparent is based upon relationship more than anything else, and second marriages need even more commitment to the marital relationship. Christians experiencing a second marriage can be sure that God expects the same level of commitment to his principles, regardless of the number assigned to a particular marriage.

As a remarrying couple becomes aware of the extra burden they are assuming by starting a marriage with children already in place, the need for time alone, a time to be intimate and develop a special degree of caring for one another beyond what they feel for the children is critical. Perhaps Mom and Stepdad need to make special arrangements for a night out at least once a week *without children.* My experience is that the primary reason a night away from children does not happen is that both parents are reluctant to suggest the idea to the other for fear of being misunderstood or appearing selfish. The stepparent particularly does not want to suggest some time away from the children for fear that they will be misunderstood as not wanting to be with the children. The biological parent may be reluctant to make the suggestion because of not wanting to appear less than perfect as a parent. Counselors can be helpful in giving permission to the remarried couple to take time to be away from the children.

Building a parenting coalition. Research clearly indicates that considerable stress in children is created by the unwillingness of biological parents and stepparents to cooperate in the home in a manner that facilitates the stepchild's development.[16] Stress of this kind in children can produce a variety of physical, psychological, and spiritual reactions. Depression, eating disorders, acting out, and psychosomatic complaints are common in children and adolescents whose parents, whether in a nuclear family or a stepfamily, have failed to form a cooperative child-building coalition.

What is needed is to get the new stepfamily parents committed to forging a united front through which they can support *and* control their children. The "divide and conquer" truism is clearly applicable to the stepfamily. The stepparent in particular feels vulnerable to accusations of any type from the children. In order to avoid losing their already marginal power with their children, the newly married couple must come to the point where they can decide to disagree on many things but always present a united, we-have-decided front to the youngsters in the home. Parents can be reminded that God intended families to be led by two parents, and he made no distinction, so far as we can tell, between biological parents and stepparents.

Accept continual changes in family composition. The stepfamily is not a *normal* family unit in many ways, yet it is not *abnormal* either. The stepfamily simply experiences change of a magnitude experienced by few intact families. Children will come and go as visitation arrangements are made and kept. The stepfather may at some point have his children from a previous marriage come to visit for a few days. As the children become older they will often be able to choose with whom they wish to live, how long they wish to remain during visitation, and under what circumstances they will visit.

If additional children are born into the new family, the previous biological children of both the husband and the wife will tend to feel displaced. This sense of being displaced may not be obvious from the parent's perspective, but it certainly is real to the kids. Imagine the feelings of a twelve-year-old boy who lives with his mother and stepfather and who has just learned that his mother gave birth to a baby boy! He may feel betrayed by his mother, who always claimed that he was her favorite (if only) son.

Parents in stepfamilies must be prepared to accept and deal with unavoidable shifts in residence and loyalty. If the couple in a stepfamily are really committed to each other and their marriage *first* and to the children *second*, the turmoil that is natural to all stepfamilies in some degree need not become disruptive to the point of ruining what may be the last chance the children will have to grow up in a family with two parents.

Taking the plunge in spite of little support. The need is to have a couple so determined to build a God-honoring family this second time around that nothing will deter them. God has a plan for each family and does not distinguish the type of family required. God ordained two married opposite-sex people to be parents to the children born into that family unit. Christians getting ready to embark on a second marriage need an extra measure of commitment to each other and to the Lord if they are going to be able to survive the rebuffs of a community that is still intact-family oriented. The need is for parents who care little of the dangers that await them on the family front and who are willing to plunge ahead and determine to do the job God's way!

THE REMARRIAGE

When a second marriage involving children is planned, what can a counselor share with the engaged couple that may make the decision more sound and the marriage more stable? The following questions are commonly asked (or should be asked) about second marriages involving children.

Should children be involved in the decision to remarry? Absolutely not! Researchers have unanimously concluded that children should be involved in making the decision work, but not in the decision itself.[17] Asking children or adolescents if they think it is okay for Mom or Dad to remarry is asking for trouble of a kind no parent would want, especially if the child says "no." While asking permission of the children may seem fair, it conveys to the children that Mom or Dad is not sure about marrying this person or that Mom or Dad is willing to let the children have an adult choice in life-changing decisions. Children and even teens are so egocentric that they are usually unable to make a rational choice from an adult perspective. It is unfair, even under the guise of fairness, for parents to transfer some of the responsibility for this grown-up decision onto their children.

When is the best time to remarry? Research on second marriages indicates that the optimal time for both children and adults is between two and four years after the divorce. Marriages that occur too soon after a divorce may not allow children the time they need to mourn the loss of their first family and to deal with all the psychological adjustments common to children of divorce. While the evidence is not quite so clear for adults, roughly the same timespan is recommended due to the need of the divorced parent to adjust out of the old relationship. Failing to allow enough time may create an overlap situation where the new husband or wife is asked to adjust to the new marriage when they have not adequately resolved their departure from the previous marriage.

Remarriages that occur too long after the divorce may allow negative patterns of behavior and methods of interacting to develop within the family. These may have the potential to become sufficiently powerful so as to discourage second marriages, thereby requiring children to continue to be raised in a single-parent family with all the expected deprivations while mother or father becomes increasingly more lonely. Second marriages long after a divorce may also provoke feelings of jealousy in children and teens.[18]

What factors predict that the second marriage may be headed for trouble? Divorce researchers have developed a list of nine warning signs[19] that have proven to be accurate in predicting problems. These predictors of trouble include:

1. A wide discrepancy in life cycles between the two families can pose a problem. If one parent has teenagers and the other young children, or if there are teenagers in the stepfamily and then babies are born into the family, problems can be expected. Similarly, wide age variations between husband and wife can predict problems on the horizon, especially if marital experience differs greatly.

2. Custody arrangements that are changed at the time of the marriage create problems for the new couple. Children coming into the remarriage family or exiting that family create additional adjustment demands that the newly married couple does not need at this time.

3. Expectations that the children will easily accept the new marriage and the new stepparent are generally not realized and create turmoil as a result. Counselors can be helpful in those relatively rare opportunities to do premarital counseling with couples contemplating a second marriage through dealing with such unrealistic expectations. Reminders should be straightforward that the children are not getting married and may not be particularly happy with the new arrangements.

4. Denial of losses in the first marriage or rapid movement to a second marriage predict problems. As previously discussed, time is needed to adequately resolve the emotional elements in losing a marriage. Quick remarriage usually signals, especially in Christian people, a need to regain one's respectability as soon as possible, even at the risk of choosing a marriage partner unwisely.

5. Excluding the other parent or grandparents reduces the support system for the children and increases stress for the custodial parent and new stepparent. What is often overlooked is that grandparents may be the most underutilized commodity in the stepfamily system and are a solid resource in time of financial or other stress.

6. Forcing primary loyalty to the new family, especially if encouraged mainly by the stepparent, is counterproductive and can have serious and family-threatening consequences. Making such demands on the children inevitably results in resentment toward the new parent and rebellion and sabotage within the family. A new stepparent, and especially a stepfather, who insists on doing this has virtually assured the dissolution of this family, too. Unfortunately, this characteristic is common among second marriages involving Christians and in which the new stepfather sees himself as something of a rescuer for the children. It will not work!

7. Inability to surrender the ideal of the intact first family will continue to trouble the stepfamily and threaten its survival. The parent or stepparent who continues to

worry over what *might* have been will have great difficulty realizing what *can* be for the new family. Unresolved guilt lies at the heart of this problem element and, unless redressed, will continue to tear away at the fabric that holds the stepfamily together.

8. Failure to resolve intense relationship issues from the first marriage will threaten the success possibilities of any new stepfamily. Not limited to husband-wife issues, relationship problems can extend to other family members and even mutual friends. This is essentially old business and cannot be allowed to continue unresolved for very long.

9. Denial of differences between the old and new family will subvert any attempts to help the new stepfamily grow and develop as it should. If the adults in the stepfamily are unable or unwilling to come to grips with the differences in a stepfamily, choosing instead to believe that this new family is no different than any other family, problems will remain hidden until an explosion of some type engulfs the family in long-smoldering anger or any number of other negative emotions.

What factors predict success in a remarriage? First, we want to acknowledge that second marriages succeed at about the same rate as first marriages.[20] Variables associated with success in second marriages include:

1. The higher the educational level for both spouses, the greater likelihood that the couple can call upon coping strategies and options of which a less educated couple may be unaware. There is also some evidence that higher intelligence, which is clearly related to educational achievement and persistence in school, is also related to desirable personality traits. One might wonder why such traits, if now present, were not effective in preserving the first marriage. We must recognize that first marriages invariably take place at a younger age than second marriages and during a time of life when impulsive decisions

are more likely to be made. Many of these impulsive decisions involve choosing the wrong person to marry.

2. Remarriage occurring roughly two to four years after the termination of the first marriage predicts a greater chance for success. Certainly there will be exceptions, but as previously discussed, there are many solid reasons involving both adults and children as to why this time period is recommended.

3. It is a good sign when both sets of parents are in favor of the new marriage. Parental support is equally, if not more, important in second marriages. Given the psychological adjustments required and the social ostracism experienced by many stepfamilies, having the support of older adults in the two families, and especially parents, is extremely helpful in succeeding in the second marriage.

4. If people in the church, neighborhood, extended family, and circle of friends are in favor of the wife remarrying, the second marriage will not suffer the negative feelings experienced by many. If the divorced wife and mother was a victim of her husband's sinful behavior, for example, the social group that is most important to the remarried woman will be more supportive.

5. A good first marriage indicates greater possibility for a successful second marriage. Again, the question arises, if the first marriage was good, why did it fail? The answer lies in circumstances that put stress on the marriage and may have led to its dissolution. Perhaps the marriage was loving, nonabusive, and appeared fine until it was discovered that the husband was leading a second life as a homosexual. This kind of situation provides a smoother lead into a second marriage than when the first marriage was abusive, violent, addictive, etc.

6. Age represents maturity, and a couple twenty years of age or older at the first marriage will probably be older than average at the second marriage, too.

7. Commitment to a supportive religious system by both partners can promote the success of a second marriage.

Religious belief provides another support structure for a new marriage, whether first or second, and if the religion is one that is practiced and has an impact on the lives of the family, the family system will be strengthened. While divorce is on the increase among Christians, it is recognized that the rate of divorce would be much higher if it were not for supportive religious involvement.

Development in Stepfamilies

A 1984 longitudinal study of stepfamilies concluded that the stepfamily experience involved seven stages of development.[21] It should be noted that there will certainly be exceptions to these rules, and such variances should not be taken to mean that something is wrong or necessarily missing from the stepfamily. What follows are simply carefully thought-out suggestions as to how a stepfamily grows and develops by stages. Counselors can help families recognize and understand these phases as they unfold.

1. *Fantasy Stage.* Typical fantasies relate to being rescued by a perfect husband and father who will support the family financially, emotionally, and spiritually and will make no demands on family members to meet his needs. Other fantasies by either parent relate to making up for errors in the first marriage, raising stepchildren right this time around, experiencing instant love from stepchildren, and having a truly equal and fair second marriage. Children also fantasize about how great the stepparent will be, and when that parent proves to be a mere mortal, smaller children will try to wish that parent away.

2. *Assimilation Stage.* During this early stage the stepparent is rejected by the children. The stepparent is attempting to become assimilated into the new family unit but is outnumbered in most cases. Patience at this stage is critical, thus the recommendation to new stepparents that they make virtually no demands nor have any nonnegotiable expectations of the children for the first several months or even years of the new marriage.

3. *Awareness Stage.* Some months into the second marriage involving stepchildren, the stepparent comes to realize that something needs to be changed within the family. Often counseling

comes into play at this point. Counseling emphases for this level of concern usually relate to encouraging patience and negotiation with the children. Perhaps a family council can be established wherein all family members have an opportunity to express themselves without fear of recrimination. It may be that the children have been harboring unspoken fears about how their absent parent will feel if they like their stepparent too much. Only a little encouragement and counsel is needed to resolve this issue.

4. *Mobilization Stage.* During this fourth stage outside forces become important to the stepfamily. Such forces may include the pastor of the church the family attends, counselors, and experienced friends and family members who are brought in to help mediate the family's problems. At this stage, actual work is entered into by the entire stepfamily but primarily by the stepparent. Several issues probably will be brought to the surface that have usually been hidden but are still disruptive. These issues can include feelings for the biological parent, the fear that that parent will not visit the children so often if there is a stepparent present, and confusion by the children as to whether they should be able to love more than two parents. The fourth stage is usually the time during which the family begins to feel that there is hope for them.

5. *Action Stage.* Recommendations from counselor, pastor, family, friends, books, and other resources on the subject begin to be applied in earnest during stage five. Decisions are made to put some plans made during stage four into effect while deciding to drop others. New family traditions are decided upon and implemented as well.

6. *Contact Stage.* Time is passing during stage six, and plans and changes are becoming routine and accepted by all the family members. What seemed to be radical new ideas that differed so dramatically from the first family now seem almost boring in their acceptance. The family is now talking about how they feel with each other, what is okay and what is not, and what each can do to help the family grow stronger. Setbacks will occur but will be dealt with in an adaptive manner.

7. *Resolution Stage.* During this final stage (which can be expected to last as long as there are children present in the home,

and in some cases even longer), parents solidify their relationship with each other, and the stepparent accepts the idea that he or she will not and should not expect to replace the children's biological parent. Some have called this stage "holding on and letting go," illustrating the need to hold onto the marriage relationship and let go of the children.

Conclusion

God said, "It is not good for the man to be alone" (Gen. 2:18). Before the fall, Adam, in his perfect sinless state still needed human companionship for inner happiness and satisfaction. The human needs divorced people and their children experience are not to be written off as unimportant. Human needs were sufficiently important for God to comment on them and create a way for those human needs to be met. Feeling lonely is not sinful, and we need to remember that God promises to meet all our needs that cannot be otherwise met: "And my God will meet all your needs according to his glorious riches in Christ Jesus" (Phil. 4:19). His means of supplying those needs is primarily through people.

Counselors and other helpers need to be careful to avoid inadvertently prohibiting a decision that may be God's will for an individual or a family. Does God want children to be raised without a father—even a stepfather? Would God want a family to sacrifice social, spiritual, and even sexual fulfillment attainable through a second marriage for the sake of what some interpret to be a strict prohibition? "It is not good for man to be alone," God said, and Christian counselors will increasingly be called upon to support decisions by divorced Christians to remarry. Competent Christian counselors can help divorced parents consider all their options and prayerfully select those that best meet the needs of the individual family.

NOTES

1. L. A. Westoff, "Two-Time Winners," *New York Times Magazine*, 10 August 1975, 10–13.

2. Report of the National Center for Health Statistics, *American Demographics Magazine*, April 1991.

3. E. B. Visher and J. S. Visher, *Stepfamilies: A Guide to Working with Stepparents and Stepchildren* (New York: Brunner/Mazel, 1979).

4. E. B. Visher and J. S. Visher, *Old Loyalties, New Ties: Therapeutic Strategies with Stepfamilies* (New York: Brunner/Mazel, 1988).

5. J. M. Theis, "Beyond Divorce: The Impact of Remarriage on Children," *Journal of Clinical Child Psychology* 6, no. 2 (1977): 59–61.

6. D. R. Kompara, "Difficulties in the Socialization Process of Stepparenting," *Family Relations* 29 (1980): 69–73.

7. R. L. Hayes and B. A. Hayes, "Remarriage Families: Counseling Parents, Stepparents, and Their Children," *Counseling and Human Development* 18 (1986): 1–8.

8. J. Kleinman, E. Rosenberg, and M. Whiteside, "Common Developmental Tasks in Forming Reconstituted Families," *Journal of Marriage and Family Therapy* 5 (1979): 79–86.

9. H. C. Lewis, *All About Families: The Second Time Around* (Atlanta: Peachtree, 1980).

10. H. C. Johnson, "Working with Stepfamilies: Principles and Practice," *Social Work* 25 (1980): 304–8; and T. Z. Anderson and G. D. White, "An Empirical Investigation of Interaction and Relationship Patterns in Functional and Dysfunctional Nuclear Families and Stepfamilies," *Family Process* (1986): 407–22.

11. K. Pasley, "Stepfathers," in *Dimensions of Fatherhood*, ed. S. M. Hanson and F. W. Mozett (Beverly Hills, Calif: Sage, 1985).

12. K. Bursik, "Adaptation to Divorce and Ego Development in Adult Women," *Journal of Personality and Social Psychology* 60, no. 2 (1991): 300–306.

13. Hayes and Hayes, "Remarriage Families."

14. S. Kupisch, "Children and Stepfamilies," in *Children's Needs: Psychological Perspectives*, ed. A. Thomas and J. Grimes (Washington, D.C.: National Association of Psychologists, 1987).

15. L. Messinger, "Remarriage between Divorced People with Children from a Previous Marriage," *Journal of Marriage and Family Counseling* 2, no. 2 (1976): 193–200.

16. J. Strother and E. Jacobs, "Adolescent Stress as It Relates to Stepfamily Living: Implications for School Counselors," *The School Counselor* 32 (1984): 97–103.

17. C. B. Reingold, *Remarriage* (New York: Harper and Row, 1976).

18. W. F. Hodges, *Interventions for Children of Divorce* (New York: Wiley, 1986).

19. M. McGoldrick and E. A. Carter, "Forming a Remarried Family," in *The Family Life Cycle: A Framework for Family Therapy*, ed. E. A. Carter and M. McGoldrick (New York: Gardner Press, 1980).

20. N. D. Glenn and C. N. Weaver, "The Marital Happiness of Remarried Divorced Persons," *Journal of Marriage and the Family* 39, no. 2 (1977): 331–37; and J. Bernard, *Remarriage: A Study of Marriage*, 2nd ed. (New York: Russell and Russell, 1971).

21. P. L. Papernow, "The Stepfamily Cycle: An Experimental Model of Stepfamily Development," *Family Relations* 33 (1984): 355–63.

Chapter 7

Counseling and the Divorce Process

It has not been my purpose to argue the merits of the case for or against divorce and remarriage but rather to acknowledge that, as counselors, the people we will be ministering to in our offices and churches *will* be divorcing and remarrying. This is reality. Christian counselors who choose to take a strict position against divorce and remarriage may obtain doctrinal purity at the expense of ministry to hurting people.

The Bible has much to say on the subject of divorce and less on the subject of remarriage. We have looked at many of these already, and such pronouncements may be disregarded at some peril by counselors, Christian or secular! The position of this book is not to disregard Bible passages but to apply them to the reality of the lives being experienced by those coming to us for counseling. A willingness to work with divorced and remarrying people should not be seen as compromise on the part of the counselor committed to biblical truth. Rather, a recognition of the power of sin in the lives of people allows counselors to better understand possible motivation. We need to be aware that sin in the lives of our clients and ourselves tends to cloud the ability to understand.

BIBLICAL COMMENTS ON DIVORCE

For edification if not empathy, we will take a brief look at biblical comments on the subject of divorce and remarriage. This section is meant to be more a sampler than exhaustive exegesis, intended more to raise issues for the counselor than to resolve them for clients.

One of the most straightforward examples of biblical teachings on this subject is when Jesus answered the Pharisees, the legalists of the day, when he made the following comments on divorce:

> "Haven't you read," he replied, "that at the beginning the Creator made them male and female, and said, 'For this reason a man will leave his father and mother and be united to his wife, and the two will become one flesh'? So they are no longer two, but one. Therefore what God has joined together, let man not separate."
>
> "Why then," they asked, "did Moses command that a man give his wife a certificate of divorce and send her away?"
>
> Jesus replied, "Moses permitted you to divorce your wives because your hearts were hard. But it was not this way from the beginning."
>
> (Matt. 19: 4–8)

The primary emphasis in this passage appears to be two-fold: First, that marriage is a special spiritual and physical arrangement ordained by God and one that should not be tampered with. Second, that God does not condone divorce even though Moses allowed it.

The prophet Malachi emphasized God's attitude toward the kind of divorces of convenience so common today when he proclaimed, "It is because the LORD is acting as the witness between you and the wife of your youth, because you have broken faith with her, though she is your partner. . . . 'I hate divorce,' says the LORD God of Israel, 'and I hate a man's covering himself with violence as well as with his garment,' says the LORD Almighty" (Mal. 2:14–16). Jesus addresses the subject again in Matthew 5:32 and 19:9 in a similar negative vein, while the Apostle Paul condemns divorce in Romans 7:1–34.

There is no scarcity of teaching against divorce, however, our job as counselors is to deal with people where they are. The reality is that people coming to us for help will, in most cases, already have made and implemented their decision to divorce and perhaps to remarry. We then have the choice between "cleansing" our counseling practice of this controversy through refusing to accept divorced or remarried Christians as clients or allowing our desire to help people overrule a need to remain uncontaminated by the sins of the world. We cannot help but consider, what would Jesus do? I believe he would help people where they are regardless of where they have been.

FUNDAMENTALS OF DIVORCE COUNSELING

There is a short list of generally accepted truisms regarding the impact of divorce on the lives of people and how counselors can therapeutically intervene in the process.[1] We should consider these suggestions as starting points for counseling rather than the final word. Individual problems and circumstances will, as a matter of course, negate any type of rules or recommendations. Each person's uniqueness and the complexity of each situation makes it impossible for any single rule of counseling to apply universally.

THE FAMILY SYSTEM CHALLENGED

The family unit functions as a system. When that system is disrupted, children as well as adults in the family can be expected to show symptoms that reflect the disorder in the family. The destruction of the family unit through divorce involves four typical features.[2]

First, individuals begin the divorcing process when the wish to leave the marriage has become so crystallized in at least one marriage partner that he or she initiates the separation process. "Two to make a marriage, one to make a divorce" remains a realistic and an accurate representation of the kind of situation common to the counselor's office. When one partner feels that he or she has had enough and is able to rationalize social, legal, and religious discouragements to beginning the separation process, the family begins to dissolve. Christian counselors have a special responsibility to recognize the likelihood that victimization has occurred in the marriage, and whether the separation was initiated by the victim or the victimizer, the choice has been made and is unlikely to be changed. The mindset of the Christian counselor working with this population should be, "Where sin increased, grace increased all the more" (Rom. 5:20).

Second, divorce is a process through which parents and children leave one family system and enter a new one. It is important to grasp that two processes are at work simultaneously when a family breaks apart. Family members are called on to accept and deal with the destruction of the family in which they had lived for some time. For the children, this is usually the only family they have ever known. Adults must adjust to the absence of a partner, and children must adjust to the absence of a parent.

Egress and ingress, exit from the old and entrance into the new, are happening at the same moment and will be stressful under any circumstances. Counselors who have worked with abused women know how frightening it is, even under life-threatening circumstances, to realistically contemplate starting over with a new and radically changed family. Though less of a threat to physical safety, we can only try to empathize with the feelings of children and adolescents who are required to accept and adjust to their new family.

Third, family members enter the separation and divorce process with their own agendas from which they devise strategies, often unconscious, for navigating the process. Experienced family counselors recognize the intense emotions involved in virtually every marital dissolution and prepare for conscious and unconscious subterfuge, sabotage, misrepresentation, and emotional blackmail emanating from and directed to each of the divorcing parties, their lawyers, and even counselors. Anger is easily displaced to those who are perceived as helping a spouse who is in the wrong, and while lawyers are more likely to be targeted, counselors are not exempt.

Extreme care must be taken by family counselors to insure their professionalism and avoid any kind of conflict of interest. The counseling profession warns against any relationships that could be perceived as dual. Specifically, section B.13 of the Ethical Standards of the American Counselors Association warns:

> When the member has other relationships, particularly of an administrative, supervisory, and/or evaluative nature with an individual seeking counseling services, the member must not serve as the counselor but should refer the individual to another professional. Only in instances where such an alternative is unavailable and where the individual's situation warrants counseling intervention should the member enter into and/or maintain a counseling relationship. Dual relationships with clients that might impair the member's objectivity and professional judgment (e.g., as with close friends or relatives) must be avoided and/or the counseling relationship must be terminated through referral to another competent professional.[3]

Such ethical requirements place great responsibility on the shoulders of the church-based family counselor who may have intimate knowledge of the divorcing couple over many years. A counselor who is a paid staff member of the church and who is expected to provide Christian counseling services to church members will find himself or herself in a difficult dilemma. The pastor expects that counselor to help, but the counselor is aware of the ethical standards of the profession and knows how difficult it would be to be impartial and objective under these conditions. Professional ethics must be the final arbiter of such a problem. The Christian counselor will find that the ethical standards of the counseling profession are not incongruent with his or her own belief system.

Fourth, family counselors become aware that the meshing of individual agendas in the divorce process creates a temporary divorcing process system that has the potential to produce behavior by the family members that could prevent the various members from successfully navigating the process. Emotional reactions may be of such intensity that the process is detoured for months or years, usually resulting in much more damage to the children than should have been anticipated.

Intervention strategies are critical at this point, and certain conceptualizations are warranted. Failure to internalize the following principles will likely result in a struggle by the counselor to accurately understand and help divorcing clients.[4]

Divorce is a disorganizing and reorganizing process that extends over time. All involved should expect years of disruption and instability to follow the breakup of a family. We will see research in a later chapter that supports the contention that divorce of one's parents remains the single most upsetting event in our lives, even more than the death of a parent, child, or spouse.

Sue Craig repeated over and over in my counseling office that she felt that her world had been absolutely destroyed and would not ever be the same again. The four Craig children, each in their own age-appropriate way echoed their mother's sentiments. The anger that all four children expressed seemed to be related to the sense of being permanently scarred by what their father had done. As I counseled with each, they repeated so often that they felt like mutants living in a two-parent world where they would never be able to have the success and happiness they felt was available to their friends from intact families.

The Craig family had many strengths they were not feeling at the time of separation and divorce—strengths that would become available to serve them in the days to come. What I was able to provide for them was the idea that they must each give themselves time to get through, not over, these experiences. I heard a speaker say that for children *love* is spelled T-I-M-E, and if this is true, I would also suggest that *healing* is spelled the same way!

The entire post-separation period is a central determinant of the well-being of those involved. The manner in which the parents function and relate to one another in the days following separation and divorce affects the children as significantly as the behaviors and interactions that may have preceded the breakup. The manner in which children adjust impacts the ability of parents to adjust. The process is reciprocal, even in the total absence of one parent.

Parents who remain separated without either reconciling or divorcing may be placing the child in a situation of unresolved stress leading to the potential for long-term adjustment difficulties. Though not an easy issue to confront for Christian counselors, encouraging separated parents to decide on the future of their marriage is probably appropriate in terms of the well-being of children involved. This is especially true if the separation period is conflictual. Research data supports the contention that continued parental conflict limits the ability of adults *and* children to adjust to their new lifestyle.

In contentious marital disruptions, the process by which one parent overtly or covertly speaks or acts in a derogatory manner to or about the other parent during or subsequent to a divorce proceeding directly impacts the children's adjustment and, in a reciprocal manner, the parent's ability to adjust. It has also been pointed out that even residual positive emotions of love and affection held by the custodial parent for the now noncustodial parent can interfere with child adjustment. It is not simply the hate and anger at the end of a marriage that limits adjustment, but the love that persists as well.[5] Dealing with residual emotional issues in a separated or divorced family may be facilitated through several counseling interventions (see table on page 143).

The child's capacity to maintain his or her developmental pace is related to the custodial parent's needs. The more the custodial parent employs the child in fulfillment of adult emotional needs and social support, the more negatively it will affect the child's course of development. This appears to be of particular importance with the oldest child. There needs to be an optimal distance required between the older child and his or her custodial parent providing sufficient space in which to develop in an autonomous manner.

About eighteen months into her single-parent life, Sue Craig found herself worrying that she was relying too heavily on her adolescent daughter Emily for emotional support. Even

COUNSELING INTERVENTIONS FOR RESIDUAL EMOTIONAL ISSUES

1. Discuss issues raised in the literature on post-divorce relationships early in the divorce adjustment process. There is an abundance of relevant professional research available to counselors willing to spend some time seeking it out. Journal articles on this subject should be readily available in a local college or university library or through one's professional associations.

2. Schedule counseling sessions specifically for negotiating post-divorce relationships. In the divorce process, the significant concern will be the welfare of the children, and it is appropriate, if the counselor has opportunity, to raise relationship issues at that time.

3. Schedule counseling sessions with custodial parent, children, and noncustodial parent if possible for at least the first year following the divorce. Counselors should resist the temptation to see divorce adjustment as no more than simply informing the parents about what they should or should not do and then dispatching them to "just do it!" Issues will evolve in the months following a divorce that did not exist or were too painful to deal with in the initial process.

4. Meet separately with each new branch of the family to discuss parent-child concerns. Counselors will want to arrange sessions with the custodial single-parent and the grandparents to discuss the needs of the new single parent and how everyone involved can be helpful during the adjustment process. Similarly, the noncustodial parent and the grandparents from that side of the family should meet with a counselor to discuss the same issues covered with the custodial side of the family. At the point a potential stepparent becomes a part of the system, a session or two with that person should be helpful. Such sessions may be possible only under the best of circumstances, but we should do as much as possible at the time.

(Source: D. G. Brown, "Divorce and Family Mediation: History, Review, Future Direction," *Conciliation Courts Review* 20, no.2 [1982]: 1–44).

though we had discussed the dangers of single parents doing too much sharing with same-sex children, Sue had slipped into a pattern of talking with Emily as a sister rather than a daughter. She knew not to let this happen and was concerned that it had in spite of her efforts. Sue was able to regroup and commit again to being Emily's mother instead of a sister or peer. We discussed the possibility that Emily might want to see a counselor for a short time again, and Sue arranged to see me on a more regular basis until she felt competent to handle her emotional needs through her adult friends.

The period immediately following the separation is crucial. As crisis theory emphasizes, opportunities for effective change are greatly enhanced in a fluid system. Following divorce, parents are usually involved in long-term, important decisions concerning the children. Even though the changes being experienced are very likely to be negative and distressing, being able to overcome such trauma and find alternate ways of living as a single person or parent can be more easily acquired now than later.

Children also tend to be amenable to adjusting their attitudes after a period of crisis. Children and teens will recognize that change is happening and they must adjust in order to survive. The critical difference is found in the circumstances of the moment. Children and teens eventually must acknowledge the need to accept some changes in their lives and it may be that the time is right to consider making *other* changes as well. Parents can carefully suggest that perhaps as long as the family is being required to move to another place to live following the separation or divorce, it just might be a good time for the teenager in the family to consider his or her choice of friends and maybe think about trying to enter a new peer group.

Loss is a common denominator in divorce and death. Divorce, like death, provokes a process of mourning and loss, but unlike death, divorce still affords the child contact with the separated parent. We can be reminded that the mourning process is roughly the same following divorce *or* death, and all members of the family must be afforded time and space to conduct their own grieving processes. Counselors can be helpful in legitimizing the need to experience all the feelings common to the grief process. It is critical for counselors to carefully consider whether to interject God's sovereignty into the emotional equation for the child. As mentioned in an earlier discussion, counselors or parents who do make such an allusion might be asked the impossible question, "If God will take care of me now that Mom and Dad have divorced, why did he let this terrible thing happen to my family in the first place?"

Emotional reactions are not limited to children and adolescents. It is well known that never-divorced adults report that they feel significantly greater happiness than those who have divorced at least once. Those same never-divorced adults reported less depression than those with a history of one divorce, who in turn reported less depression than those with a history of more than one divorce.[6]

Divorce counseling with parents and children seems relatively unaffected by the parents' participation in any other ongoing form of psychotherapy. Many participants in divorce recovery counseling have been or are concurrently in group or individual therapy for other concerns. It is not unusual to find a divorced wife struggling with a perceived lack of assertiveness or having a difficult time accepting the high level of autonomy that has been thrust upon her by the divorce. Counselors will want to follow ethical guidelines regarding dual relationships as applied to concurrent therapy, but we should also know that counseling regarding child welfare may not conflict with the personal types of counseling mentioned.

THE "CIVILIZED" DIVORCE: ADVANTAGE OR DISADVANTAGE?

It is generally accepted that post-separation and divorce conflict between parents is responsible for a major portion of adjustment difficulties in offspring of all ages as well as in the divorced parents.[7] The natural assumption that could follow might be that the more "civilized" the divorce, the easier the transition to divorce and single-parent status. However, a total or near-total absence of acrimony between divorcing parents may present children with inadequate opportunities to resolve their feelings about the dissolution of the family. Some have suggested that so-called "civilized" divorces may actually undermine the psychological processes necessary for completion of divorce work by all involved.[8]

Despite an absence of acrimony and conflict, children as well as custodial and noncustodial parents may develop symptoms in reaction to the benign but disruptive termination of their family. Aggressive acting out, poor school performance and a decline in academic achievement, night terrors, psychosomatic complaints, and restricted social and interpersonal relationships may all be manifestations of unresolved issues related to the divorce. While such "civilized" and "friendly" divorces may prevent the serious consequences of ongoing battles between bitter and angry ex-spouses, the low level of negative emotion may also deny parents and children the opportunity to work through important issues and consequently may undermine the adjustment processes necessary for completion of the divorce work.

Specific counseling treatment issues include the following:

- It is essential to the course of therapy that past and painful issues relative to life in the previous family be resolved. An unusual level of cordiality after the divorce may convince children that it would be wrong to bring up issues about the past that concern them but do not concern others who seem to be getting along well after the divorce.

- Divorced parents who seem friendly may, as a matter of course, stifle such feelings by withdrawing permission to talk about them. It is crucial that children be given the opportunity, which must involve open and complete permission on all matters, to discuss their feelings of rejection and isolation as well as their anger over the divorce.

- Children often harbor guilt and shame over the divorce. These feelings, along with depression and separation anxiety, must be expressed and dealt with in a therapeutic manner. Divorced families for whom religion is a significant factor will contain children whose guilt and shame component is higher than those with less religious involvement.

- Divorced parents will also have unresolved feelings and issues that demand attention. For divorced adults with a preexisting religious belief system that was relevant to their daily lives, the post-divorce period often involves a falling away from religious practice by one or both parents. This seems to stem from a mixture of guilt, embarrassment, and an unwillingness to continue to be associated with the religion of the former spouse.

• Civilized divorces allow children to continue to hold onto their reconciliation fantasies. For all the negatives involved in an acrimony-filled divorce, one positive side effect is that the anger and bad feelings evident in parents helps to discourage the unrealistic hopes of children that their parents may reconcile some day.[9]

MEDIATION TO MINIMIZE DIVORCE TRAUMA

When the divorcing couple is able to cooperate sufficiently to facilitate a voluntary agreement regarding custody, property distribution, and visitation arrangements a lose-lose scenario for the family may be avoided.[10]

Divorce mediation is based on five beliefs:[11]

1. Mutually acceptable solutions are available.
2. Possible solutions are desired by those involved.
3. Each party is valued and respected and has the right to be heard and understood.[12]
4. Superordinate goals of children and family exist that transcend special interests.
5. The mediator is fair and impartial.

CUSTODY

Custody of children following a divorce is one of the most troublesome problems facing everyone involved. There can be no greater stress placed on children than that experienced when one parent leaves their daily lives and they are left with only one parent. Regardless of acrimony or cordiality between divorced parents, children and adolescents care most about how the adult decision to terminate their family of origin will impact their own lives. Egocentrism is rampant and normal in growing children and teens. Adults trying to intervene should not assume that this apparent self-centeredness is evidence of adjustment difficulties. Egocentrism requires a focus on self and a partial or complete disregard for any impact on others. Thus, when custody becomes an issue in resolving the post-marital family arrangements, we should expect children and teens to be unhappy with *any* arrangement, regardless of how appropriate it seems to adults.

Most custody arrangements are made through stipulated agreements. In only 10 percent of the cases does a judge or referee decide who shall get custody. Even though judges decide only a small portion of custody cases, the criteria used lead to expectations on the part of lawyers and parents about what will happen if custody arrangements are challenged.[13] In those 10 percent of custody settlements where a court official is called upon to decide the residence of children, an inordinate amount of pain and anger can result no matter what the decision may be.

CRITERIA FOR CUSTODY DECISIONS

Keeping in mind that the welfare of the child is always dominant in custody decisions, twelve criteria for reaching a decision are suggested. Based on several research projects carried out over several years,[14] the child's best interests were defined as requiring the following:

1. The moral fitness of the parents.
2. Love and affection between parent and child.
3. The permanence of the home as a family unit.
4. The capacity to meet the physical needs of the child including medical care, food, clothing, shelter, and education.
5. The amount of time the child has already lived in a stable, satisfactory environment, and whether the custody decision would remove the child from that environment.

6. The ability of the parents to express love and affection to the child, provide guidance, and continue to raise the child in their present religion.

7. The mental health of the parents.

8. The home, school, and community record of the child to date.

9. The preference of the child including the age and reasonable ability of the child to express such desires.

10. Ties to extended family.

11. Parents' history of working with the child's school, community agencies, etc.

12. Information received from significant others in the child's life.

COMMON ASSUMPTIONS REGARDING CUSTODY[15]

Counselors working from a conservative Christian perspective need to become aware of the common-knowledge assumptions regarding custody typical of American divorce courts today. While many of the following statements will be found to be consistent with conservative, family-oriented counseling, others will not. We will see that the bases for custody decisions are often questionable and based more on secular humanistic principles than traditional family experience.

It is also noteworthy that custody following divorce was not much of an issue prior to 1920, because children were traditionally considered to be property of the father and would remain in his care. It was generally assumed that the father would be best able to provide for the child's welfare and academic and spiritual development. It is interesting to note that the first known instance of custody *change* for the welfare of children dates to 1817 when the poet Shelley lost custody of his children after his wife's suicide because he was a self-acknowledged atheist and was known to be engaging in immoral conduct.[16] That the world of divorce settlements should change so dramatically in so few years is consistent with other changes impacting and threatening to impact the traditional family unit. These days it seems that the divorced parent most able to offer the best of traditional family living for the children can be in the weakest position when it comes to custody settlements.

Following is a list of custody assumptions of American divorce courts with comments and explanations.

1. *Generally speaking, the family itself, more than anyone else, knows what is best for it.* Court officials can be expected to give great weight to what the family members believe about how to provide for the needs of children. Family includes parents, children, grandparents, and other family members as well.

2. *The way parents cope with divorce will, in large part, determine how the children will cope as well.* Research suggests that divorce is associated with poor adjustment of children primarily in two ways: parenting skills and parental functioning in the post-divorce period.[17] Further, children and adolescents who exhibited some form of behavior pathology tended to come from families headed by parents with greater pathology. Specifically, mothers of depressed children were more chronically depressed than mothers of other children, and children receiving services from a mental health clinic reported significantly more negative perceptions of their post-divorce family than divorced families whose children had not received such services.[18]

3. *Children need two parents.* Continuous and meaningful contacts between the children and both parents lessen the traumatic impact of divorce and facilitate the process of growth and development. From a custody perspective, then, it should be assumed that the children need continued contact with both parents *even if one parent has entered into a dysfunctional lifestyle such as homosexuality or other forms of social deviance not determined to be criminal.*

4. *Most adults and children of divorce have the ability to deal with the crises of divorce and to grow with them.* However,

some may need help to arrive at adaptive solutions rather than maladaptive, self-defeating ones. A basic Rogerian perspective exists among divorce court personnel—a self-actualizing, self-growth philosophy leading to an acceptance of lifestyles Christians and other conservative people would find unacceptable. Having a homosexual parent, in other words, may be seen as an opportunity for the children to experience personal and social growth and tolerance rather than something that may place them at risk in the future.

5. *The problems of children of divorce are not necessarily due to the divorce: they may be normal developmental problems.* Family counselors of just about any theoretical orientation would acknowledge the challenge of helping parents sort out those child or adolescent problems that may be arising out of the divorce process and those coming from the challenges of normal growth and development.

6. *It is possible for the law and the behavioral sciences to cooperate and communicate with each other.* Counselors will find not only a willingness of lawyers and mental health professionals to work together, but what appears to be a symbiotic relationship where one does not appear able to function without the other. Litigation seems the normal way to resolve disputes these days, and very little litigation is accomplished without some form of mental health testimony.

7. *The rights of children of divorce must be protected at all times.* Children are people too, of course, and have the same right to legal service, informed consent, limited confidentiality, and safety as any client of any age. This point may appear obvious to those unfamiliar with the more extreme element of conservative Christianity. Sadly, there remains a segment of Christianity that still views children as property of their parents until the age of majority. Implied within this perspective is the notion that minors really have no rights, especially in comparison with the needs of the family as a whole.

8. *Parenting is a learned behavior. Nothing in the genes ensures effective parenting.* The comprehensive philosophy on the subject of how parents got that way is at one and the same time helpful and hurtful in the eyes of those interested in child welfare after a divorce. This notion is helpful in the sense that it is obviously true that what we know we have learned somewhere, sometime, and what has been learned can be unlearned and relearned. Thus, in the eyes of many divorce court officials, there is no such thing as a hopeless case. What has been missing in a given family can be corrected by parenting classes and other forms of instruction. This is helpful. The hurtful element lies in the possibility that almost no matter how bad a parent has behaved, he or she is always potentially recoverable, thus leading to parents demanding that their children visit them in prison, at the residence of their homosexual lover, and so on.

9. *The adversarial system, though suited for other areas of law, is not suited for divorce law.* The adversarial system, where one party must be found at fault, places children of divorce at risk of injury through being called upon to choose sides in a contested custody case. Though not common, true custody battles when they occur can be deadly to a child's psychological well-being. While recognizing the possible negative side of cordial divorce settlements, by comparison with acrimonious divorces, we would opt for the quieter resolution.

10. *Self-determination in developing custody plans is more desirable than court-imposed plans.* The more divorcing parents can cooperate to reach an amicable custody settlement, the more effectively stress will be reduced for the children. The sense of control appears to be especially important to fathers without custody but relates to the feelings of both partners regarding the divorce proceedings in general, visitation arrangements, child support equity, and property distribution. The more decisions on these matters that can be reached without court mandate, the easier the transition for the children *and* adults.[19]

11. *Joint custody works when properly planned and implemented.* We will discuss the specifics of the various custody possibilities a little later, but for now I want to emphasize the desirability of divorced parents sharing custody of their children in a voluntary arrangement. We will see that joint custody in acrimonious settlements may not be the answer. But when well planned and executed, joint custody is preferred.

12. *Mediation is an effective method of helping families develop joint custody plans.* Arriving at an equitable decision regarding custody and visitation is best accomplished by two divorcing parents more concerned about the welfare of their children than themselves. Too often, though, this is not the case and mediation is the next best option. The goals of mediation include helping the family come to an amicable settlement, protecting the children's rights, and helping the divorcing parents understand that they are still parents.[20] (Mediation will be explored more thoroughly in the next section.)

TYPES OF CUSTODY

Probably no single issue of divorce has more long-term impact on all involved than custody of children. The options available to a divorcing couple with children are extremely important and worthy of careful consideration.

Sole custody. Historically during the modern period, the legal responsibility for the care of dependent children has been assigned to one parent. Prior to the development of joint custody arrangements, mother received custody about 90 percent of the time, father about 7.5 percent, and others (usually relatives) about 2.5 percent.[21] The pervasive belief seemed to be that mothers were instinctively and constitutionally better prepared to provide for the emotional needs of the children.

Split custody. When interpersonal relationships in the home are determined to be destructive to the child's welfare, the court may decide to assign one or more children to one parent and other children to the other parent. This is seen as the *least* desirable alternative and is essentially a last resort while still trying to continue some form of family system for the good of the children.

Conflict between siblings may lead to a split custody decision if the conflict is seen to be sufficiently severe as to threaten the welfare of the child. Frequently, split custody decisions will involve provisions for visitation and periodic review by the divorce court to determine if the destructive factors have been resolved and the child can be moved to a more traditional custody and visitation arrangement. The needs of the children are paramount in such cases.[22]

Joint custody. It is common to find people confusing the issue of joint custody with physical living arrangements. Joint custody refers, in most cases, to legal and financial responsibility for the child while one residence serves as primary home for the child. Approximately thirty states have some provision for joint custody[23] and the trend appears to be moving strongly in that direction in most other states. Many states have ceased assuming that one parent was automatically better than another and have instituted comprehensive methods for evaluating parenting skills and related issues in each case.

The issue of post-divorce conflict is of significant importance. When a couple appear unable or unwilling to discontinue the battles that led to the divorce, a judge may decide that it would be in the best interest of the child to assign sole custody to one parent and then periodically review the custody arrangements to see if the absent parent can be brought back into the life of the child.

The major concerns with joint custody include:

• Disruptions in the continuity of childcare.

• Disruptions in the child's physical and social environment.

• Difficulty in maintaining close emotional relationships with both parents.

Research on these concerns is encouraging, however. A 1985 study of joint custody found:

• Children in joint custody arrangements reported a significantly greater number of positive experiences than children in sole maternal custody.

- Children in joint custody reported higher levels of self- esteem.
- No difference in child misbehavior or emotional disturbance was found.
- Children had more contact with the parent with whom they did not primarily reside.[24]

Pros and Cons of Joint Custody

The desire is to have children of divorce continue contact with both parents if at all possible. The following criteria are offered in hopes of better decision making.[25]

Positive parental criteria:

1. Parents who are each committed to making joint custody work because of their love for their children and desire to be involved in their children's lives.
2. Parents who have a good understanding of their respective roles in a joint custody plan and are willing and able to negotiate differences.
3. Parents who are able to give priority to their children's needs and are willing to arrange their lifestyle to accommodate these needs.
4. Parents who are able to separate the husband/wife roles (where the anger started) from their parental roles.
5. Parents with a reasonable level of communication and willingness to cooperate.
6. Parents who have the potential flexibility to make changes in the joint custody arrangements as the developmental needs of the children change.

Negative parental criteria:

Joint custody is not for every divorced family. If the following negative factors are present, joint custody may be contraindicated.

1. A history of addiction in one or both parents.
2. Family violence, including child abuse (emotional, physical, or sexual).

3. Child neglect.

4. A family history indicating inability of the parents to agree regarding rearing of children.

5. Parents who are unable to differentiate between their needs and their children's needs.

6. Mental illness in either parent.

7. Children who are likely to be unresponsive to joint custody arrangements or rebel against joint custody.

8. Families with a severe history of disorganization.

9. Families in which both parents are unalterably opposed to joint custody.

10. Logistics (geographic distance, incarceration) working against a joint custody plan.

The attention we have given to joint custody reflects both the reality of current divorce settlements and the high priority placed on the need of children to have continued contact on a regular basis with both parents. Joint custody affirms that parents are forever. Though the divorce ends the legal relationship between husband and wife, the parent-child relationship should, and in most cases does, continue. Joint custody tends to equalize the balance of power between parents, providing each with a sense of control over their relationship with the children. Such a sense of shared control is expected to reduce the occurrence of child kidnapping and other reactions by parents who feel frustrated and impotent.

THE UNPLEASANT BUT NECESSARY TASK

Working with Sue and Ron Craig as they transitioned out of their marriage was not a happy experience. I have never worked through a family dissolution and reorganization that was in any sense pleasant, and the Craig case was no exception. I did feel, though, that through careful attention to the issues raised in this chapter, the mental health of everyone involved was enhanced and protected. In the months between separation and divorce, I found that Sue and Ron Craig not only conformed to time sequencing expected but to typical emotional reactions as well. Knowing what to expect was a tremendous benefit as I worked to help the family survive their divorce trauma.

I believe it is important to emphasize to divorcing parents that God expects them to continue to carry out their responsibilities as parents regardless of the circumstances. For all the pain and negative emotions experienced by Sue, Ron, and their children, the Craig parents were committed to their children. They just did not realize how difficult it was going to be. We find no provision in the Bible allowing a parent to escape his or her responsibilities after a divorce. Counselors work to deal with the stress of family dissolution, but we must also focus on maintaining parenting continuity for legal and biblical congruence. Even in the most challenging of situations, parenting must continue.

Consider the case of George Blake. George was a father of three, married for thirteen years, and in prison for the last five of those thirteen years. George became a Christian while in prison and communicated with me by mail as encouraged by the prison chaplain, a former student of mine. George was as determined as anyone I have ever seen to be a good parent while in prison and when he was released. His chaplain worked with him in person, and I helped by mail and telephone. For two years George practiced and rehearsed how he was going to be a better father when he was free.

What I learned from George, in addition to the success as a father he experienced when he was out of prison, was that he became a better father and husband even while still behind bars. He wrote to his kids almost daily. He dated his loyal wife, Ellen, by mail and telephone. He read books and took correspondence courses on the family. When he was released after seven years of being gone, George was a better husband and father than many who have never been separated from their family.

I learned from George that, with God's help and personal determination, divorced parents, who do not face anything like the challenges George faced, *can* be good parents in spite of the difficulties in their marriage. God expects nothing less. I also learned that I had been far too pessimistic with some of the families with whom I had worked. I learned again that God is ever able.

NOTES

1. J. S. Wallerstein and J. B. Kelly, "Divorce Counseling: A Community Service for Families in the Midst of Divorce," *American Journal of Orthopsychiatry* 47, no. 1 (1977): 4–22.

2. M. B. Isaacs, "Helping Mom Fail: A Case of Stalemated Divorcing Process," *Family Process* 21 (1982): 225–34.

3. B. Herlihy and L. B. Golden, *Ethical Standards Casebook* (Alexandria, Va.: American Association for Counseling and Development, 1990), 30.

4. Wallerstein and Kelly, "Divorce Counseling," 6.

5. W. H. Berman, "The Role of Attachment in the Post-Divorce Experience," *Journal of Personality and Social Psychology* 54, no. 3 (1988): 496–503.

6. L. A. Kurdek, "The Relationship between Reported Well-Being and Divorce History, Availability of a Proximate Adult, and Gender," *Journal of Marriage and the Family* 53 (1991): 71–78.

7. C. M. Hansen, "The Effects of Interparental Conflict on the Adjustment of the Preschool Child to Divorce," (Ph.D. diss., University of Colorado, 1982); and J. R. Johnston, L. E. G. Campbell, and S. S. Mayes, "Latency Children in Post-Separation and Divorce Disputes," *Journal of the American Academy of Child Psychiatry* 24, no. 5 (1985).

8. E. H. Futterman, "After the Civilized Divorce," *Journal of Child Psychiatry* 19 (1980): 525–30.

9. Ibid., 525; and N. Kalter, J. Pickar, and M. Lesowitz, "School-Based Developmental Facilitation Groups for Children of Divorce," *American Journal of Orthopsychiatry* 54 (1984): 613–23.

10. W. F. Hodges, *Interventions for Children of Divorce: Custody, Access, and Psychotherapy* (New York: Wiley-Interscience, 1986).

11. D. G. Brown, "Divorce and Family Mediation: History, Review, Future Direction," *Conciliation Courts Review* 20, no.2 (1982): 26–28; and O. J. Coogler, *Structured Mediation in Divorce Settlement: A Handbook for Marital Mediators* (Lexington, Mass.: Lexington Books, 1978).

12. L. K. Girdner, "Adjudication and Mediation: A Comparison of Custody Decision-Making Processes Involving Third Parties," *Journal of Divorce* 8 (March/April 1985): 33–47.

13. R. S. Weiss, "Issues in the Adjudication of Custody When Parents Separate," in *Divorce and Separation: Context, Causes, and Consequences,* ed. G. Levinger and O. C. Moles (New York: Basic Books, 1979).

14. J. F. Charnas, "Practive Trends in Divorce Related Child Custody," *Journal of Divorce* 4, no. 4 (1981): 57–67; E. P. Benedek, "Child Custody Laws: Their Psychiatric Implications," *American Journal of Psychiatry* 129 (1972): 326–28; J. Goldstein, A. Freud, and A. Solnit, *Beyond the Best Interests of the Child*

(New York: Free Press, 1973); and M. Elkin, "Joint Custody: Affirming That Parents and Families Are Forever," *Social Work* (January/February 1987): 18–25.

15. Ibid., 20–21.

16. H. H. Foster and D. J. Freed, "Life with Father," *Family Law Quarterly* 1, no. 40 (1978): 321–42.

17. R. Forehand et. al., "Role of Maternal Functioning and Parenting Skills in Adolescent Functioning Following Parental Divorce," *Journal of Abnormal Psychology* 99, no. 3 (1990): 278–81.

18. N. J. Kaslow et al., "Depression and Perception of Family Functioning in Children and Their Parents," *The American Journal of Family Therapy* 18, no. 3 (1990): 227–35.

19. R. C. Bay and S. L. Braver, "Perceived Control of the Divorce Settlement Process and Interparental Conflict," *Family Relations* 39 (1990): 382–87.

20. H. H. Irving, *Divorce Mediation: The Rational Alternative* (Toronto: Personal Library, 1980).

21. Hodges, *Interventions*, 89–90.

22. R. Chasin and H. Grunebaum, "A Model for Evaluation in Child Custody Disputes," *American Journal of Family Therapy* 9, no. 1 (1981): 43–49; and S. Ramos, *The Complete Book of Child Custody* (New York: Putnam, 1979).

23. N. D. Repucci, "The Wisdom of Solomon: Issues in Child Custody Determination," in *Children, Mental Health, and the Law*, ed. N. D. Repucci et al. (Beverly Hills, Calif.: Sage, 1984).

24. S. A. Wolchik, S. L. Braver, and I. N. Sandler, "Maternal Versus Joint Custody: Postseparation Experiences and Adjustment," *Journal of Clinical Child Psychology* 14 , no. 1 (1985): 5–10.

25. Elkin, "Joint Custody," 21.

Chapter 8

Counseling Children of Divorce

KEVIN WAS ONLY NINE WHEN HIS FATHER LEFT his mother for another woman. Kevin did not know or understand why this happened. Not knowing left him with a sense of being betrayed not only by his father, but by his mother and older siblings as well who knew the truth but did not want to tell him or his little sister Alicia. Kevin would be told many times that it was for his own good. He was told that he would not understand anyway because he was only nine. All Kevin knew was how he felt—rejected, embarrassed, lonely, guilty, and most of all, angry.

As is typical with younger children, Alicia at five was clearly upset that something bad was happening to her family but did not ask many questions in the beginning because her mother was so upset. Like most little girls her age, Alicia judged her world on the basis of the people closest to her, especially her mother. If Mom was feeling okay, then things in general must be okay. If Mom was upset Alicia was upset, too, even though she would not usually know why. Alicia was becoming frightened and insecure simply because her mother was frightened and insecure. When Sue felt angry or sad after Ron left, Alicia felt it was her duty to feel the same way. When you are only five, you try to help your mom any way you can!

Kevin was developing problems in school. Alicia was beginning to show signs of growing separation anxiety, particularly when she had not seen her father for more than a few days. The two younger children in the Craig family were going to need professional help adjusting to the separation and divorce of their parents. It was going to be a long-term process.

CHILDREN AT RISK

Children who lose a parent for any reason experience what some have termed a loss in social definition or the sense of who and what one is.[1] The meanings of divorce for children are based on the socially ascribed meanings and functions of marriage and family within a given culture. For children in particular, disruption of the family for any reason constitutes a crisis of meaning and belonging. When the complex issue of a parent voluntarily exiting the family is introduced into the equation, even greater turmoil is experienced. Children going through the divorce of their parents often need some form of temporary buttressing to shore them up while they formulate and establish new patterns of meaning, belonging, and relatedness for themselves.[2]

While accepting the idea that the good years experienced by children like Kevin and Alicia are important, some have suggested that there may be a hidden negative in moving quickly from an intact, functional home such as that experienced by the Craig children into a single-parent family with all the stressors involved. Research has shown that children such as Kevin and Alicia, who have not experienced anything other than a two-parent intact family, may have more difficulty adjusting to a different form of family structure. While the good years may have served as a form of emotional battery charge, they have also set a pattern of expectations that can be extremely difficult to surrender to the reality of divorce and single-parent status.[3]

WHERE HAVE ALL THE FAMILIES GONE?

The past three decades have brought American children into a new world of being raised by one parent. The percentage of white children living with one parent has almost tripled during the past three decades to 19.2 percent and has more than doubled among blacks, to 54.8 percent. About half of all marriages now end in divorce, and out-of-wedlock births have skyrocketed. It is fair to say that *most* American children born today will spend some part of their youth in a single-parent home. Children of the current decade are more likely than their predecessors to be raised by one parent who is poor, never married, female, undereducated, and underemployed.[4]

The National Institute of Mental Health noted that younger children such as Kevin and Alicia Craig going through a divorce are three times more likely than older children or teens to need psychological services of some kind while growing up.[5] Of particular concern are those elementary and younger children whose parents:

- did not function well prior to the divorce;

- continue to focus on their marital problems and are unable to negotiate a new post-divorce relationship for the benefit of the children;

- are unable to develop a support system of friends and relatives following the divorce; or

- were unable to arrange father visitation or another form of male influence on young boys.[6]

A committee of The American Psychological Association's Division of Counseling Psychology defined counseling as a process "to help individuals toward overcoming obstacles to their personal growth, wherever these may be encountered, and toward achieving optimum development of their personal resources."[7]

The National Conference of State Legislatures and the American Association for Counseling and Development defined counseling as "a process in which a trained professional forms a trusting relationship with a person who needs assistance. This relationship focuses on personal meaning of experiences, feelings, behaviors, alternatives, consequences, and goals. Counseling provides a unique opportunity for individuals to explore and express their ideas and feelings in a nonevaluative, nonthreatening environment."[8]

Christian counselors have the advantage of being reminded of what Jesus said about caring for and helping children: "Take heed that ye despise not one of these little ones; for I say unto you, that in heaven their angels do always behold the face of my Father, which is in heaven" (Matt. 18:10).

It is noteworthy that ethical standards of the counseling profession do not conflict with the biblical emphasis of protecting children. But how would we be guilty of "despising" children in any case? Perhaps by not taking them or their problems seriously. Or by assuming children to be stronger and more resilient than they are, or in assuming that they are unable to understand that which they need to learn. There are many ways a counselor or other helper can "despise" children and a few ways counselors can demonstrate a genuine concern for their welfare and a willingness to put some personal effort into helping.

LISTENING TO CHILDREN

There are many avenues that can lead a counselor to the place where a child can be helped. What follows represents one such avenue. Let me suggest that a child who is brought to a counselor for help needs that counselor to listen for three important keys to what is troubling the child.

1. *The felt problem or concern.* What is it that is uppermost on the child's mind at the moment, and what is causing the greatest concern? Is the felt problem loneliness, rejection, depression, anger, or guilt? How does the child at his or her age express that problem or concern to the counselor? How children express what they are thinking helps the counselor determine the level of understanding possible.

2. *The child's feelings about the problem or concern.* Beyond children's ability to understand what has been happening to them, the feelings associated with their problems are central to helping. Emotions reveal the inner child to the counselor more accurately than any test or observation. Emotions are very hard to fake, especially for children. Are the feelings negative, positive, or ambiguous? Are the feelings focused or dispersed? Are the feelings accepted by the child or repressed? Each answer will focus counseling on a different target.

3. *The child's expectations about the counseling process.* Careful counselors will listen for a client to state what he or she expects to take place. Counselors will then have an opportunity to respond, clarify, and redirect the focus of counseling. Though not as sophisticated as adults, children will express themselves in their own way on this subject if given permission by the counselor. How long do I have to come here? What will I have to tell you? Do I have to tell you secrets I have promised to keep? Will you tell my parents what we talk about? Will you get upset with me if I say the wrong thing? Depending on age and experience, children *will* have anxieties and fears that need to be dealt with if progress is to follow.

Most problems brought to the counselor concerning children can be classified into one or more of five categories. Each of the areas identified represents a beginning point from which to work with the child of divorce.[9]

1. *Interpersonal conflict, or conflict with others.* Following separation or divorce the child has increased difficulty relating with parents, siblings, teachers, or peers and is seeking a better way of dealing with these important people. We know that anger is the emotion most commonly experienced by children of divorce. We also know that boys are more likely to exhibit angry acting out behavior upon the loss of a father. Frequently, the child is described as no longer getting along with anyone, always grouchy,

disagreeable, obstinate, and stubborn. The child of divorce is likely to feel angry and will turn that emotion outward, becoming hostile as a result.[10]

2. *Intrapersonal conflict or conflict with self.* The child of divorce exhibits trouble with decision making and needs help to clarify alternatives and consequences involved in what he or she has experienced. The typical child of divorce struggles with feelings of responsibility and guilt for the divorce. The child seeks answers as to what was done to deserve such severe punishment as losing a parent from the home. The child is depressed, has trouble going to sleep, and suffers from loss of appetite, fatigue, and weariness, and play is less frequent.

3. *Lack of information about self.* The child of divorce needs to learn more about his or her abilities, strengths, or values. During this time of family turmoil, the child may need help in determining if he or she is really strong enough to be able to deal with the tearing apart of the family. Many times hidden strengths and abilities surface only when needed, and the child may not have been so challenged as yet. This was the case with all four of the Craig children who, in differing degrees, showed unusual resiliency in coping with the divorce of their parents.

4. *Lack of information about the environment.* The child of divorce needs information about what it takes to succeed in school, neighborhood, church, or home. Most children experience a change in physical environment after a divorce. The child is required to adapt to a new (and usually less comfortable) home, a new school filled with strangers, a new neighborhood in which to try and find friends, and possibly a new church to get to know as well. Counselors working with children of divorce must be prepared to take an active role in providing needed information while retaining a therapeutic stance with the client.

5. *Lack of a variety of skills.* The child of divorce needs to learn specific skills related to making new friends, dealing with a reduced budget at home, explaining his or

her family situation to others, and finding appropriate ways to deal with emotions. Counselors will need to be practical rather than theoretical in the teaching of such skills. Role-playing, role reversal, and paradoxical methods can be valuable tools in the process.

Individual counseling with a child from a divorced family is combined, whenever possible, with counseling with one or both parents. While combining counseling efforts is often helpful, individual rather than family counseling, is expected to be helpful and is recommended under the following circumstances.[11]

- *When parents are psychologically unavailable for counseling in family therapy.* Due to intense emotions or unresolved conflicts, it may not be feasible or safe to bring parents together for a counseling session.

- *When the child's maladaptive behavior is related to past misinterpretations of events and is not corrected by less stressful interactions ongoing in the present.* Bringing the child into contact with stress-producing interactions with or between parents may only intensify the child's discomfort.

- *When the child needs to learn to separate his or her identity and problems from that of the parents.* The child may need to feel more in control of his or her life and circumstances. This may be best accomplished by treating the child as much like an adult as possible, thus the benefit of individual sessions focusing on the child's perceptions alone.

- *When the child could benefit from a consistent, predictable counselor in the midst of a chaotic family situation.* The child may need exposure to adult role models who are not exhibiting the type of characteristics that may have led to the divorce. The counselor can provide stability and safety while teaching more adaptive coping strategies than those the child has seen at work in the home.

- *When the child needs someone who does not have divided loyalties and can provide needed advocacy.* The child may simply need an adult who is clearly and unambiguously on his or her side.

Counseling with children of divorce necessarily involves parents. Parents have extensive knowledge of the child and have attempted a variety of strategies over the years to help the child develop properly. Though the marriage may be at an end, the power of parent knowledge is indispensable to the counseling process. Helping children of divorce overcome the burden parents have placed on their immature shoulders requires comprehensive knowledge of the child's background as well as an eclectic framework for counseling. A multimodel has been developed in order to help the counselor focus on the issues likely to be a problem in children, especially in children from stressed or broken families. The eclectic counseling process as it is applied to counseling children of divorce is called the BASIC ID model and describes seven problem areas most often treated in counseling.[12]

The Lazarus BASIC ID model covers most counseling problems with children of divorce. Others have verified the effectiveness of the model with children experiencing a variety of difficulties including family dissolution.[13] I found the model to be helpful with all the Craig children because it provided me with a useful method for organizing complicated counseling plans and notes with four children of different ages and concerns.

Psychological Tasks and Resolution

In addition to the general framework suggested by the BASIC ID model, children of divorce face significant personal and family reorganization challenges. Some of these challenges involve primarily cognitive issues such as believing things will happen that will not, being incorrect in their assumptions about causes, and assuming responsibility for the divorce. Others are mostly emotional, psychological, or spiritual in nature.[14] Counselors may find their child clients to have differing levels of concern from case to case, but there is not much doubt that each of the following issues will surface in some form and intensity.

Task 1: Acknowledging the Marital Disruption

Children fear abandonment more than death. Every child has to some degree experienced the anxiety and fear of feeling

BASIC ID Model

B—BEHAVIOR

Fighting   Disruption

Talking   Stealing

Procrastination

A—AFFECT

Anxiety   Phobias

Depression   Expression of anger

S—SENSATION/SCHOOL

Headaches   Backaches and stomachaches

School failure   Perceptual/motor problems

I—IMAGERY

Nightmares   Low self-concept

Fear of rejection

Excessive daydreaming and fantasizing

C—COGNITION

Difficulty in setting goals   Decision-making problems

Problem-solving difficulties

I—INTERPERSONAL RELATIONSHIPS

Conflict with adults   Conflict with peers

Family problems

Withdrawing from others (shyness)

D—DRUGS/DIET

Hyperactivity   Weight-control problems

Drug abuse

Addictions to tobacco, alcohol, and other drugs

lost when separated from a parent or wondering if the parent who is late picking him or her up is really going to *ever* show up. Both Kevin and Alicia Craig had trouble admitting to themselves that their father had really left and was not going to return—not ever! Children their ages often fantasize and create make-believe reasons for a parent's absence from the family; the pain of facing reality is just too much to bear.

Parental support is clearly the most important variable in controlling the strong negative feelings of young children of divorce. In this case, the Craig children had a significant advantage because both Ron and Sue, despite their intense negative feelings for each other, were completely committed to helping their children through the trauma of their divorce with the least amount of damage. With parents supplying needed support and reality testing for the children, all four Craig children were helped to acknowledge reality in spite of their fears.

Recovery from feelings of abandonment, desertion, and rejection as experienced in the Craig family can best be accomplished by supportive counseling techniques. These include active but uncritical listening, careful reflection, clarification and interpretation at their intellectual level, and problem solving.[15] In some cases, stress-reduction techniques such as guided imagery and conscious relaxation are helpful. Counselors can be helpful as well by building on the information already (we hope) supplied by the parents as to the reasons for the marital problems. Counselors may need to be reminded that too many parents incorrectly assume their children are unable to understand what happened.

Task 2: Accepting the Permanence of the Divorce

Children will fantasize about the possibility of getting Mom and Dad back together again, and they will continue such wishful thinking in the face of the most overwhelming evidence to the contrary. While death affords clear and incontrovertible evidence that the past will not be regained, continued contact with the absent parent, while advantageous in many ways, serves as a constant reminder that the child's wishes for reconciliation may be realized. Children need verbal reminders of the true state of affairs, and they need such reminders repeatedly and gently offered by parents and other important adults.

TASK 3: RESOLVING ANGER AND SELF-BLAME

Children always seem to blame themselves for the divorce that has impacted their family. It is primarily the voluntary nature of the divorce that causes so much confusion and bad feelings in children. The fact that Mom or Dad chose to leave the home in which they continue to live is abundant proof to young minds that a parent cared more about their own needs than the needs of the children. Children of divorce are at the same time angry at parents and discouraged with themselves that something they might have done could have led to all this turmoil.

Counseling emphasis is on helping the child forgive himself or herself and others in the family for what has happened and move forward with the challenges of a changed lifestyle. If the child has not seen much forgiveness practiced in the family (and this is not an unusual component in divorces), he or she may not know how forgiveness happens. Counselors and parents will want to be careful to deal with acting-out behaviors within a framework of understanding the child's reason for being angry in the first place. Children may benefit from counseling that employs role-playing, play therapy, story telling and writing, and group activities with other children facing the same challenges. The child will need to learn how to forgive himself or herself *and* others.

TASK 4: BREAKING FREE FROM PARENTAL CONFLICT

I worked with a teenager some time ago who had attempted suicide as a result of parental fighting. Eventually the parents divorced, but before that happened, Ellen nearly succeeded in taking her life through an overdose of prescription medication.

When she was released from the hospital and reentered therapy as an out-patient with me, Ellen quickly told me that she was better and would not be needing to do herself harm again. In response to my question as to what had changed for her, she replied, "I have just learned that their problems are their problems, and I am not going to punish myself anymore for the life my parents have chosen to lead."

And this from a fifteen-year-old!

If only we could get children of divorce of all ages to gain this insight. Counselors can facilitate this process by encouraging teachers, adult family friends, church staff, and others to provide as much stability for these children as possible. Stability tells children that there is a foundation under their shaky world and that eventually the shaking will stop and they will once again be able to get about on their own without worrying about what will happen to them. Consultation between counselor and significant adults is essential if the child is to be able to escape the burden of family conflict.

TASK 5: RESOLUTION OF WHAT HAS BEEN LOST

If we were to ask the person on the street what children lose when their parents divorce, we would probably get a response such as, "Well, I suppose the most important thing children with divorced parents lose is the parent who doesn't live with them anymore." The loss of a parent cannot be minimized, but a parent is not the only important loss that occurs. Children must also adapt to the loss of income, loss of a familiar school, neighborhood, and old friends.

This powerful sense of loss the child of divorce experiences may be mitigated by continued contact with the noncustodial parent. In cases where this does not happen, children frequently face a childhood filled with disappointment and dejection.[16] Counselors can facilitate growth and adaptation through methods mentioned previously including role-playing, puppetry, writing and drawing, and storytelling. If the child has changed home and school as a result of the divorce, helping the child connect with a friend can be a major boost to the child's self-concept.

TASK 6: FINDING REALISM IN RELATIONSHIPS

Counselors will focus on bringing the child of divorce back to a more realistic perception of the family situation, even if that reality is more unpleasant than the child seems willing to accept at the moment. It is not effective to feed the child's sense of fantasy by agreeing that anything is possible after all and that Mom and Dad *could* get back together again, even though the chances are remote. Walking the balance between reasonable optimism and damaging pessimism is the challenge facing any counselor working with this group of clients.

Low self-esteem is the common denominator with children and adolescents. Children will express their damaged self-esteem by withdrawing into a fantasy world of television, video games, and reading. Adolescents will try to self-correct by moving even more into the peer group in hopes of finding ways of feeling good about themselves again. Risks may be taken to obtain acceptance by peers. Sexual acting out, alcohol and drug abuse, running away, or over-identification with heavy metal, biker, or surfer subcultures may be observed in these adolescents. We will consider adolescents further in the next chapter.

COUNSELING CLUES FOR PARENTS

Message Carrying. Help parents understand the danger in asking the children to carry emotionally powerful messages back and forth between custodial and noncustodial parents. The danger lies in subverting the child's important need to think well of both parents. Counselors will find some difficulty in accomplishing this task with a mom or dad who has been abused or who is presently being taken advantage of. In spite of the justifiable nature of their complaints, parents on both sides should be strongly encouraged to leave the children out of adult matters.[17]

Communication. Encourage parents to talk with their children about the divorce. Children at even very young ages can benefit from being told what has and is happening to their family and what they can reasonably expect in the future. Encouraging parents to keep the channels of communication open is extremely important. Children who are led to feel that they have broad permission to talk if they need to are going to have an easier time adjusting to any type of family turmoil, including divorce. Again, this encouragement may not be consistent with the parent's own upbringing and may be difficult to get started, but it is worth the effort.

Visitation. Educate parents on the continued value of consistent and regular contact with children. Asking conflictual divorcing parents to set aside their own agendas for the benefit of the children is easier said than done! Counselors can use books and other reading material to support this position. If feasible, including a divorce-recovered former client in a session to discuss what did or did not work with the children can be helpful. (Issues of confidentiality are important and should be explicitly dealt with before such an arrangement is made.)

Stability. Encourage parents to make the child's life as stable as possible during the divorce turmoil. By taking an authoritative stance regarding what is best for the child, even bitter parents can be brought to a position where the child's needs are paramount. Encourage parents to retain as much of the child's history, brief as that history may be, in the new living environment. Having memory stimulators in the home should have a positive impact on the child's adjustment.

Appropriate information. Instruct parents on the need to tell the children what is happening to them and what will or may happen to them in the future. It is equal parts hurtful to tell the child too much or too little. Who is the expert on what the child can handle? Only the parents, but with important input from the counselor where needed. There are no rules on what is appropriate for a given age, because there is just too much variability in maturity levels. But working together, parents and counselor should be able to determine what the children can hear that will help them.

Let children be children. Encourage parents to insist that the children continue to be children. Household responsibilities are appropriate as long as the child retains sufficient playtime as a balance. The stressed-out single parent is vulnerable to using children excessively for chores such as cleaning, meal preparation, and babysitting. While this may not be a problem under normal circumstances, the already emotionally burdened child may begin to wilt under the additional responsibility.

GROUP WORK WITH CHILDREN

Group counseling with children of divorce is most likely to take place within the school structure. The requirement of identifying children at risk while obtaining sufficient numbers of group participants necessitates involvement of the school at some level. Often provided in a joint effort with classroom teachers, school-based counseling is a trend that will continue to grow in acceptance and frequency.

DEFINING GROUP WORK WITH CHILDREN

A group is often defined as "two or more individuals who (a) interact with each other, (b) are interdependent, (c) define themselves or are defined by others as belonging to a group, (d) share norms concerning matters of common interest and participate in a system of interlocking roles, (e) influence each other, (f) find the group rewarding, and (g) pursue common goals."[18]

Group counseling with children includes the following elements:

- Children identify thoughts or behaviors that are self-defeating and set goals for themselves with the help of the counselor/facilitator and other group members.

- The counselor and the group assist children in setting specific and attainable goals.

- Children try new behaviors in the safe atmosphere of the group and make commitments to try the new behaviors in the real world.

- Children report the results of homework assignments during the session and decide either to continue the new ways of thinking and behaving or to reject them for further exploration of alternatives.[19]

General structuring of the children's group is based on the research-determined needs of the typical child of divorce. Research follow-up of divorce-recovery groups for children found the following curriculum components to be essential:

- The group must foster a supportive environment.

- The group must facilitate identification and expression of divorce-related feelings.

- The group must promote understanding of divorce-related concepts and clarify divorce-related misconceptions.
- The group must teach problem-solving skills.
- The group must enhance positive perceptions of self and family.[20]

More specifically, a session-by-session program for group counseling with children of divorce has been developed. While the emphases are not to be applied dogmatically, the format has proven to be generally successful.

Once a broad structure has been determined and an appropriate setting arranged, the group leader must determine participant characteristics. Age, sex, grade level, present living circumstances, and major concerns are among those to be carefully considered. For example, children of five and six years of age have a short attention span and are unable to give much attention to the concerns of others. Older children, pre-adolescents, and mid-to-older adolescents will each need a group suited to their abilities and developmental stage.

Session-by-Session Program

Session 1: The activities planned for the first session should be designed to establish an appropriate atmosphere, to get acquainted, and to introduce divorce as a common influence in each of their lives.

Session 2: Promote discussion about family structure and the changes caused by divorce.

Session 3: Encourage discussion of possible causes of divorce.

Session 4: Help the children identify and express how they felt about their parents' divorces and how they were told of their parents' decision.

Session 5: Deal with memories of favorite family vacations and family traditions. This is to encourage mourning the lost family.

Session 6: Discuss the sources of self-esteem.

Session 7:   Discuss threats to self-esteem.

Session 8:   Focus on how the children see themselves in the future. What kind of family do they hope to be a part of?[21]

Early Elementary School Interventions

It is critical to emphasize confidentiality when establishing groups for children of early elementary age. Being egocentric and rule-bound, children in this age group will readily accept a statement from the group leader to the effect that secrets are to stay within the group. Additional rules regarding teasing and hurtful comments must be emphasized at the outset. Children unable to conform to these requirements should be moved to individual therapy.

Ethical requirements of professional counselors as cited in Ethical Standards of the American Counselors Association (1990) section B.8 state:

> The member must inform the client of the purposes, goals, techniques, rules of procedure, and limitations that may affect the relationship at or before the time that the counseling relationship is entered. *When working with minors or persons who are unable to give consent, the member protects these client's best interests.*[22]

Section B.10 states:

> The member must screen prospective group participants, especially when the emphasis is on self-understanding and growth through self-disclosure. The member must maintain an awareness of the group participants' compatibility throughout the life of the group.[23]

Thus, one overriding concern of the counselor working with children in a group is their safety and protection from any kind of harm. Once provisions for safety have been instituted, the group process for children of divorce may get underway.

Examples of group building with elementary-age children include suggestions by Joan Levine and Norman Dewhurst of a mental health team in the Cherry Hill School District in Colorado:

- *The name game.* Add a word to your name that says something about yourself. Then repeat what the previous person said about himself or herself.

- *Car wash.* The children stand in a line. Each child in turn goes down the line, looks at each person and says something positive (a potentially difficult exercise). The child being complimented can only say, "Thank you."

- *Reverse fantasies.* Draw four pictures: a happy time with your family; a sad time with your family; what you would like to happen now; what you would like to happen in two years. The pictures are then used for discussion.

- *Group murals.* Every child draws something important happening in their family on a large sheet of paper.

- *Family tree.* Each child draws his or her own family tree as he or she knows it.

- *Picture completion.* The therapist gives a topic and each child draws a part of the picture and then passes it on. For example, children may draw a composite picture of the day the family split up.

- *Bibliotherapy.* Read from books that talk about children going through divorce.[24]

Other suggestions include dressing up like adults, using a playhouse or dollhouse in which to act out feelings, hand puppets representing adult and child characters, musical instruments, punching toys, and clay for modeling.[25] Younger children especially need help communicating their true feelings, which range from anger to depression to shame.

LATER ELEMENTARY INTERVENTIONS

Children in fourth, fifth, and sixth grades possess higher-level expressive skills, which makes it easier for them to talk about their experiences and feelings. Groups of seven to nine children may benefit from the following activities:

- *True/false game.* Say three things about yourself, making one of them false. Have the group guess which one is false.
- *Role-playing the courtroom divorce scene.* Children who were in the courtroom often have strong feelings about the event, and children who were not there have strong fantasies. Re-enactment can help a child think about and work through the feelings about divorce.
- *Write a book about the divorce.* One chapter is written per session. The therapist suggests the topics, which may include: telling the children about the divorce; parent's dating; family secrets; family spying; remarriage; money; or visitation. A variation on this approach includes giving advice to other children going through a divorce or giving advice to parents on how to help children.
- *Use sentence stems to encourage verbalization of feelings.* Stems might include: "My mother gets angry at me when————" or "I get sad about————." Each child writes his or her answers in private, and the answers may be kept private if the child wishes. However, after the writing is finished, the therapist brings up a stem and invites any child who wishes to read his or hers aloud.
- *Role playing a divorcing couple.* This works particularly well if a male and female therapist are available. The children write the script for the problem. The therapist(s) can role-play appropriate problem solving or have the children suggest solutions to the problem that the couple is struggling with.[26]

The South Carolina Department of Education developed a counselors' guide for children of separation and divorce. While originally designed for use with children from kindergarten to twelfth grade, it has found its greatest applicability among late elementary and junior-high/middle-school children. The authors divided the activities into warm-up and group-process activities.

The following is an abbreviated description of these activities; complete details can be found in *Parting: A Counselor's Guide for Children of Separated Parents.*[27]

Warm-Up Activities

- *Houses my family lives in.* Drawing pictures of the houses including figures (stick figures are acceptable) of family members. Be careful to protect children who do not know where family members are or who have a parent in jail or a hospital. Provide discussion questions after the drawings are completed.
- *Scrambled feelings.* Children are asked to unscramble letters of feeling-oriented words. Words such as *thea* (hate), *yollen* (lonely), and *dashema* (ashamed) can be used to get things started. Discussion follows the game.
- *Coping with feelings.* Provide each child with a paper cut in the shape of a cloud and ask them to write on it the feelings they are experiencing. Discuss constructive coping skills. Help the children think about how to cope with different feelings in ways that do not cause problems or hurt anyone.

Group-Process Activities

- *Getting to know you.* Children are asked to find someone in the group that fits each of thirteen categories (for example, "loves to eat vegetables"). Have that person sign a sheet. No person can sign the sheet more than twice. Leaders check the sheets when finished.
- *Changes.* Group members are asked to list changes in their families and themselves. Feelings about those changes are also listed.
- *Things that bother me.* A list of thirty potentially bothersome problems is provided. The child is asked to check those that bother him or her and circle the check for those that are the most distressing. One problem is then selected to discuss how to solve it.

- *Coping with feelings.* Discuss displacement of angry or frustrated feelings and better coping.

- *Communication.* This exercise is a list of nine questions for the children to discuss. The questions focus on feelings about divorce such as whether parents divorce children, why divorce occurs, could the child get the parents back together, and whether the child gets caught in the middle.

- *New rules since there has been a change.* Discuss how things have changed since the parents separated.

- *Happiness is———.* Discuss what makes the child and parents happy.

- *Mixed feelings.* This exercise provides a vignette about having mixed feelings and discussion of those feelings.

- *From me to you.* Communication to parents through a note or picture to make them feel happy.

- *Home responsibilities.* An exercise about who has what responsibilities at home.

- *Make believe.* This exercise provides ten short vignettes in which the child is asked to role-play the situation and imagine how each person feels and acts.

- *What should Sara do?* This exercise provides a vignette of a twelve-year-old girl with mixed feelings about her mother's starting to date. The group is asked to answer questions as if they were Ann Landers or Dear Abby.

SENSITIVITY TO CHILDREN

Counselor personality is never more important to success in the counseling process than when working with children. Children seem to possess extra sensitivity when dealing with adults and can spot a phony immediately. It is true that children who have been abused or badly treated in other ways seem to lose some of this ability over time, but in most children absolute transparency on the part of the counselor is essential.

Part of being transparent is having personal issues from one's own past resolved or in the process of being resolved. Counselors who share experiences with the child client should experience greater levels of empathy but only if the issues being raised are no longer roadblocks to health for the counselor. Counselors working with children should have experienced therapy themselves at some level in preparation for working with this age group in order to determine if there are such unresolved issues that may interfere with counseling. I am reminded of the emphasis on protecting children Jesus repeated so many times in the Bible: "'I tell you the truth, anyone who will not receive the kingdom of God like a little child will never enter it.' And he took the children in his arms, put his hands on them and blessed them" (Mark 10:15–16). "See that you do not look down on one of these little ones. For I tell you that their angels in heaven always see the face of my Father in heaven" (Matt. 18:10). Counselors, be careful that you do no harm!

CONCLUDING SUGGESTIONS

Effective counseling must be appropriate for the developmental level of the client. The following suggestions are most applicable to younger clients but may be adapted to children through middle school.[28]

- Use relatively brief sentences. Three to five words with preschoolers and fewer than ten words per sentence with middle-schoolers.

- Use names rather than pronouns. This helps the child know exactly who is being discussed. Children of divorce will have more than one person occupying a labeled position such as father, grandmother, etc.

- Use terminology compatible to the child's level of understanding. No psychobabble allowed.

- Do not ask, "Do you understand?" It is the counselor's responsibility to make himself or herself understood. Instead ask the child to repeat your message.

- Do not repeat questions the child does not understand. This implies that it is the child's fault, and the child may feel a need to agree with the counselor to gain acceptance and approval. Instead, rephrase the question.

- Avoid time-sequence questions. Adapt chronology issues to the child's ability to understand and follow.

- Children, and especially younger children, are strongly literal and may give answers that are easy for an adult to overinterpret.

- Do not respond to every answer with another question. Try summarizing followed by open-ended questions that cannot be answered with a "yes" or "no." Avoid questions that may imply an expected answer.

Conscientious Christian counselors will experience a strong need to meet the child where he or she is and to empathize as much as possible. We continue to ask ourselves, "What would Jesus be saying and doing if *he* were the counselor instead of me?"

NOTES

1. R. Freeman and B. Couchman, "Coping with Family Change: A Model for Therapeutic Group Counseling with Children and Adolescents," *School Guidance Worker* 40, no. 5 (1985): 44–50.

2. E. Hancock, "The Dimensions of Meaning and Belonging in the Process of Divorce," *American Journal of Orthopsychiatry* 50, no. 1 (1980): 18–27.

3. A. Scherman and L. Lepak, "Children's Perceptions of the Divorce Process," *Elementary School Guidance and Counseling* (October 1986): 29–35.

4. "Where Have All the Children Gone?" *Business Week*, 29 June 1992.

5. M. Adams, "Kids and Divorce: No Long-Term Harm," *USA Today*, 20 December 1984, 1, 5D.

6. J. H. Brown, P. R. Portes, and D. A. Christensen, "Understanding Divorce Stress on Children: Implications for Research and Practice," *The American Journal of Family Therapy* 17, no. 4 (1989): 315–25.

7. Report of the Committee on Definition, American Psychological Association, Division of Counseling Psychology, *American Psychologist* 11 (1956): 283.

8. H. Glosoff and C. Kopowicz, *Children Achieving Potential: An Introduction to Elementary School Counseling and State-Level Policies* (Alexandria, Va.: American Association for Counseling and Development, 1990), 8.

9. C. L. Thompson and L. B. Rudolph, *Counseling Children* (Pacific Grove, Calif.: Brooks/Cole, 1992), 20.

10. J. A. Seltzer, "Legal Custody Arrangements and Children's Welfare," *American Journal of Sociology* 9, no. 4 (1991): 895–929; and W. J. Reid and A. Crisafulli, "Marital Discord and Child Behavior Problems: A Meta-Analysis," *Journal of Abnormal Child Psychology* 18, no. 1 (1990): 105–17.

11. W. F. Hodges, *Interventions for Children of Divorce: Custody, Access, and Psychotherapy* (New York: Wiley, 1986), 292.

12. A. Lazarus, "Multimodal Applications and Research: A Brief Overview and Update," *Elementary School Guidance and Counseling* 24 (1990): 243–47.

13. D. Keat, "Change in Multimodal Counseling," *Elementary School Guidance and Counseling* 24 (1990): 248–62; and E. Gerler, N. Drew, and P. Mohr, "Succeeding in Middle School: A Multimodal Approach," *Elementary School Guidance and Counseling* 24 (1990): 263–71.

14. V. Roseby and R. Deutsch, "Children of Separation and Divorce: Effects of a Social Role-Taking Group Intervention on Fourth and Fifth Graders," *Journal of Clinical Child Psychology* 14, no. 10 (1985): 55–60.

15. J. S. Wallerstein and S. Blakeslee, *Second Chances* (New York: Ticknor and Fields, 1989).

16. Ibid., 202.

17. J. R. Johnston, "Role Diffusion and Role Reversal: Structural Variations in Divorced Families and Children's Functioning," *Family Relations* 39 (1990): 405–13.

18. D. Johnson and F. Johnson, *Joining Together: Group Theory and Group Skills*, 3rd ed. (Englewood Cliffs, N.J.: Prentice-Hall, 1987).

19. W. Dyer and J. Vriend, *Group Counseling for Personal Mastery* (New York: Sovereign Books, 1980).

20. L. J. Alpert-Gillis, J. L. Pedro-Carroll, and E. L. Cowen, "The Children of Divorce Intervention Program: Development, Implementation, and Evaluation of a Program for Young Urban Children," *Journal of Consulting and Clinical Psychology* 57, no. 5 (1989): 583–89.

21. S. E. Bonkowski, S. Q. Bequette, and S. Boomhower, "A Group Design to Help Children Adjust to Parental Divorce," *The Journal of Contemporary Social Work* (1984): 131–39.

22. B. Herlihy and L. B. Golden, *Ethical Standards Casebook* (Alexandria, Va.: American Association for Counseling and Development, 1990): 24–25 (italics mine).

23. Ibid., 26.

24. Hodges, *Interventions*, 250.

25. E. A. Drake, "Helping Children Cope with Divorce: The Role of the School," in *Children of Separation and Divorce: Management and Treatment*, ed. I. R. Stuart and L. E. Abt (New York: Van Nostrand Reinhold, 1981).

26. Hodges, *Interventions*, 252.

27. A. Bradford et al., *Parting: A Counselor's Guide for Children of Separated Parents* (Columbia, S.C.: South Carolina Department of Education, 1982).

28. J. Garbarino and F. Stott, *What Children Can Tell Us* (San Francisco: Jossey-Bass, 1989).

Chapter 9

Counseling Adolescents and Young Adults

ADOLESCENTS AND YOUNG ADULTS EXPERIENCING THE DIVORCE of their parents face a dilemma of major proportions. At the time when they should be moving out of the home and into the realm of building an individual life and a family structure of their own, one of their parents is interfering by asking for a divorce. Parents who divorce when the children are teenagers or young adults face the accusation that they are placing their own needs above the normal developmental needs of their own children. Unlikely to be heard from younger children, older offspring even complain of competition from their parents—competition for independence, freedom, starting over, and being the one to break away first. Teenagers and young adults resent the fact that the decision made by their parents may prevent them from attending the college they had chosen. They resent the reality that the car expected as a graduation gift will not be arriving because of the added expense of the divorce. They resent so many losses they are forced to face for no other reason than Mom and Dad have decided not to remain married.

Stated simply, adolescents and young adults resent their parents' divorce because it gets in their way. Certainly they are upset because of the turmoil being inflicted on the family, but they are often *more* upset because of what the divorce is doing to them and the life they are trying to begin.

Should young people react with such resentment when they are old enough to understand why parents are doing what they are doing? Should the bitterness that is so common be there? Feelings are just feelings and cannot be done away with through rationalization and argument. The kids feel the way they feel!

SPACE-AGE CONCEPTS

Counseling adolescents and young adults requires an understanding of the developmental nature of this age group. Understanding the normal processes of development facilitates better counselor awareness of the underlying issues that are likely to be involved and, if compassionately shared with parents struggling to let go, can help the older generation understand what is happening to the family. After discussing the concept of developmental issues, we will apply the understanding to children of divorce.

SATELLIZATION

As soon as an infant is able to realize he or she is outside the womb, something to grab onto is sought. Anything placed into the infant's hand will be grasped, often with surprising strength. We are told this is nothing more than a reflex, an unconscious physical reaction to the palm of the hand being touched. Certainly this is true, but this early grasping reflex also serves to illustrate an instinctual awareness on the part of the infant that at this age separation is the primary danger.

We continue to see this behavior in older infants and toddlers who seem to have no ability to understand that Mother will return once she has moved out of the child's line of sight. Little children gravitate to their parents as the planets gravitate to the sun. In the natural science realm, if gravitational pull weakens, disaster and cataclysm result. If the child's ability to hold onto the parents is broken, panic follows. If the bond is not reestablished, the unattached or unbonded child may grow up to be psychologically disturbed and possibly a threat to himself or herself or to others.

The child orbits the parent as the earth orbits the celestial sun. The younger the child, the closer the orbit. The child is as interested in making sure the gravitational force continues as are the parents. If parents are not working to continue their bond with their children, they may be accused of child abuse or neglect. Children who do not have parents with whom they can establish their satellite status suffer developmentally as orphans have always suffered. Failure to thrive, failure to bond, lack of a sense of attachment, and conduct disorders are the common fate of those children who do not become satellites to their parents.

DESATELLIZATION

During adolescence, the second stage is observed. *Desatellization* is the term applied to the teenager beginning the process of breaking away from home and parents and moving into a different orbit, that of the peer group. Desatellization will begin the child's awareness of approaching adulthood and will continue until adult status is realized. Desatellization is generally traumatic for all parents but is particularly keen for those parents who do not understand the necessity of moving into another orbit.

For the majority of American adolescents, the teenage years are not especially troubling. For parents, however, the years when their children are adolescents can be a difficult period. Whatever we remember as pleasant about our own adolescence probably relates to the success we experienced breaking away from family. That is, if our parents did not fight our developing demands for independence, we probably remember having a pretty good time while teenagers. If, however, parents inappropriately fought the independence needs of their teenagers, then adolescence will likely be remembered by both parents and grown children as an unhappy time.

RESATTELIZATION

As teenagers we stretched the orbit. Some of us moved to and beyond the breaking point. Perhaps we moved so far away from the parental planet that we could not find our way home when the time was right to return. Perhaps the process of stretching the orbit was so painful for us or our parents that our parents were not willing to let us come back into the same orbit. "Not so close," we may hear our older parents say. "You hurt us badly once with your demands for freedom and independence; we will keep you at a safe distance now to protect ourselves. You may come back into our neighborhood but not into the home of your childhood. We can't be hurt like that again!"

For most, however, the orbit was not pushed so far that family was permanently alienated. Most parents will let prodigals come home again (metaphorically speaking only), but neither we nor our parents want the orbit relationship to be as close as it was during childhood. What is natural and healthy for a little child becomes codependent and destructive for a young adult. The orbit established is to be close but not too close, distant but not out of touch, connected but still free and voluntary.

THE CHILD'S NEED FOR SATELLIZATION

For the younger child, divorce pulls Mom or Dad's finger out of the tiny fist. Divorce, separation, death, even long-term illness or involuntary separation force the child to search for something else to hold onto—something or someone to replace the parent no longer there for the child.

The child may find a grandparent to take the place of Mother or Father. The child may find that the one remaining parent possesses sufficient strength and has enough time to make up for the absent parent so that he or she can, in effect, be both parents. An older brother or sister, if older by a large margin, may fill the void of the missing parent.

The child may become sufficiently desperate, however, that he or she welcomes unsuitable parent substitutes into his or her young life. The child may turn to the single, middle-aged man next door who seems to like little children so much. Another child may turn to food and become grossly overweight in an attempt to plug the emotional hole in his or her heart. Children a little older may use alcohol or drugs to meet the needs left unfilled by the absent parent. By whatever means, the child will find a way to meet his or her needs. The child will see these behaviors as dangerous, destructive, or illegal *only* when there are more acceptable ways to meet needs. The young child of divorce knows that he or she might need to fend for himself or herself when Mom or Dad walks away, so meeting needs is all that matters.

INDEPENDENCE IMPACTED BY DIVORCE

We have already examined the impact of divorce on adolescents. We turn now to a brief discussion of the confluence of desatellization and parental divorce.

Adolescents are striving to prove to others and themselves that they can make it on their own. Even while only in the preparation stage of breaking away, independence becomes the sole focus of their time and energy. Teenagers talk among themselves and compare notes on the relative amounts of freedom being experienced by peers. Howls of complaint, admiration, and jealousy emanate from groups of teens doing nothing more than talking about how free or imprisoned each feels. The car so diligently saved for, entering college or the service, dating or planning to get married with or without the consent of parents, moving into an apartment with friends upon graduation, all illustrate the mind-set of American adolescents who cannot wait to get their post-family life started.

Then Mom and Dad announce their separation and plans for divorce! All of a sudden, the teenager planning to go into outer orbit hears that the flight has been canceled. The car will have to wait. Mom will need the money to get a car to get back and forth to work. College becomes less likely, except at the boring, unglamorous, too-close-to-home community college! Entering the service now becomes an issue of loyalty to the custodial parent. "Can Mom make it if I go into the army? Perhaps I should remain at home, get a job after graduating high school, and just stick around and try to help out the family."

All choices confronting the adolescent in this situation are unhappy and unwelcome choices. All choices diminish the adolescent's drive to greater autonomy. And all choices for the adolescent are forced by decisions being made by parents who are supposed to be willing to put the needs of their children above their own needs. Not only is the orbit not going to be stretched for a while, the teenager may even turn inward and seek internal escape through alcohol, drugs, or promiscuous sex. The final escape, suicide, is more common among teenagers who have experienced a parental divorce.

Older adolescents, though typically more mature and better able to deal with crises, also struggle with parental divorce. How well or how poorly older adolescents adjusted depends upon their age and the length of time (if any) they had been out of the home since the divorce. Religious belief mitigated to some extent the negative impact of parental divorce as did the relative amount of parental conflict prior to and following the divorce. The following problems were seen as statistically more likely for older adolescents facing the divorce of their parents compared to those from intact families:

difficulty concentrating on studies

drug use

sleep problems

eating problems

withdrawal

dependency on roommates

difficulty with intimate relationships

depression

anxiety

sexual identity problems

fears of abandonment

finances

loyalty conflicts

feelings of insecurity[1]

Other researchers have investigated the long-term effects of parental divorce on college-age young people. For those who were between the ages of eighteen and thirty when their parents divorced, it was found that:

1. Fathers, more often than mothers, were blamed for the divorce. Several years after the divorce, the adult child-father relationship was still strained.

2. Divorce forced the adult child to struggle with acceptance of each parent as a separate person and caused the child to differentiate himself or herself, sometimes prematurely, from the family of origin. In some instances, parental divorce pulled the child back into the family, thus hampering separation.

3. Most of the young adults, despite sadness and worry, eventually continued on their delayed developmental paths.[2]

The conclusions of available research inevitably lead to the recognition of a disruption of the expanded orbit aspect for older adolescents. Anger over their lives being interfered with can lead to more long-term problems including depression, increased stress, and increased feelings of insecurity. The strongest negative reactions appear to be in the daughters and are directed primarily at the father.[3] Details not withstanding, when adolescent movement toward independence is detoured, time lost by the adolescent may not be made up for years if at all.

Hypermaturity

The term applied to a child or adolescent moving up to a developmental level beyond what is reasonably expected is *hypermaturity*. This accelerated growth and psychological development should not involve a solely negative connotation. Hypermaturity is seen in young people in many different areas and functions, and while the concept contains many positive elements, risks to the hypermature young person exist as well.

When comparing adolescents from intact and divorced homes, for example, we note that those from divorced homes had an easier time adjusting to college life away from home and reported feeling more separated than their college-age peers from intact families.[4] Other studies have supported the hypothesis that college students from divorced homes demonstrate greater functional, emotional, and attitudinal independence from parents, especially from fathers.[5] At first glance this might appear to be an advantage, but in families where the transmission of values is seen as important, independence implies less successful passage of those values from parent to children.

Divorce may accelerate most forms of parent-young adult separation and promote earlier individuation, ego maturity, and courtship activity.[6] Research also implies that these benefits may come at the expense of lowered opinion of both parents, especially the father. Counselors working with college students from divorced families would do well to gather background information on the family's divorce experience and to assess the young person's current relationship with his or her divorced parents.[7]

Prospects for the future are often clouded for children of divorce. One commonly accepted hypothesis, which is supported by current research, suggests that disruptions experienced in the family of origin constitute a risk factor for persons who in adulthood are facing similar situations involving the breaking of a social bond. Those men and women with more evidence of childhood disruptions demonstrated greater difficulty in letting go of the former relationship and in entering new relationships. Background data on stalkers and former husbands who seem unable to let go of their previous marriage indicate a common trait of childhood experiences with disruptions such as divorce. Thus, when confronted with a client whose reaction to a disruption appears excessive, the counselor should carefully investigate that person's background.[8]

HIERARCHY OF SEPARATION TASKS

Problems of separation for adolescents and young adults who have experienced a parental divorce tend to organize themselves into a hierarchy or time-line.

1. Those concerns likely to be faced and hopefully resolved during the first post-divorce year include:

   Acknowledging the reality of the marital rupture.

   Disengaging from parental conflict and distress and resuming customary pursuits.

2. Concerns likely to be faced and resolved or continually reworked concurrently or later are:

   Resolving the loss.

   Resolving anger and self-blame.

   Accepting the permanence of the divorce.

3. Concerns likely to be faced and resolved into later adulthood include:

   Achieving realistic hope for relationships.

   Communicating relationship values to children.[9]

ADDITIONAL CONCERNS FOR THE ADOLESCENT AND YOUNG ADULT

Life-long adjustment difficulties should be anticipated as a result of parental divorce. It is well known that inappropriate sexual orientation and other gender-based concerns are more common in children who have lost a same-sex parent for any reason. Divorce is extremely potent in negatively impacting the child, primarily because of the perceived voluntary nature of the parent's departure from the home. Given that the majority of absent parents are fathers, counselors would expect greater adjustment challenges in male clients from divorced families.[10]

Counselors need to be alert to male clients expressing problems handling anger and aggression, as was the case with fourteen-year-old Scott Craig. Such clients also tend to struggle with separation/individuation issues and gender identity/sexual orientation.[11]

Young people old enough to understand adult issues in parental divorce often feel caught between parents. Having a close relationship with both parents helps relieve this burden, so counselors will want to encourage reasonable contact between grown children and their divorced parents.[12]

THE COUNSELING PROCESS

There are several counseling theories appropriate to working with adolescents and young adults from divorced families. Rather than attempt to exhaustively discuss those theories, I will present more general counseling principles known to be important when counseling with this broad age group.

Principles for Counseling Adolescents and Young People

1. Adolescents are always potentially psychologically ill and not just going through a phase. Reports from the National Institute for Mental Health indicate that adolescents are among those groups with the greatest risk for psychological and emotional breakdown serious enough to warrant hospitalization. When a parent says, "My daughter is just going through a difficult time right now," counselors cannot make such an assumption.

2. Parents, family, and concerned others are important in assessment and treatment. Family background and life experiences are important to the counselor's knowledge base, and proper diagnosis and treatment planning depend as much on anecdotal material as on formal assessment.

3. Any adequate assessment of an adolescent must include:

   Biological maturation status and associated feelings including body image and self-esteem.

   Intrapsychic conflicts. Specifically, is the adolescent or young adult at war with the self over appearance, personality, income, etc.?

   The young person's position in relation to developmental tasks (i.e., preparing for home-leaving, preparing for marriage and family life, preparing for career).

   Information from outside the family (i.e., school, church, neighborhood, employer).

4. The goals of counseling include the attainment of psychological independence, a reduction of symptoms, and improved orientation to reality.

GUIDELINES FOR COUNSELING ADOLESCENTS AND YOUNG PEOPLE

The first contact is important. Specifically, who made it (parent, young person, pastor)? When was the appointment made, and did the caller appear to be upset?

Adolescents often do not present themselves or their problems willingly. The important issue is that they come for the appointment. Adolescents often feel a need to protest *any* decision made for them by authority figures regardless of the extent to which they feel a need for help.

Do not promise complete confidentiality. Most adolescents will be minors in the eyes of the law, and an ethical counselor will explain limitations on confidentiality. Counselors must report instances of suspected child (adolescent) abuse, threats to self or others, etc. Counselors may also be subpoenaed. The counselor should not be constrained from consulting with professional colleagues in difficult cases. We want to put our youthful clients at ease but cannot go so far as to promise what we cannot deliver.

Professional counselors must be prepared to inquire into virtually all areas of the adolescent's life. What information may appear peripheral at first consideration can prove to be very important as the counseling process continues.

Attempts at manipulation by the young person should be expected and dealt with as they arise. Specifically, even though parents request help from the counselor, they may be reluctant to go further if necessary. "Tough love" is a concept foreign to many parents. Unfortunately, some adolescent clients may have learned to react to threats by getting into even greater amounts of trouble. Threats such as suicide, pregnancy, and running away must be dealt with head-on by the counselor with hospital, police, and alternate living arrangements available if needed.

Counselors must remember that adolescents may not be able to handle adult responsibilities and obligations. Adults often confuse physical growth with emotional and psychological maturity, and counselors may be prone to such a false assumption as well. Be careful not to assign homework to adolescent clients lacking sufficient maturity to follow through on such tasks. Counselors working with teenagers will also want to avoid trusting physical appearance as an adequate gauge of other types of growth. If the teenager comes from a dysfunctional family, it would be reasonable to assume that there may be a deficiency in learned skills related to family problem solving. Though the orientation of Carl Rogers and client-centered therapy may be somewhat out of favor with some Christian and non-Christian counselors, his emphasis on knowing and accepting the client's frame of reference and avoidance of unfounded assumptions should be helpful when working with adolescents.

Counselors should be careful to be aware of physical appearance, clothing, and personal hygiene, noting rapid and unexplained changes. Anyone working with adolescents knows how quickly a clothing or hairstyle fad can sweep through the teen subculture. Part of being able to relate well to adolescents is learning not to overreact to these changes. However, there is a difference between being carefully and methodically sloppy in appearance and being disheveled and unconcerned about how one looks. Teens are manifestly self-conscious, and lack of personal hygiene and sloppy appearance are more likely to indicate some form of personal adjustment difficulty (such as depression) rather than a mere fashion statement. Counselors should be particularly concerned if they see a rapid and unexplained deterioration in personal appearance in adolescents.

Counselors will note that confrontation and argument are standard operating procedures for American teenagers. The teenage client who comes to the counseling office with a chip on his or her shoulder should be viewed as normal. Teens learn to deal with authority figures defensively if not aggressively. Challenge and debate from an adolescent client are not to be seen as true confrontation but rather as a form of self-defense in an anxious situation. The challenge is for the counselor to see the individual person underneath the chip on the shoulder.

Counselors and other mental health professionals must be prepared to share personal values, ideals, and beliefs. It has been accepted by the counseling profession for some time that personal values are a helpful adjunct rather than a hindrance to counseling. Though required to conform to ethical guidelines regarding appropriate self-disclosure and recognizing that there may be some limitations on values disclosure in public facilities such as mental health agencies and schools, such ethically guided sharing of values can be helpful. Adolescent clients will be looking for evidence of trust by the counselor, and personal sharing of relevant information can be helpful in building a good relationship.

It is useful to combine family counseling with individual counseling when working with an adolescent. Even in dysfunctional family situations, parents and other family members will possess valuable information that may not be available anywhere else. Information regarding friends, attitudes, typical activities, and reactions to authority figures can be best gained through first-hand information from family members. In cases where a parent is unavailable or unwilling to participate in family counseling (as is often the case in single-parent families), that person's absence may be as revealing and important as what might have been learned if they had been in the counselor's office.

What the Adolescent Client Needs to Experience

Much of what we are discussing pertains to counseling with adolescents in general rather than just single-parent adolescents. Good counseling has basic tenets, of course, and what follows are important attributes of effective counseling with adolescents regardless of family situation.

Adolescent clients need to experience the counselor as understanding them and their situation. The intimacy of the family situation and resultant embarrassment in the adolescent makes it very difficult for the young person to share openly. It will be assumed that adolescent functioning will be limited following divorce, especially in the face of three sets of stressors: (1) separation and divorce of parents, (2) poor relationship with mother, and (3) poor relationship with father.[13] Counselors will need to be prepared to extend themselves to demonstrate support and advocacy as well as empathy. Withdrawal is a common experience for adolescents going through a parental divorce, and acknowledgement of the need to leave the family temporarily will enhance the counseling relationship and build empathy.[14]

Adolescent clients need to experience the counselor as having similar experiences or of concurrently sharing their experiences. Core conditions as outlined by Carl Rogers include:

1. Two persons are in psychological contact.
2. The first, the client, is experiencing incongruence.
3. The second, the counselor, is congruent or integrated in the relationship.
4. The counselor experiences unconditional positive regard for the client.
5. The counselor experiences an empathic understanding of the client's internal frame of reference and endeavors to communicate this experience to the client.
6. The communication to the client of the counselor's empathic understanding and unconditional positive regard is to a minimal degree achieved.[15]

The realization of these prerequisite conditions should enable the counselor to communicate at least a minimal level of empathy and should facilitate the counseling process. Failure to attain a minimal level of any of these conditions will seriously impair any counselor's ability to build a therapeutic relationship.

Adolescent clients need to experience unconditional positive regard. Clients generally have a felt need to experience in their counselor what they have been missing in other areas of life. Unconditional positive regard is caring that is unconditional in that it is not contaminated by evaluation or judgment of the client's feelings, thoughts, and behavior as good or bad. This acceptance should not be understood as an *absence* of values on the part of the counselor but rather a *temporary suspension* of comments that could be taken as an evaluation by the client. The counselor possesses an attitude of "I'll accept you as you are" rather than "I'll accept you when————." Unconditional acceptance is a recognition of the client's right to his or her feelings; *it is not the acceptance or approval of all behavior.*

Adolescent clients need to experience a degree of satisfaction from the counseling session. Relief is an important component in establishing a therapeutic relationship with an adolescent. If the teenager feels better or has the hope of feeling better in the near future, the counseling process can be expected to continue to a beneficial outcome. Counselors should not emphasize intake information to the exclusion of getting to know the client during the first session. If the client does not feel better in the first session, he or she is unlikely to return for the next.

Adolescent clients need to feel safe in the counseling relationship. The difference between *being* safe in counseling and *feeling* safe is important. The issue is client perception rather than counselor intention. Effective counselors know they will do no harm. Adolescent clients typically do not trust adult authority figures, and no matter how dedicated a counselor may be to the proposition that he or she is no more than a highly trained equal, it will take more than attitude to convince the adolescent that this is really the case. Feeling safe means:

- knowing and believing that confidentiality will be maintained;
- knowing what your counselor will and will not do;
- the counselor is perceived to be an advocate as much as an expert, for the client at least as much as for the client's family;
- feeling protected from criticism and evaluation during the sessions;
- feeling no threat.

Adolescent clients need to feel a sense of togetherness in the counseling relationship. The client must experience empathy on the part of the counselor to such an extent that he or she truly feels understood. The client experiencing togetherness feels as if he or she is sharing problems with someone who knows what to do, and that client and counselor are, in fact, in this thing together.

ADDITIONAL RESOURCES

Several anticipatory counseling strategies for use with adolescent and young-adult clients have been formulated.

Anticipatory counseling is preventative in focus and accepts the proposition that major personal reorganization will follow a family trauma as significant as divorce.[16] Counseling strategies to be discussed accept the following tenets:

1. The family's organization (or reorganization) governs the individual functioning of its members such that a viable organization sustains adequate individual functioning.

2. The data refute the notion of a unitary and necessarily catastrophic response of adolescents and young adults to the divorce of their parents.

3. Divorce is probably within the realm of adaptation for many families and adolescents.[17]

A study of post-divorce reorganization of family relationships between children of any age and their divorcing parents concluded that adjustment involved one or all of the following:

• A reassertion of the solidarity of the parent-adult child relationship.

• The divorced individual's retreat within the privacy of the nuclear family unit.

• Mobilization of an expanded network of friends and relatives of which parents are only a part.[18]

A 1983 study of the need for preventative counseling in high school suggested the following strategies for conducting such counseling with adolescents and young adults experiencing family divorce.

1. Sharing frustrations and concerns with peers.

2. Identifying coping mechanisms and developing new ones.

3. Improving communication patterns and interpersonal relationships with parents and others.

4. Discussing expectations about future relationships, marriage, and divorce.

5. Developing available resources and support systems.[19]

When dealing with combative, arbitrary, and argumentative conflict, certain resolution strategies have been proposed and tested. Important elements include:

1. Cognitive description that strictly avoids emotional overtones.

2. Description of the feelings generated.

3. Formulatation and description of a situation favorable to everyone.

4. Changes that are agreed to rather than imposed.

5. Follow-up plans and specific dates for accomplishment are established.[20]

These formulations were suggested in the hope that ongoing turmoil might be avoided. This seems to be a reasonable expectation when effective counseling is a part of the divorce recovery process.

THE PARENT PERSPECTIVE

Single parents with adolescent or young-adult children tend to react to parenting challenges in one of three ways: capitulation, rigidity, or realignment. We do occasionally find some combinations and overlapping of responses, but from a counseling perspective, most parents will react in one predominate manner.

Capitulation. Parents surrender to the demands of their children in the face of the apparently overwhelming challenges of single parenthood. At times this type of parental reaction is perceived to be a return to adolescence by the custodial parent and is usually harshly judged and criticized by friends and family members. Capitulation is the most extreme fear reaction short of abandoning the family altogether. Capitulation is a stress response and may represent poor parenting skills on the part of the custodial parent—a deficiency that may have been compensated for by the other spouse until the marriage ended.

Legalistic rigidity. Also a fear reaction, legalistic rigidity is often seen in families that were once strong and together in their childrearing. Upon the departure of one parent, the remaining parent attempts to rebuild the family fortress. This is done through a return to rules and regulations perceived to characterize previous better days. The custodial parent tends to think, "If this or that rule was good when the children had two parents, then toughening the rule should be better now that I am the only one in charge." Counselors will recognize this as more common in single-parent families with teens or young adults still at home. We should note that while structure and strength are to be commended, legalistic rigidity tends to unfairly punish family members for what a parent did.

Adjustment. Unlike the two preceding reactions, adjustment is not fear-based but is characterized by the ability of the custodial parent to listen, negotiate, and respond appropriately to the needs of teens and young adults at home. Adjustment by single parents tends to be very much a reflection of their own experiences as children. The single parent who can feel confident in the face of great challenges will communicate that confidence and personal power to the children in the family who will in turn respond more positively to their own challenges. Adjustment tends to be characterized more than anything else by reasonable boundary-setting, a significant ability when raising adolescent and young-adult children as a single parent.

HELPING PARENTS UNDERSTAND ADOLESCENT AND YOUNG ADULT DEVELOPMENT

Parents are often confused by what they see in their adolescent and young-adult children. This confusion may stem from a lack of clarity regarding what parents want from their children. Similarly, parents express concerns regarding what they hope does *not* develop in their adolescents and young adults. The following table shows the most common desires and concerns of parents as well as the areas of greatest conflict.

Parent-Adolescent Conflict: What Do We Want?

1. WHAT DO PARENTS REALLY WANT FROM THEIR ADOLESCENTS?

be responsible   use common sense

be reliable   value their education

be respectful   appreciate parents

be thoughtful   control sex

be honest   act mature

dress appropriately

2. WHAT DO PARENTS *NOT* WANT FROM THEIR ADOLESCENTS?

back talk   embarrassment

premarital sex   alcohol/drug use

bad friends

Parent-Adolescent Conflict: What We Fight About!

1. SCHOOL

study habits and study attitudes attendance

grades and level of performance

attitudes toward school personnel

2. FAMILY RELATIONSHIPS

relationships with relatives   immature behavior

problems with siblings

attitude toward and respect for parents

3. SOCIAL ACTIVITIES

choice of dates and friends   hair and clothing styles

curfew   frequency of going out

going steady   acceptable places to go

4. RESPONSIBILITY FOR

household duties   use of the telephone

use of the family car   earning and spending money

working outside the home

taking care of room and personal belongings

5. VALUES AND MORALITY	
honesty	sexual behavior
language	obeying the law
alcohol, tobacco, and drug use	
attending church and Sunday school	

DEALING WITH THE ADOLESCENT SUBCULTURE

Most adolescents and young adults recognize that it is not in their best interest to become involved with one of the many subcultures available to American young people today. However, there are those who for whatever reason do join a subculture. Depending on the part of the country one lives in, teenagers might choose the bikers, headbangers (heavy-metal music), surfers (on the West Coast), druggies (including alcohol and *all* forms of drugs), jocks (athletics and chewing tobacco), skinheads (racial bigots), rappers (as in rap music), turf gangs, and many more that are common to limited geographical areas. The most prevalent and worrisome to the average family is probably the druggie subculture.

Counseling adolescents and young adults who have turned to a subculture as a defense against the insecurity brought on by family breakup can be difficult. Several considerations are important.

First, for adolescents and young adults there are basically three options. The young person can remain in the mainstream adolescent and young-adult culture. Or the young person may select an alternative subculture that is not particularly negative or hostile to mainstream culture, such as jocks, rappers, or headbangers. As unwelcome as the latter two might be in the typical Christian home, youngsters can be expected to survive the music and grow up anyway.

The third option available to young people is the negative subculture. Kids in this category tend to come from two forms of experience. The first group includes those who are *dropping out* or severing their relationship with the mainstream culture. These youngsters have had experience, sometimes extensive, with the main adolescent and young-adult culture and are choosing to go in another direction. The second group is made up of young people who have never been a part of the mainstream culture. This multigenerational group is not so much leaving as deciding not to join at all. An example of this might be children born into the hippie movement who are now grown and may have only a limited idea of how straights live.

COUNSELING AND THE ADOLESCENT SUBCULTURE

The challenge to counselors and other concerned adults is to provide an alternative subculture sufficiently attractive so as to draw young people to it. This will not be possible until we become aware of what the negative subcultures are offering American youth.

MEETING NEEDS

What do American young people get from subcultures? Why are they going outside the mainstream to find what they are looking for? Consider the following table.

Needs	Subculture Provides
A sense of competence	A place to feel competent
Effective coping skills	A place to use street smarts
Commitment to norms	Alternative norms
Social bond with institutions	Social bond with subculture
Positive self-esteem	Positive self-image
Independence and autonomy	Pseudo autonomy

SYMBOLS OF A SUBCULTURE

Symbols are important to young people and should not be written off as irrelevant or evidences of nothing more than a phase the young person is passing through. Understanding these symbols will help parents and other concerned adults recognize a young person's involvement in a subculture for the threat it is.

Folk heroes and folk stories. Those committed to a movement such as drugs, radical politics, or abusive music will trade stories about subculture leaders who have engaged in various antisocial and rebellious acts in the name of their cause. Reading material such as newsletters and magazines are common evidence of such involvement.

Special language. It has long been common to adolescents to invent a language that authority figures would not understand even though the words were in plain English. What was once called slang has now been transformed into many forms unique to the gang, interest, or geographic area of those employing it. One need only to try to understand lyrics of some forms of rap music to experience the potency of a special language.

Membership. We recognize gang membership and the various initiation rites associated with joining as typical of other types of antisocial activities. What we have often overlooked is that there are equally important, if not so obvious, membership obligations for those involved in the heavy-metal head-banger subculture and drug/alcohol subculture. It is just that the signs of initiation tend to be more subtle. Drinking to passing out, getting stoned on drugs, experiencing an LSD trip, and engaging in random and unprotected sex are all common initiation acts required to enter the more informal subculture groups.

Group names. Members, whether formally or informally initiated, will quickly come to identify themselves as skinheads, headbangers, deadheads, bikers, surfers, and so on. Parents should watch for evidence that their young person has started labeling clothing and school books with group names or even gone to the extreme of self-inflicted tattoos of the group name.

Group dress. Members of a subculture tend to take what appears to be an inordinate amount of pride in dressing consistent with other members of the subculture. Regardless of the amount of consternation caused for parents and other adults, young people indoctrinated into a subculture will exhibit intense loyalty to other members and feel like traitors for dressing straight, even for special occasions.

Rituals. Subculture members tend to develop rituals connected with their group. This may involve getting stoned every

Friday night or attending sports events, rock concerts, or general gatherings as faithfully as others attend church. Rituals may include special handshakes or other coded ways of greeting others in the subculture.

Values. Over time, young people involved in a subculture will come to accept the values of that group as their own. There is a significant risk that if parents or other significant adults fail to take this seriously and intervene, the young person may become lost to the mainstream culture permanently. Evidence for this permanence can be seen in the large number of unreconstructed hippies and flower children approaching retirement age but still "living the life."

DIRECTIONS FOR COUNSELING

The needs of sixteen-year-old Emily and fourteen-year-old Scott controlled the counseling process and directed that process differently for each. Emily struggled with a sense of abandonment by her father and turned her negative feelings inward, developing depression and eating disorders. Scott turned his anger outward and began to become something of an aggressor at school and at home. For each of these young people counseling is an ongoing process and has not yet achieved the levels of adjustment we hope to attain. Their parents and I remain optimistic about the future for these two, believing that the underlying love of *both* parents and the pre-divorce strength of the family will eventually pay good dividends in mental and spiritual health.

Some general suggestions for counseling can be offered here, with the caveat that what works with one young person will often not work with another. The absence of specific treatment regimens in this chapter recognizes the need to be truly eclectic in counseling. Some general directions and goals might include:

1. Promote *reciprocal tolerance* within the family.
2. Develop and enhance *self-awareness* by and for all family members.

3. Raise the *level of motivation* to help and support one another. Some have called this "team building."

4. Increase the ability to *resist frustration*.

5. Understand the application of *biblical principles* to family problems.

6. Recognize the importance of the counseling *relationship*.

7. Maintain *flexibility* in determining whose behavior needs to be altered and to what extent.

8. Establish and strengthen *communication* between all parties involved in the process.

9. Consider the *developmental status and needs* of the focus young person.

10. View the entire counseling process as one of *reeducation* and possibly also *reparenting*.

WHEN CONFRONTATION IS NEEDED

In situations where parents feel the problems arise because of friends, the following recommendations to parents often prove helpful:

1. Do not challenge directly. Recognize that confrontation and argument are normal defenses for young people. Counselors and parents need to avoid being placed in the position of directly challenging the young person.

2. If the issue is friends, encourage parents to try to control the contacts rather than outright forbidding them. Recognize, too, that there are certainly times when totally disallowing any contact is appropriate. Situations that could become dangerous or exploitative are in this category.

3. If questions are appropriate, ask questions that are open-ended (not supplying or implying the expected answer) and from an open-minded orientation. For example, a parent might say, "What does John's father do for a living?" rather than, "I suppose John's dad is unemployed like most of those folks who live in that part of town."

4. Do not make threats unless prepared to carry them out. Counselors will try to avoid this position routinely, but parents may need to be encouraged to only warn or threaten when they are prepared to back up their words with action.

5. Be evangelistic. Christian parents, even stressed-out single parents, can be encouraged to see the spiritual needs of their children's adolescent and young-adult friends. As difficult as this may be when under stress, our responsibility to witness the love of God to the friends of our children is not diminished by marital status.

CONCLUSION

I am confident that Emily and Scott will continue to make improvement in days to come. Although I know I am being used of God to help, I recognize that I am not the most important element in their recovery.

Emily and Scott have two parents who continue to love and support them and who, with considerable difficulty, have been able to place the needs of their children above their own need to do battle with each other. Emily and Scott have been well taught in a Bible-based church that provides support as well as good preaching and teaching. They have many Christian friends of several different age groups to call on when they need help.

Most importantly, they have a God they love and who loves them. They know this God to be one who has been there in the difficult past days and whom they can rely on to be there in the less-difficult days ahead.

NOTES

1. S. S. Farber, J. Primavera, and R. D. Felner, "Older Adolescents and Parental Divorce: Adjustment Problems and Mediators of Coping," *Journal of Divorce* 7, no. 2 (1983): 59–74.

2. S. E. Bonkowski, "Lingering Sadness: Young Adult's Response to Parental Divorce," *Social Casework* (April 1989): 219–23.

3. J. Bales, "Parent's Divorce Has Major Impact on College Students," *APA Monitor* 15, no. 8 (1984): 13.

4. S. F. Allen, C. D. Stoltenberg, and C. K. Rosko, "Perceived Separation of Older Adolescents and Young Adults from Their Parents: A Comparison of Divorced Versus Intact Families," *Journal of Counseling and Development* 89 (September/October 1990): 57–61.

5. F. G. Lopez, V. L. Campbell, and C. E. Watkins, "The Relation of Parental Divorce to College Student Development," *Journal of Divorce* 12, no. 1 (1988): 83–98.

6. A. Booth, D. B. Brinkerhoff, and L. K. White, "The Impact of Parental Divorce on Courtship," *Journal of Marriage and the Family* 65, no. 4 (1984): 85–94.

7. F. G. Lopez, "The Impact of Parental Divorce on College Student Development," *Journal of Counseling and Development* 65 (1987): 484–86; and P. R. Amato, "Parental Divorce and Attitudes toward Marriage and Family Life," *Journal of Marriage and the Family* 50 (1988): 453–61.

8. D. Chiriboga, L. Catron, and P. Weiler, "Childhood Distress and Adult Functioning during Marital Separation," *Family Relations* 36 (1987): 163–67.

9. S. S. Coffman and A. E. Roark, "Likely Candidates for Group Counseling: Adolescents with Divorced Parents," *The School Counselor* (March 1988): 246–52.

10. R. R. Sears, E. E. Maccoby, and H. Levin, *Patterns of Child Rearing* (Evanston, Ill.: Row, Peterson and Co., 1957); H. B. Biller, "Father Absence, Divorce, and Personality Development," in *The Role of Father in Child Development*, 2nd ed., ed. M. E. Lamb (New York: Wiley, 1981), 489–552; and J. W. Santrock and R. A. Warshak, "Father Custody and Social Development in Boys and Girls," *Journal of Social Issues* 35 (1979): 12–15.

11. N. Kalter, "Long-Term Effects of Divorce on Children: A Developmental Vulnerability Model," *American Journal of Orthopsychiatry* 57, no. 4 (1987): 587–600.

12. C. M. Buchanan, E. E. Maccoby, and S. M. Dornbusch, "Caught between Parents: Adolescents' Experiences in Divorced Homes," *Child Development* 62 (1991): 1008–29.

13. R. Forehand, K. Middleton, and N. Long, "Adolescent Functioning as a Consequence of Recent Parental Divorce and the Parent-Adolescent Relationship," *Journal of Applied Developmental Psychology* 8 (1987): 305–15.

14. J. S. Wallerstein and J. B. Kelly, "Responses of the Preshool Child to Divorce: Those Who Cope," in *Child Psychiatry: Treatment and Research*, ed. M. F. McMillan and S. Henao (New York: Brunner/Mazel, 1974).

15. C. Rogers, "The Underlying Theory: Drawn from Experiences with Individuals and Groups," *Counseling and Values* 32 (1987): 38–45.

16. L. Asmussen and R. Larson, "The Quality of Family Time among Young Adolescents in Single-Parent and Married-Parent Families," *Journal of Marriage and the Family* 53 (1991): 1021–30.

17. D. Abelsohn and G. S. Saayman, "Adolescent Adjustment to Parental Divorce: An Investigation from the Perspective of Basic Dimensions of Structural Family Therapy Theory," *Family Process* 30 (1991): 177–91.

18. C. L. Johnson, "Postdivorce Reorganization of Relationships between

Divorcing Children and Their Parents," *Journal of Marriage and the Family* 50 (1988): 221–31.

19. Y. Camiletti, "Anticipatory Counseling for Adolescents of Divorced Parents," *The School Guidance Worker* 39, no. 1 (1983): 20–23.

20. S. G. Coffman, "Conflict-Resolution Strategy for Adolescents with Divorced Parents," *The School Counselor* 38 (1988): 61–66.

Chapter 10

Counseling Single Parents

THERE IS NO REASON TO EXPECT THE NUMBER of single-parent families to decline. Research cited in chapter 1 demonstrates a trend toward more and more nontraditional families. The concepts of traditional and nontraditional have undergone radical transformations in recent years and, as discussed earlier, the "traditional" family of two biological parents raising their two children now accounts for less than 50 percent of American families. The concept of "broken home" as well has been largely discarded and replaced with a kinder, gentler way of thinking about single-parent families. The quiet acceptance of the term *single-parent family* as a replacement for *broken home* illustrates the change in current thinking related to what is traditional and normal.

Our concern in this chapter is not so much the family unit or children but the single parent. It is no longer assumed that children raised in single-parent families will inevitably develop some form of pathology. Sufficient numbers of single-parent children have grown up successfully so as to contradict what has been for many years a doomsday-type assumption of problems ahead. Focusing attention on the needs of the single parent is not only appropriate but balanced when considering the crucial role parental mental health plays in the future of the entire family as well as the broader community and culture.

NEEDS OF THE SINGLE PARENT

Single parents often feel overwhelmed by the mundane, day-to-day tasks of simply living. Housekeeping chores, child management, school, work, financial responsibilities, and relationships constitute the majority of presenting problems for single parents seeking help. Single parents typically describe themselves as "exhausted" and "lonely," and the help they seek needs to be practical rather than theoretical or preachy.

SPECIFIC FELT NEEDS

Most divorced single parents will spend considerable time reflecting on the following questions. Researchers have found that these are specific needs that single parents face.

1. How do I parent alone? Parenting without a partner in a society that too often continues to assume two-parent homes to be the norm can be stressful and anxiety-producing. Single parents want help from the counselor regarding disciplining children, paying bills, finding employment, and dealing with developing relationships as a single person.

2. Is it acceptable to feel as lonely as I feel? And how long will I feel this way? Single parents describe themselves as exhausted first, but feeling lonely is always near the top of single-parent problem lists.

3. How do I cope? The divorce experience is among the most traumatic of all experiences, and it is common to hear single-parent clients express doubt about their ability to successfully cope with a transition of such significance.

4. How will I manage financially? We have found that the standard of living declines for both partners following a divorce, but the decline is much more severe for a single mother with children. Again, the issue of practicality in providing advice and information on finances is noteworthy. Many of my single-parent clients who have seen church-based counselors following their divorce complain that the information they received on finances was long on principles (continue to tithe, do not go into debt) but short on *how* to manage on a day-to-day basis.

5. Is there life after divorce? More emotional than rational, this question tends to be an expression of the intense worry experienced by single parents regarding their hopes for the future. Single parents worry about getting married again, obtaining some degree of financial security, providing for the needs of growing children, and finding happiness.

6. What will my family become? Now that singleness has begun to sink in, custodial parents worry about family relationships. Will I be accepted by other family members? Will my son have problems establishing a male sex-role identity now that his father has left us? Will my daughter be at risk for teen pregnancy because I have to go to work and may not be able to properly supervise her after school? Will my children eventually have to go through their own divorces because of my divorce?

7. Am I a strong enough Christian to really trust God to meet our needs? I have never had my faith tested like it is being tested now. Will God be pleased with the measure of faith I have, or will I fall short? What will the pastor and others in the church think about my Christianity in the next few years as I try to manage as a single parent?

8. What can I learn from Bible characters who lived single lives? Is it right for me to try and compare myself with them, given differences in historical timing, culture, education, etc.? Am I being unfair to myself and my family by expecting specific answers from the Bible?

9. Will I ever again be accepted as a full citizen of my church? Or will I always be burdened with being seen as different by the people who were my friends before the divorce?

10. What resources are available to me? Who or what can I call on in time of need to help with my finances, the children, finding employment, developing friendships to combat my sense of loneliness, and eventually finding someone to marry and spend my life with? Who or what can help me do these things?[1]

My contacts with Sue Craig and many other single parents, mostly mothers with child custody, confirm the relevance of these concerns. Counselors need to affirm the importance of such expressed concerns, even in the face of what appears to the counselor to be strong evidence that the concerns will not be as serious as the client expects.

A FRAMEWORK FOR THERAPY

Single parents continue to live in the family system thought to have been dismantled with the divorce. Terms such as "unfinished marriage" and "unfinished divorce"[2] have been employed to illustrate the ongoing adjustment typical in post-divorce families. I have found it helpful to raise questions such as "Is your marriage really as dead as you seem to think? Are there not some unresolved issues left over from your marriage that are still bothering you? Is it possible that some of the troubles you are now experiencing are related to unfinished business from the marriage?"

The same type questions could apply to an unfinished divorce. Many clients assume, usually incorrectly, that when the divorce became or will become final, they will feel free to move on with the rest of life. This is an unreasonable expectation in the great majority of divorces and needs to be confronted in counseling. The client needs to be encouraged to think of his or her marital transition as an ongoing process that may take many years to fully conclude, and in some cases, it may *never* be completely finished.

To encourage clients to confront important issues that may be as yet under the surface, I have found questions assigned as homework or interjected into the counseling sessions to be helpful. The following questions serve as a focus of attention rather than as prescriptions for counseling. Counselors using this method should use care in phrasing and timing of these questions and assignments so that clients respond from their own perspective rather than what they think the counselor wants or expects to hear.[3]

1. Describe what you would like to accomplish in the following areas in the next five years:

   a. financially

   b. socially

   c. vocationally

   d. emotionally

   e. spiritually

2. Describe steps you are taking in each of the areas listed above to make your dreams a reality.

3. Describe how you will reconstruct your spiritual life as a single parent in terms of worship, service, and witness.

4. Describe ways you can change your thinking and feeling about yourself and others.

5. Describe ways you can reconstruct your social life in terms of terminating some relationships, maintaining present relationships, and starting new relationships.

6. Describe your dreams for your children. What are some of the ways you can help make those dreams a reality?

7. Describe ways in which you will love yourself, others, and God.

8. Describe what you are doing to forsake destructive past attitudes and actions toward yourself, others, and God.

9. Describe what you are going to do to help yourself grow personally, socially, and spiritually.

MEN AS SINGLE PARENTS

NONCUSTODIAL FATHERS

Fathers are never so irrelevant to children that continued contact becomes unimportant. Though relationships between father and children will surely change when they no longer live in the same home, Dad is always important.

The noncustodial father may be able to develop new relationships with his children that can be independent of the family of origin. He may be able to become more nurturing and caring once the marital stresses are resolved. Father may be able to develop a "friend" type relationship to supplement his standard role as authority figure. Now that he is, to some degree, free from family pressures and the constant presence of children, the noncustodial father may make time spent with his children more special and intimate.

Noncustodial fathers, however, must also face loss of income, loneliness, and loss of relationship. It is more expensive to maintain two homes than one, and if remarriage occurs, men who continue to support the first family can find themselves in debt. This can be compounded by the burden of legal costs.

Men without their children often find they have too much time on their hands. This can leave the father feeling lonely and lost. The loss of relationship with his children can deepen over time, especially in the presence of continued conflict between parents[4]

CUSTODIAL FATHERS

The ranks of fathers with custody has grown from approximately 600,000 in 1980 to an estimated one million today.[5] While most fathers with custody report feeling comfortable in their single-parent roles, the minority who felt uncomfortable felt that way primarily due to different and more negative experiences with the marital and parental role. Counseling interventions are needed for those single fathers bringing their own problems to the parenting role or who were simply struggling to manage their new responsibilities. For those custodial single fathers who reported feeling some level of discomfort with their parental responsibilities, it was found that the father's discomfort decreases:

- as the number of years of sole custody increases;
- as satisfaction with the father's social life increases;[6]
- if the father has no religious affiliation or preference (presumably due to the absence of ostracism for his role from church people);
- as the father's income increases;
- as the father's rating of himself as a father increases.

The custodial father's discomfort increases:

- as the father's relationship with his children deteriorates;[7]
- if visitation decisions are handled less than amicably as opposed to very amicably.[8]

Counseling Recommendations with Custodial Single Fathers

1. Reassure the father that his situation will likely improve with time.
2. Provide concrete services.
3. If allowed, use sliding-fee scales that are sensitive to economic pressures on the client.
4. Provide flexible counseling hours.
5. Inquire about religious influences that may be producing stress.
6. Focus on his relationship with his children and his ex-wife.
7. Focus on his social life.

WOMEN AS SINGLE PARENTS

CUSTODIAL MOTHERS

Mothers typically have the most intimate, nurturing relationship with children. When mother becomes the sole resident parent, stresses and strains may test her resolve to be a good mother, but most single mothers with custody are reasonably successful being mother and father. The advantages of being a single mother with custody can include learning competence and confidence. Women find that they can manage, take charge of their lives, and care for their children. They can also become closer to their children. As they are forced to make adjustments together, the family can become more loving and cooperative. Despite the extra demands, the family tone can be more peaceful.

However, there are distinct disadvantages for the custodial single mother. The loss of income can affect lifestyle, entertainment, and freedom of choice regarding childcare and work.[9] Time is also a problem since women as single parents have barely enough time to do all that they must and have little or no personal time. The custodial single mother also may have no other adult to turn to for help. Even an irresponsible or unloving adult takes some of the burden of responsibility off a woman who now has to make all decisions alone. If the stress is too great, the single mother may abdicate the parental role.[10] Blurred intergenerational boundaries may lead to the mother removing herself from the parental role and moving into a more peer-oriented role.

NONCUSTODIAL MOTHERS

Several reasons are offered to explain the small but significant increase in mothers relinquishing custody of children following divorce.[11] It should be noted that mothers without custody continue to represent a very small proportion of custody situations, and comprehensive research, especially of a longitudinal nature, is only now beginning to surface. Preliminary findings regarding mothers without custody reveal the following:

1. There is greater societal acceptance of women's independence in recent years leading to less social ostracism.

2. There is less felt need by women to remain financially tied to former husbands through child support.

3. Fathers are increasingly seeking custody, and their requests are being supported by research that shows a child can be nurtured adequately by an adult other than the mother.[12]

4. More children are choosing to live with the father, and more courts are agreeing.

THE NONCUSTODIAL MOTHER OR FATHER: DILEMMAS AND INTERVENTIONS

For either parent, losing custody of his or her children can be traumatic. Part of the reason for the negative impact of loss of custody is that the noncustodial parent faces many dilemmas not experienced by custodial single parents or parents in intact families.[13]

DILEMMAS

In many ways the noncustodial parent can be in a "lose-lose" situation. Although noncustodial parents are labeled as irresponsible when they do not pay child support, they are also often criticized for trying to "buy" their children if they give them money or gifts. If they do not visit their children, noncustodial parents are accused of being bad parents, yet they are also criticized for being a bad influence when they *do* see their children.

Noncustodial parents often are told that they are not important as parents, and particularly if the children are doing well, they may accept this as true. However, if the children are not doing well, they are frequently blamed by others for the children's problems and may themselves feel guilty for not being there. While being criticized for not caring or being involved in the lives of their children, noncustodial parents may not be informed of what is occurring with the children. And although unemployed noncustodial parents are criticized for being unable to provide financially for the children, if they are employed they frequently are criticized for caring more for their career than their children.

The area of visitation poses many possible dilemmas for the noncustodial parents who may find that no matter how they approach visitation, they encounter difficulty. If they do not plan ahead, they are told they did not inform the custodial parent enough in advance; if they plan ahead, they are told that they are interfering with something already planned at home.[14] Criticized for being weekend or "Disneyland" parents, they are excluded from day-to-day contact with their children. Although noncustodial parents are told that the child support and visitation are separate issues, they usually are not permitted to see their children if they do not pay child support. Sadly, when post-divorce problems continue and no resolution seems realistic, attorneys often advise noncustodial parents to "wait until the children get older."

INTERVENTIONS WITH NONCUSTODIAL PARENTS

Counselors and other support people can help noncustodial single parents in many ways. The following is a short list of some of the most common interventions.

1. Assist noncustodial parents to control, reduce, or eliminate emotional reactions. This can be accomplished most readily by listening uncritically and through validating the feelings being expressed.

2. Assist noncustodial parents to accept the reality of their situation. Specifically:

   a. They are in a position that discounts the parental role.

   b. The court has the power to award custody, determine visitation, and order child support payments.[15]

   c. There are consequences of disobeying court orders, regardless of their feelings or whether they are permitted to see their children.

   d. The award of custody and determination of visitation are usually permanent and irreversible.

3. Assist noncustodial parents to stop behaving in self-defeating ways.

4. Assist noncustodial parents in realistically assessing their situation and negotiating an effective level of parental involvement without custody.

PITFALLS OF SINGLE PARENTING

The phrase "single-parent family" may lead one to think of the post-divorce family as having only one parent. Our discussion to this point has emphasized the continuing importance and necessary involvement of both custodial and noncustodial parents. The "single parent" label may serve to perpetuate the erroneous notion that a parent who no longer lives in the home is no longer a parent at all. Nothing could be less true, but while accepting this reality, we must also come to accept the unique pitfalls or traps that await a single parent unprepared for this new family status. The following comments represent some but not all of the pitfalls confronting the single parent.[16]

When a child is seen as the embodiment of the absent parent. If a happy marriage is suddenly terminated by the accidental death of one parent, the child may be looked upon by the surviving parent as the last remnant of the deceased spouse. The child may be placed in a position so close to the surviving parent that the child is unable to move into his or her own individual sphere at the proper developmental time. While closeness has significant advantages for children, the negatives of this situation seem obvious.

In the case of divorce, the child may serve as a reminder of a hated former spouse and become the recipient of negative verbal and emotional messages. One of my clients had gone through a difficult divorce from a husband who had gradually begun to give the appearance of one who was becoming mentally ill. My client received custody of her two sons, aged ten and twelve but within two years had relinquished custody of the older boy because, as she told it, he was so strikingly similar to her ex-husband that she could not bear to have him around.

While extreme, this case impressed me with the potential problems awaiting children who serve as reminders of their noncustodial parent. Most cases counselors face will be much less obvious, but the potential for harm is there, especially for children of the same sex as the ex-spouse who may possess many of the same physical and behavioral characteristics. There probably is no better example of the idea mentioned earlier of an unfinished marriage and divorce than when the child is punished for the actions of a parent. Single parents who appear unable to separate their feelings for their child from those for their former spouse are in serious trouble and will need intervention.

When a parent marries the child. A problem well known to counselors of children of divorce is the child's moving into the parental bed. The child feels lonely, frightened, and rejected, and all these feelings are intensified when the lights go out and the bedroom door closes. Counselors generally see this problem as being internal to the child, motivated by those dark and scary fears known to follow trauma.

What is often overlooked is that it may be the parent who is bringing the child into his or her bed. The parent who is alone will frequently turn to the child for emotional support and physical companionship. I know from personal experience leading single-parent workshops and seminars that three topics can be counted on to get the participants involved and emotionally interested in what is going on. These topics are child masturbation, not defending yourself when the ex-spouse attacks, and insisting on children sleeping in their own beds. It is clear that many times the child is sleeping in the parental bed *mostly* because it makes the parent feel better.

While parent and child moving closer together following a divorce or death is generally seen as a positive development, when the relationship goes beyond the point of being healthy and functional and becomes problematic and burdensome to the child, we know it has gone too far. Counselors are faced with the challenge of discriminating between healthy closeness and pathological dependency. Measures of pathological dependency include:

- The parent initiating extreme togetherness such as sleeping in the same bed or insisting that the child sit with or on the lap of the parent while watching television, talking, etc.

- Conversations between parent and child in which the level of the communication appears to be too grown-up for the child's age.

- The parent's unburdening himself or herself of emotionally heavy issues such as dating, financial problems, and problems with the former husband or wife.

- The parent and child always being together. Examples would include a parent wanting the child to sit with him or her in the adult Sunday school class rather than be in a class for the child's own age group.

• The parent excessively emphasizing the accomplishments of the child. A never-married single mother I briefly worked with signed her only child up for every "Little Miss" beauty contest in the area and insisted that her pastor announce in church how her daughter had done. The child was always with her mother in church and always overdressed as if the contest was being held during church. This lady was clearly struggling to find some significance for herself through the manufactured accomplishments of her daughter.

• Extreme upset over what would appear to be minor failures by the child. Not winning the contest (any contest), getting dirty while playing, *any* disobedience (especially if it was observed by others), and apologizing for the child's "fail-ure" as if it was the parent's own all indicate excessive closeness and dependency on the part of the single parent.

• Overreaction to apparently minor scrapes and bruises ac-quired through play. As with discipline, this will tend to be more pronounced if the parent believes someone may be observing.

• Shared decision making that is inappropriate to the child's age and level of understanding. The custodial mother or fa-ther may try to demonstrate a desire for democracy in the home and fairness with the child by involving the child in decisions that would normally involve a husband and wife only. This tends to be more apparent if the parent believes someone may hear about their parenting behavior or be ob-serving how the children are adjusting.

When the child is seen as an overwhelming burden. While the presence of children in the home following a divorce can be therapeutic and helpful in reducing a parent's sense of shock and grief over the terminated marriage, the need to provide care and discipline may be perceived as too great a burden to manage without help. Just as some people will see a problem as nothing more than a temporary detour while others will see the same obstacle as insurmountable, single parents will see the challenges of childrearing in the same way. Some will feel so overwhelmed with child care that they feel incompetent and inadequate in *all* areas of life, not just parenting.

Single parents typically experience problems with self-esteem. The presence of children can add to the single parent's sense of self-worth, even under less than ideal conditions. If the parent is sufficiently consumed with anger, grief, and self-pity, the children are at risk for becoming targets for these negative parental feelings. In that case, therapeutic intervention is mandated.

Enhancing self-esteem in single parents can be accomplished through counseling interventions[17] targeted at the following:

1. *The client's thought processes.* Counselors should focus on replacing negative self-talk with positive self-talk, changing self-defeating negative beliefs, creating and using positive affirmations, and focusing on the positive and on their successes.

2. *The client's imagination.* Help can be provided by creating positive mental images with the client, using guided imagery for mental rehearsal of difficult concerns, using imagery to access his or her God-given wisdom as well as finding more resources within the client's own experiences.

3. *The client's physical state.* In some cases the counselor will need to attend to how the client is feeling physically. It may be that the client needs some ethical and carefully monitored physical touch (an arm around the shoulder or a hug after tears, for example). Counselors may want to implement stress reduction techniques so the client can control difficult feelings or just to relax at the end of the day. Some clients will need help learning how to energize themselves when necessary and to love and appreciate their bodies by nurturing themselves in ways that are not self-destructive (overeating, substance abuse, sexual addiction).

4. *The client's emotional condition.* Many Christian single parents struggle with accepting their emotions as legitimate.

Some will need help understanding that emotions are a natural part of their personality and that emotions can be expressed in nondestructive ways. Others will need help learning how to talk about their emotions while eliminating the need to create guilty feelings, harbor resentment, or fear the future.

5. *The client's intuition.* Parents often say they have developed a sixth sense about their children. Single parents may need permission from the counselor to trust that intuition and overcome the pervasive self-doubt that is so common in parents after a divorce.

6. *The client's will.* Many single parents feel that their will has been disabled as a result of the divorce trauma. Counselors can help by emphasizing the need to take full responsibility for their lives while learning how to make more responsible choices. In many cases clients have lost the ability to exercise self-discipline, set *reasonable* goals for the family, and act with the kind of integrity they possessed prior to the divorce.

7. *The client's spiritual state.* Christian counselors should routinely take spiritual matters into account when counseling Christian single parents. This may include helping the client to accept God's forgiveness, his unconditional love, and the responsibility to live as a Christian while understanding and applying God's principles for living.

Each of the areas identified above should be routinely addressed in the course of competent Christian counseling.

When perspective is lost in the struggle for survival. Parents faced with double responsibility for raising their children and maintaining employment struggle with priorities every day. Single parents are faced with the reality that their children need a parent on call, and children are asked to remember that their parent may not want to go to work but has to anyway. Parents worry that their children are not being given the chance to have a real childhood. Sensitive children begin to worry that their parent is over-stressed and feeling guilty for being gone so much.

When problems arise, as they inevitably will in any family, perspective tends to be lost as parents and children react emotionally and often excessively to what would be seen by most as typical everyday family challenges. Small problems tend to be seen as larger and more pathological than reality warrants, and a normal family evening without turmoil becomes a special event. When such problems cause a family to come in for counseling, it is the conscientious counselor's responsibility to facilitate their understanding of the true magnitude of their problem. When I suspect one of my clients is in this situation, I usually ask, "How often do you think a problem like this happens in families with *two* parents?" Upon reflection, the answer is usually, "Very often, I guess!"

When the burden of guilt impedes effective functioning. Our discussion of the impact of divorce on children and adolescents explored the powerful impact parental guilt has on parental functioning. Guilt-ridden single parents will be less likely to provide the necessary structure through discipline required by youngsters and will tend to feel guilty and even apologize when they do discipline. Studies indicate that separation and divorce are associated with significantly higher levels of major depression in both men and women,[18] that it limits the ability of parents to function in the post-divorce family, [19] and that the guilt will be felt more intensely and earlier by the spouse who initiated the divorce.[20]

When reentry into the social scene is experienced as a return to adolescence. Within four months of the sudden and unexpected death of her husband, a thirty-six-year-old widow had acquired a tattoo, begun to associate with bikers who would arrive at her home at all hours of the day or night and park their motorcycles on the lawn in the middle-class neighborhood where she and her two teenage children lived, had been arrested for having marijuana in her home, and had experienced court proceedings that eventually resulted in the custody of her two children being placed in the hands of their paternal grandparents. This person is known to me personally and represents the clearest example I have ever seen of a single parent returning to his or her adolescence at the first opportunity.

In less sensational cases, the single parent who begins to date stands a good chance of doing so at or around the same time that one or more of the children are beginning to date. The single parent in this situation is faced with the dilemma of being, in a sense, both parent and teenager. The dating single parent is likely to be experiencing most of the uncertainties of dating for someone who has probably not dated in many years *and* is responsible (as a parent would be) for deciding whom to date, where to go, what to do, when to come in, and what to tell the children. Reentering the social scene carries with it the implicit risk of bringing a third party into the family system. It is the worry over this risk that seems to plague single moms and dads who are considering expansion of their social life.

When the single parent becomes dependent on the family of origin. When a divorce or death occurs or when a woman bears a child out of wedlock, the single mother frequently finds herself back at home living with her parents. Even if she lives outside her parents' home, she may be dependent on them for financial and other types of support. Grandfathers may be asked to become surrogate fathers to grandsons without a father. Grandmothers may be asked to become full-time babysitters while Mother goes to work.

The single parent may regress and return to asking his or her parents for advice, a potentially problematic situation in that the advice may serve as a further threat to the single parent's sense of self-confidence already shaken by the divorce. Counseling needs for the single parent living with parents or being supported by them revolve around depression (based on the return to dependence) and anger (that he or she was forced to ask for help in the first place).

RECOVERY PROCESS PHASES

Both Sue and Ron Craig are well into their recovery process at this point. For Ron, the second marriage appears to have complicated and slowed down his work toward getting on with a new life, but he is maintaining his commitments to Sue and the children as he promised and seems satisfied that the slower movement is just the price he will have to pay for his post-divorce decisions. Sue has not yet begun to date but is thinking about it. She has acknowledged that the children remain her first priority and seems content to wait for her social life to develop rather than push for more of a social life than she might be prepared to handle at this time.

Ron and Sue's post-divorce experiences have followed a four-phase process[21] with one or two of the phases yet to be completed.

PHASE 1: THE AFTERMATH

This phase follows the formation of a new family unit once the former unit has been dissolved through divorce or death. *Aftermath* has a generally negative connotation, and such an emphasis applies here. The period following *any* change in family status can result in intense emotions including confusion, anger, depression, and ambivalence. Single parents seeking counseling during this phase frequently experience intense rage, despair, anxiety, and worry about the future. Single parents in this early phase tend to be consumed with doubt about their own ability to cope with the new family situation. Friends may withdraw during this phase due to conflicting loyalties and uncertainty about how to talk with and try to help their friend. The concept of an "unfinished marriage" is relevant in this phase as a means of encouraging the single-parent client to mourn the loss of the previous family appropriately.

PHASE 2: REALIGNMENT

This second phase relates primarily to the regrouping or re-aligning that takes place in any family attempting to adjust to the loss of a parent. Major realignments during this phase include:

Economic. In most families, the standard of living is reduced following the loss of a parent. Both custodial and noncustodial parents tend to feel greater financial stress and need to find new sources of income and economizing measures to conserve resources.

Reduced access of children to both parents. Since the mother is the custodial parent in most cases and is likely to return to work full time to support her family, and since the noncustodial parent no longer lives with them, children typically suffer some reduction in parental contact. Babysitters and day care for younger children and proper after-school supervision for older children and teens becomes a major worry. The children need to have a good relationship with both parents, beyond mere contact, if they are to develop normally.[22]

Changed social life. Most people report a severe alteration in their social network following divorce. Women seem to resent the loss of social relationships more than men, probably because they have been more dependent on friends prior to the divorce. Having lived and socialized as a couple, single parents typically find themselves in a state of social limbo, not knowing where they fit in.

Changed spiritual life. Christians experiencing the loss of a husband or wife typically report a change in their feelings about their church home. Divorced people, as discussed in chapter 5, often feel like outcasts, ostracized for the divorce and feeling unwelcome in church activities once participated in as a couple. Widows and widowers do not tend to feel this rejection, obviously due to the nonvoluntary nature of the departure. Because of the insensitivity of some in church leadership, single parents often experience a need to change church homes in order to get their spiritual life back on track.

PHASE 3: REESTABLISHMENT OF A SOCIAL LIFE

This phase refers to a family's readiness to establish a new social life according to a new reality. A single parent may feel ready to attempt the establishing of new and more intimate social relationships, and the children may express their readiness to consider a new family with a new parent. Sexually responsible behavior may become a challenge for a now-dating single parent who has been sexually active for a long period of time. Those who work with Christian single parents will acknowledge that sexual issues are at the top of the worry list for both single parents and pastors.

Concerns for the family during this phase relate to questions about what level of intimacy is acceptable for Christian single parents, how the children will feel if they become aware that Mom or Dad is developing a close relationship, and future prospects for marriage and a functional family life. Problems surface and present themselves to counselors as sudden but typically relate to the single parent's beginning of dating or follow an announcement that Mom or Dad has a "new friend" who might also become a new parent.

PHASE 4: SEPARATION

The job of parents is to raise and release children as functional adults. Separation, the fourth phase in the post-divorce process, refers to the single parent and child (of any age) successfully letting go of each other. The children, adolescents, or young adults are able to trust their parents enough to let them make their own decisions about how their lives should be managed. This development will invariably follow years of adjustment, depending on the age of the child at the time of the divorce.

Adolescence and young adulthood is typically a time of letting go in intact families as well, and counselors know that this period can be traumatic and full of turmoil. Counselors should be reminded that problems over separation develop in all types of families, and the particular problem being presented to the counselor may be independent of the marital status of the parent.

As we consider this four-phase process, we need to be reminded of the significant individuality of each client and the presenting problem that brings that client to counseling. We must remember that problems and challenges are not unique to single-parent families and resist the temptation to assign *any* type of dysfunction to the one-parent status.

GROUP WORK WITH SINGLE PARENTS

Support groups for single parents have become an accepted part of the services provided by many churches. The orientation of a growing number of churches is to see the church as hospital as well as sanctuary and single parents and their children as full members of the spiritual community and deserving of full status within that community. The following suggestions for support groups for single parents are based on the assumption of need as well as provision of services within the church.

Choosing a Leader

Group leaders, also called "facilitators," must possess certain attributes. The group leader or facilitator must:

1. *Be knowledgeable about the needs of single parents.* He or she need not be or have been a single parent, but the leader *must* be keenly aware of the problems and challenges facing single parents and their children. The leader must be academically informed and unburdened by commonsense approaches to problems that have not been tested and proven effective. In other words, the leader must be an expert on the subject, either through intensive personal experience, academic training, or both. For the Christian embarking on such a leadership task, the challenge includes possessing Bible knowledge relevant to the marriage-divorce-remarriage issue.

2. *Be knowledgeable about community resources.* Single-parent families are typically multiproblem families. The conscientious group leader must be informed of services available in the community that might be required by group participants beyond the scope of services provided by the church and support group. Such community services would include social services, free legal aid, transportation, and special services in the schools such as free breakfast and lunch for those with limited incomes.

3. *Be knowledgeable about group dynamics.* Any group properly led will quickly develop a personality of its own based on the principles of group dynamics. Factors that control liking, attraction, coalition formation, and group process must be part of the knowledge base for anyone taking on the responsibility of group leadership.

4. *Be knowledgeable about ethical standards for group practice.* Protecting the well-being of group members requires sensitivity to the no-harm principle of protecting everyone's welfare. Issues of confidentiality are important and need to be reinforced periodically in the group. It is not ethical for a group leader to allow socialization between members while the group is in existence. Leaders should refer

to the ethical standards established by organizations such as the American Counselors Association for guidance. [23]

In some groups it may be wise to choose a cofacilitator to balance the leader in terms of academic training or personal experience. If the leader is an academician, the coleader could be a single parent or one who has extensive practical experience with single parents.

Choosing Group Members

Recruitment of group members is done through announcements in the home church as well as other churches in the community (depending on space available), using the local network of pastors and church-related groups, word of mouth, newspaper and radio advertisements, and others that may be specific to an area such as a cable Christian television channel.

Application and Prescreening of Group Members

If the group is to focus on single-parent concerns, exclusions would include unwed teenage mothers, remarried and blended families, and ex-spouses. Other exclusions may be appropriate based on interview data indicating unsuitability for group work. Such applicants may be encouraged to participate in individual counseling to resolve their concerns.

Interview Screening

In the screening interview, application information is reviewed and discussed as needed, and the function, procedures, and purposes of the group are elaborated and clarified. Applicant expectations are discussed with special attention paid to unrealistic hopes and questions from the applicant. Referral is made if the group experience would not be in the best interest of the applicant. If the applicant is suitable, information on the first session is provided. An appointment is made for an initial pregroup meeting.

Pregroup Meeting

The basic purpose of conducting a meeting before the group actually begins is to screen potential participants, prepare them for what will probably happen in the group, and begin the process of rapport building. Discussion topics at this meeting might include goals and objectives, group norms and expectations of members, developing a commitment to the counseling process, and potential risks such as disclosing personal information in the group. As a part of this initial process the group leader will work to instill hope and optimism, establish a sense of universality among members, and encourage open questioning.

GROUND RULES

Group participants are provided with an informal list of expectations as a condition of group membership. For example, group members are expected to be present for all sessions and to refrain from self-abusive behavior such as drugs and alcohol, family violence, or self-injury. Confidentiality must be strictly honored, and no romantic or sexual involvement with other group members is allowed for the life of the group. Membership in the group is voluntary, and members may leave the group at any time, though reentry may not be possible. It is up to the group leader to assure the safety of all members while the group is in session and to make all efforts to minimize risks.

LEADERSHIP ISSUES

A trained person accepting responsibility for leading a divorce-recovery/single-parenting group must be knowledgeable of single-parent concerns. These concerns would include issues of child care, limited time, money, energy, the need for emotional support, struggles with role ambiguity (parent or pal to the children?), and how to discipline.

In many cases group members will hold myths about single parenting that need to be debunked. One common myth is that the only "true" family is a two-parent family and anything other than that *must* be insufficient. Group leaders will also share factual information on single parenting while working to build skills necessary for single-parent living. The group leader will need to clearly establish and set forth goals and objectives of the group, provide for ongoing evaluation and follow-up, and facilitate eventual termination.

GROUP OBJECTIVES

Suggested objectives include:

1. Reducing social isolation and negative feelings by establishing group meetings for single parents.

2. Providing social support and encouragement by developing group cohesiveness through relationship-building activities.

3. Educating clients regarding life management skills, parenting, and other relevant issues. This can be accomplished by providing informational seminars on relevant topics (e.g., discipline and money management).

4. Facilitating personal growth by providing opportunities to learn and practice necessary skills.

5. Dealing specifically with issues and stressors unique to single parents by asking for feedback on desired topics for sessions.

6. Monitoring group members for signs of pathology and concerns that might warrant individual counseling.

7. Developing leadership from within the group by periodically sharing leadership functions.

GETTING STARTED

Initial stages of a single-parent group are focused on relationship building through leader modeling and the use of icebreakers. Standard icebreakers might include:

"What is your name and the names of your children?"

"Where do you live and work?"

"What is your favorite————?" (television show, sport, food, etc.).

"If you had all the money you needed, where would you go for a vacation?"

"If you could talk to any one person from your past, who would that person be?"

"If you could live your life over again, what is the one thing you would change?"

"What is the one thing you hope to accomplish in this group?"

Feelings Identification

A list of feeling words (e. g., *sad, happy, anxious*) are distributed to encourage group members to identify the way they most typically feel. Members name the feeling, tell if it is positive or negative, and explain how they deal with the feeling.

An alternative form involves a large wall chart or handout with "happy-face" type illustrations showing the widest possible range of feelings. Group members are asked to choose the one or two that they feel characterizes them best. A group member may select "worried" and then explain what he or she is worried about and then receive feedback from group members as to *their* worries and how they cope with them.

Working Stages

Once some level of relationship has been established, members may be invited to participate in role-play. One example is the empty chair that allows them to talk to anyone they wish. As homework, members may be asked to keep a journal or write an autobiography. The working stage typically constitutes the longest phase of the group and should be approached patiently.

Final Stages

During the final stage it is assumed that most relevant issues have been ventilated and resolved, goals and achievement plans have been established, evaluation of group process and individual growth have been put in place, and termination procedures have been discussed. Follow-up is often desired and, with the agreement of group members, periodic follow-up sessions may be scheduled during which progress will be monitored and individual counseling may be initiated.

The Unfinished Divorce

As I worked with Sue Craig throughout her separation and divorce from Ron, I was careful to keep the goal of *finishing* the divorce before her. I know from experience and study that one of the primary obstacles to a client getting on with life is the hope, however unreasonable, that somehow the marriage will be healed, the errant spouse will see the folly of his or her ways, and all will be well again. Sue was not unusual in this regard. She was compelled, especially in the early days of Ron's departure, to hope and wish for reconciliation. I have found this reconciliation preoccupation to be most common in divorced men and women who have led committed Christian lives. They just will not believe that God would leave them in this predicament.

Sue, as others, had to be encouraged to accept reality no matter how unpleasant. I experienced great difficulty in facilitating this element of post-divorce growth in Sue *until* she decided to move from individual to group counseling. It appeared to be the acceptance of the other women in the group coupled with listening to their stories of surviving a divorce that brought her to the point of accepting her reality and making appropriate plans for the future. Counselors are indebted to those who have recovered from their own divorces and who are willing to share their lives with those who are still struggling.

NOTES

1. S. Atlas, *The Parents without Partners Source Book* (Phildaelphia: Running Press, 1984), 192; and S. Bayrakal and T. M. Kope, "Dysfunction in the Single-Parent and Only-Child Family," *Adolescence* 25, no. 97 (1990): 1–7.

2. A. Morawetz and G. Walker, *Brief Therapy with Single-Parent Families* (New York: Brunner/Mazel, 1984), 112.

3. D. Thompson, *Counseling and Divorce* (Dallas: Word, 1989), 188.

4. M. L. Borrine et al., "Family Conflict and Adolescent Adjustment in Intact, Divorced, and Blended families," *Journal of Consulting and Clinical Psychology* 59, no. 5 (1991): 753–55; and M. B. Isaacs, G. H. Leon, and M. Kline, "When is a Parent Out of the Picture? Different Custody, Different Perceptions," *Family Process* 26 (1987): 101–10.

5. G. L. Greif and A. DeMaris, "Single Fathers with Custody," *The Journal of Contemporary Human Services* 71, no. 5 (1990): 259–66.

6. C. A. Richards and I. Goldenberg, "Fathers with Joint Physical Custody of Young Children: A Preliminary Look," *The American Journal of Family Therapy* 14, no. 2 (1986): 154–62.

7. R. S. Benedek and E. P. Benedek, "Post-Divorce Visitation," *Journal of*

the American Academy of Child Psychiatry 16 (1977): 256–71; and R. S. Weiss, "Issues in the Adjudication of Custody When Parents Separate," in *Divorce and Separation: Context, Causes, and Consequences*, ed. G. Levinger and O. C. Moles (New York: Basic Books, 1979).

8. M. A. Koch and C. R. Lowery, "Visitation and the Noncustodial Father," *Journal of Divorce* 8, no. 2 (1984): 47–65; and B. L. Bloom and K. R. Kindle, "Demographic Factors in the Continuing Relationships between Former Spouses," *Family Relations* 34 (1985): 375–81.

9. J. A. Seltzer, N. C. Schaeffer, and H. W. Charng, "Family Ties after Divorce: The Relationship between Visiting and Paying Child Support," *Journal of Marriage and the Family* 51 (1989): 1013–32.

10. D. S. Glenwick and J. D. Mowrey, "When Parent Becomes Peer: Loss of Intergenerational Boundaries in Single-Parent Families," *Family Relations* 35 (1986): 57–62.

11. G. L. Greif and F. Emad, "A Longitudinal Examination of Mothers Without Custody: Implications for Treatment," *The American Journal of Family Therapy* 17, no. 2 (1989): 155–63.

12. M. Rutter, *Maternal Deprivation Reassessed* (Baltimore: Penguin, 1972).

13. J. R. Wilbur and M. Wilbur, "The Noncustodial Parent: Dilemmas and Interventions," *Journal of Counseling and Development* 66 (May 1988): 434–37.

14. S. Goldstein and A. J. Solnit, *Divorce and Your Child* (New Haven: Yale University Press, 1984); G. A. Awad and R. Parry, "Access Following Marital Separation," *Canadian Journal of Psychiatry* 25, no. 5 (1980): 357–65; M. Dishon, "Psychological Aspects and Factors in Planning Visitation," *Family Law News* 8, no. 3 (1985): 36–39; D. Skafte, *Child Custody Evaluations* (Beverly Hills, Calif.: Sage, 1985); and J. A. Seltzer, "Relationship between Fathers and Children Who Live Apart: The Father's Role after Separation," *Journal of Marriage and the Family* 53 (1991): 79–101.

15. C. R. Lowery and S. A. Settle, "Effects of Divorce on Children: Differential Impact of Custody and Visitation Patterns," *Family Relations* 34 (1985): 455–63.

16. Morawetz and Walker, *Brief Therapy*, 13.

17. J. Canfield, "Self-Esteem in Adolescents" (Handout for the Fourth National Conference of Advances in Testing Survivors of Sexual Abuse, *U. S. Journal Training*, 3–6 March, 1993).

18. M. L. Bruce and K. M. Kim, "Differences in the Effects of Divorce on Major Depression in Men and Women," *American Journal of Psychiatry* 149, no.7 (1992): 914–17.

19. R. Forehand et al., "Role of Maternal Fuctioning and Parenting Skills in Adolescent Functioning Following Parental Divorce," *Journal of Abnormal Psychology* 99, no. 3 (1990): 278–83.

20. C. Buehler, "Initiator Status and the Divorce Transition," *Family Relations* 36 (1987): 82–86.

21. Morawetz amd Walker, *Brief Therapy*, 17.

22. M. Wierson et al., "Buffering Young Male Adolescents against Negative Parental Divorce Influences: The Role of Good Parent-Adolescent

Relations," *Child Study Journal* 19, no. 2 (1989): 101–14; A. L. Stohlberg and J. P. Bush, "A Path Analysis of Factors Predicting Children's Divorce Adjustment," *Journal of Clinical Child Psychology* 14 (1985): 49–54; B. K. Stanley, W. J. Weikel, and J. Wilson, "The Effects of Father Absence on Interpersonal Problem-Solving Skills of Nursery School Children," *Journal of Counseling and Development* 64 (February 1986): 383–85; L. A. Hoyt et al., "Anxiety and Depression in Young Children of Divorce," *Journal of Clinical and Child Psychology* 19 , no. 1 (1990): 26–32; and W. J. Doherty and R. H. Needle, "Psychological Adjustment and Substance Use among Adolescents Before and After a Parental Divorce," *Child Development* 62 (1991): 328–37.

    23. B. Herlihy and L. B. Golden, *Ethical Standards Casebook* (Alexandria, Va.: American Association for Counseling and Development, 1990).

Chapter 11

Counseling and Remarriage

Barbara and Felix Goines explained to the receptionist at our counseling center that they needed to talk to someone "as soon as possible" about the unexpected problems they were experiencing as a remarried couple. Information on the intake form was sketchy. This was the second marriage for Felix and the third for Barbara, and each of these professing Christians were struggling with the possibility that their record of failure, as Felix stated it, was never going to end. Felix had been married for eleven years to a woman who left him, as he told it, because they could not have children together. Barbara had gone through two previous marriages, the first lasted nearly ten years and produced her only child, Ricky, now twelve years old. Her second marriage was described by Barbara as a rebound relationship that should never have happened and lasted less than one year.

As we met in my office for the first session, I was impressed with how much additional information I was going to need if I was to help this family. In addition to the issues explained by each on their separate intake forms, Ricky, Barbara's preadolescent only child was offered as the real reason for seeking counseling. Knowing from experience that presenting problems are rarely the true source of the need for help, I listened carefully as they explained their adjustment difficulties and concerns.

Barbara and Felix were relatively new Christians. Each was somewhat uncertain exactly when and how they came to a commitment to Christ, and each had a lifetime of marginal Christianity characterized by sporadic involvement in church and occasional thoughts that there might be more to life than they were then living, but without any noticeable change. They had been social drinkers all their adult lives, and Felix said that he might have been considered an alcoholic at one point in his life. While Felix and his first wife had been church members for most of their marriage, neither of Barbara's first two husbands ever attended church. Ricky had attended church only when his mother took him, which at best was once or twice a month.

Each, however, had made a new commitment to follow the Lord through the rebuilders ministry at the church where they were married and that they now attended. Since their marriage the Goines family had become "three times a week Christians" who seemed sincerely dedicated to their new faith in Jesus Christ. Ricky had also made a profession of faith shortly after the marriage. This family, on the surface, seemed to represent the best likelihood for a success story after such a disastrous record of marital failure. But there was a cloud on their horizon, and its name was "stepfather"!

The Goines family had begun to experience an affliction common to stepfamilies—unrealistic expectations. Felix had been taught by their pastor that he should be able to step in and become Ricky's father in all areas including discipline. At twelve, Ricky believed himself to be too old for spanking anyway and especially from a man he had known for only a year and who was not his real father. Ricky had announced to Felix and his mother that the next time Felix tried to spank him, he would run away, and they would never see him again. Not to be discouraged, Felix (never a father, remember) slapped Ricky for talking back, and Ricky, true to his word, disappeared.

Now Mom and Stepdad were in my office. Ricky was found at his grandparents and had returned home under an uneasy truce with his stepdad. Felix had promised not to strike Ricky *only* for a brief time while they talked with me. Ricky, I was told, kept his suitcase packed and under the bed just in case.

I listened to Felix and Barbara tell their stories, and while I listened, I grew increasingly uncomfortable with what I was hearing. Felix seemed to be saying that he would be the man of the house or he would not remain in the house at all! Barbara was clearly on the side of her son, and though she professed love for Felix, I did not doubt which one would leave if there was another confrontation. Felix would be out of there! This remarriage was in serious trouble and in only a year.

I told Felix that the Bible has little to say on the subject of how stepfamilies are to be managed, and while he was welcome to his opinion, in my experience the marriage would only work if he agreed to keep his hands off Ricky *permanently* and be content with leaving most discipline up to his mother. I told Felix point-blank that if he hit Ricky again, the boy would either run away or go to the police and accuse him of child abuse. After thee more sessions with Felix and Barbara and two with Ricky, they stopped coming.

Thirteen months later the name *Goines* again appeared on my appointment book. I am not a prophet nor the son of a prophet, but I guessed correctly what I was going to hear. Sure enough, Felix and Barbara explained that Ricky had walked to the police station and charged his stepfather with child abuse following another slap to the face during an argument. Felix was insulted and angry by the charges, even though he agreed that the slap had occurred. Barbara was angry at Felix for being "so dumb" as to allow himself to be baited by Ricky into hitting him. I think Barbara was also angry at herself for marrying Felix in the first place and for failing to be more sensitive to the needs of her son when she chose to get married again.

The Goines family and I have a lot of work to do, and I am not overly optimistic about the long-term survivability of this remarriage. I believe that there is hope for any marriage, and with a commitment to counseling that was missing a year ago, Felix, Barbara, and Ricky may find a way to save their new family and avoid sullying the testimony of Christ through another divorce. The process of healing or dissolution is ongoing at this writing.

BASIC CONCERNS IN REMARRIAGE

Some recent studies on the frequency of divorce among remarried couples have shown a disturbingly high failure rate, in some cases approaching 50 percent. Even though this divorce rate is a slight improvement when compared to rates for previous periods, the magnitude of the difficulties for parents and children in these families seems to be greater. Currently, over 40 percent of marriages involve the *remarriage* of one or both partners, and almost half these marriages eventually end in divorce.[1]

As we begin an investigation of the concerns confronting remarried couples, we will examine divorce and remarriage myths that are often encountered by members of the various professions servicing divorced and remarried people.[2] Understanding these myths can help couples establish more reasonable expectations for second marriages, with or without stepchildren.

Marriage Myths

- Everything will work out well if we really love one another.
- Always consider the other person first.
- Emphasize the positive; keep criticisms to yourself.
- If things go wrong, focus on the future.
- See oneself as a part of a couple first and as an individual later.
- What's mine is yours.
- Marriage makes people happier than they were before marriage.
- What is best for the children will be best for us.

Divorce Myths

- Because we no longer love each other, nothing can work out for us.
- Always consider oneself first.
- Emphasize the negative and criticize everything.
- If things go wrong now, focus on the past.
- What's yours is mine.
- Divorce makes people unhappy.
- What is best for us must be devastating for the children.

Remarriage Myths

- This time we'll make it work by doing everything right.
- Always consider everyone else first.
- Emphasize the positive and overlook the negative.
- Think of what went wrong in the past and make sure it does not happen again.
- Depending on one's personality, one might duplicate the marriage or divorce myth and see oneself as part of a couple first *or* as an individual first.
- What's mine is mine and what's yours is mine.
- Marriage makes people significantly happier than they were before marriage.
- What is best for us must be harmful to the children.

Granted, some of these myths possess an element of tongue in cheek, but the reality of the widespread belief in such myths warrants consideration by any serious counselor. I believe we might all be surprised by how common these myths really are. Whether we agree or not, the importance of relationship experiences *prior* to the remarriage cannot be doubted. [3]

Second marriages involving children lead to what one researcher called "acquired parent-child relationships."[4] Without the time to build an intimate marital relationship prior to the appearance of children, husband and wife in a second marriage must quickly (or so too many believe) adapt to one another *and the children.* Honeymoons are not the norm for second marriages, and when an official honeymoon is taken, most prove to be short trips away for no more than a weekend.

Counselors called on to assist in the adjustment process must be careful to consider the unique characteristics brought to the stepfamily by *both* marriage partners.[5] People of all ages generally respond to questionnaires about the stepparent role with caution and suspicion. It is generally believed that stepparents have less of an obligation to the family than biological parents, even though stepparents are the most likely to be criticized when a family problem occurs.[6] It is the worst of both worlds for the stepparent, who is not trusted in the first place and who then comes in for extra levels of criticism if a problem does arise.

GENERAL CONCERNS IN REMARRIAGE

At least five issues must concern counselors who work with remarried couples.[7]

1. *Complexity of family networks because of poorly defined roles.* Neither society nor biblical tradition speaks very much to the role of a stepparent. In earlier times, second marriages were almost exclusively due to the death of a spouse. The involuntary nature of the loss of a first marriage made it much easier for extended and close family members to accept the new marriage and the new spouse. The typical voluntary characteristic of the majority of current divorces has removed that support structure leaving the new couple largely on their own, but with the children.[8]

2. *Unresolved emotional issues from previous marriages.* Felix Goines struggled with the stepparent role primarily, I believe, because he saw his marriage to Barbara as his last opportunity to be a father. This, coupled with careless or misunderstood messages from the pulpit, led Felix to make mistakes that put the marriage at risk. But Felix was not alone in this. Barbara related to me in our individual sessions that she was worried that even though she was trusting the Lord for leadership now, she had once again married unwisely.

3. *Children's adjustment to the remarriage.* If Ricky could not be won over to accepting Felix as a father to some limited degree at least, the marriage was doomed. Initially, Ricky was not included in the *process* of making a marriage decision, thus it was easy for him to fight the marriage once it took place. While it is not wise to allow children or teens to make the final decision,[9] they should be a part of the process.

4. *Financial concerns.* Second only to problems with children,[10] finances trouble remarriages. Common to remarriages is the hope that finances will be more abundant. Unfortunately, the degree of improvement does not usually meet expectations primarily due to alimony and child support payments and other residual expenses from the previous marriage.

5. *Legal concerns.* Property rights, the disposal of jointly held assets, wills, and insurance policy provisions often make hiring a lawyer one more financial necessity. As previously noted,[11] a remarried family with three children now involves 131,054 possible paired combinations with extended family, many of which have legal ramifications.

SPECIFIC ISSUES IN REMARRIAGE COUNSELING

Counselors working with divorced parents struggle with many issues simultaneously.[12] It may assist the counselor to be able to consider issues one at a time while working with the family.

ISSUE 1: NAME FOR THE NEW PARENT

Children struggle with an appropriate name to assign to the person who has just married into their family. Age is not much of an issue here, as adolescents and young adults find this issue about equally as disconcerting as younger children. Some have suggested "Mother II" or "Dad II" or "my new father," "my second dad," and even "the man who married my mother." Of course, the issue is not the name selected but that the children are given the freedom to select a name with which they are comfortable. Counselors can be helpful in encouraging such freedom for children. The Craig children decided as a group to simply call their new stepmother "Rebecca," which seemed to suit everyone just fine. But note that it was *their* decision.

ISSUE 2: AFFECTION FOR THE NEW PARENT AND THE ABSENT PARENT

The expression of love in the stepfamily seems to be unavoidably intertwined with the issue of loyalty to the absent parent. Studies have shown that stepfathers and stepmothers are uncertain about how much affection is appropriate and how to deal with the loyalty issue. Children and teens tend to worry about whether they are acting appropriately with their stepparent and whether the expression of affection with their biological but absent parent has changed since that parent moved out.[13]

Children whose identification with the absent parent is strong, as might be expected in boys with absent fathers, may cling to a fantasy of somehow reuniting with that parent and can have their hopes shattered when the absent parent remarries. Thus, children may be cautious in expressing the same level of affection to the absent parent for fear of being hurt twice.[14] Counselors will want to be careful to give the child permission to talk with parents and stepparents about their feelings and may benefit from some rehearsal of how to discuss this issue with grownups.

ISSUE 3: LOSS OF THE NATURAL PARENT

Many researchers have noted the similarity between the loss of a parent to divorce and the loss of a parent to death. It has been pointed out that not only may the child be holding unresolved mourning for the now-changed family but may also be developmentally unable to mourn such a loss.[15] Others have emphasized that remarriage usually occurs before a child has had adequate opportunity to resolve the grief associated with the divorce.[16] Expecting the child to need adult permission to express grief coupled with counseling to reassure them that such grief is normal should go a long way toward bringing the child to health.

ISSUE 4: INSTANT LOVE OF NEW FAMILY MEMBERS

The belief that love can be created at will is common among many adults. The idea that one can commit to loving a person is appropriate and acceptable to adults with normal adult maturity and intelligence. A child, on the other hand, cannot comprehend this! Children see love as a feeling that just happens, and one cannot decide to love as one can decide to obey, respect, or pay attention. Counselors can help by encouraging family members to learn about the developmental nature of love and to allow the child with a stepparent time and space in which to grow those feelings. Most important is the counselor encouraging parent and stepparent to avoid expecting *any* level of emotional response for at least *two years* after the marriage. Time is the issue in developing healthy affection for one another.

ISSUE 5: FANTASY ABOUT THE OLD FAMILY STRUCTURE

Children of divorce are disappointed when their fantasies and hopes for the reconciliation of their parents do not come true. Research indicates that reconciliation fantasies are common, enduring, and prevalent even when the pre-divorce family was conflictual and hostile. It appears that children of all ages have a unique ability to quickly forget (suppress?) unpleasant memories.[17]

Counseling recommendations focus on assisting the child in his or her attempts to face and deal with the reality that the reconciliation fantasies may not come true. This must be done with the utmost compassion and sensitivity to the child's cognitive processes and defense mechanisms and in consideration of the child's developmental position. Patience on the part of the counselor is critical as this type of intervention may involve very limited movement for some time.

ISSUE 6: DISCIPLINE

It will come as no surprise to experienced family counselors that conflicts over discipline and childrearing top the list of problems in remarriage. Many stepparents take one of three approaches to the discipline issue. Some are inattentive to problems and disengaged from conflicts that arise. This type stepparent could be called a "bystander" in that he or she (usually he) steps back and waits for the children's biological parent to administer the discipline.

A second type is the parent who becomes actively and assertively involved in the discipline of his or her stepchildren. This type stepparent could be termed a "headmaster" stepparent. Felix Goines would fit this category and, as we have seen, without success. The third type is the stepparent who appears tentative and cautious when it comes to discipline, as if he or she were walking on eggshells. This third type could be labeled the "diplomat" stepparent, who tries to avoid alienating either spouse or children. Each of these strategies involves risk because each may act to inhibit the development of an open and trusting relationship between stepparent and stepchildren.[18]

Discipline seems to be most effective in stepfamilies when parents have thought ahead and worked out rules in advance and have been able to support one another when enforcement was needed.[19] Stepfathers are more likely to be successful disciplinarians when they take a *slow, gentle, flexible* approach and develop a *friendship* with the child that later may lead to acceptance of discipline.[20]

We should be reminded that the Bible does not speak directly to the issue of stepparent discipline. In my experience with scores of remarried Christian families struggling with this concern, I have learned that assumptions made by parents, usually the stepfather, about what they *believe* the Bible means often get these families into difficulty. We should be careful to remind Christian stepfathers that it takes time to earn the respect of children and respect *must* precede discipline. This is the advantage birth parents have over adoptive parents or stepparents. Patience and flexibility are the keys to successful stepparent discipline. Discipline works only when the person receiving it cares about the reactions of the adult administering it.

ISSUE 7: CONFUSION OVER FAMILY ROLES

Roles are expectations of a person occupying a given position, in this case, in the family. Fathers are expected to behave in a certain way, mothers another, and children and teenagers others still. Remarried families bear a burden not experienced by intact families, that of blending roles that were already established in a previous family. Confusion over what is expected of a family member is a problem in role definition or role understanding and acceptance. Poorly articulated role definitions within a family imply contradictory expectations of various family members and will invariably lead to stress and conflict.[21]

American fathers and stepfathers have been socialized to be in control. If they are Christian, they are also likely to have been taught that God himself expects them to be in charge. Thus, stepfathers often find themselves in the awkward position of trying to enforce discipline when they have no apparent authority. Stepmothers are also socialized, of course, but in the direction of burden bearing and soothing conflicts rather than administering discipline or being in charge. Familiar forms of family process must be reconstructed in remarriage families in order for the child to be able to form workable attachments and functional solutions within the stepfamily.[22]

ISSUE 8: SIBLING CONFLICT

Blended families involving custodial children from both remarried partners is relatively rare and provides great opportunities for conflict. Sibling rivalry and conflict in nonstep families occurs at a predictable level. But in families that bring together children from both sides of the remarried family, the level of conflict potential is exponential. Territorial battles in blended families are common and are usually settled on the basis of age. Stepsibling relationships are critical to the eventual success of the marriage and need to be dealt with expeditiously and, if possible, *prior* to the marriage.

Stepsiblings are likely to have experienced differing degrees and levels of family socialization, attachment, and bonding in their individual prior families and will inevitably bring those concerns to the remarriage. Ongoing counseling is almost assured in these cases because expectations will have been developed in stepchildren that are likely to go unmet initially, leading to conflict on many levels. Counseling interventions include focusing on communication styles and patterns developed on each side of the remarried family and developing motivation in the children and teens to work together to solve their common problem. In stepsibling conflicts, two or more counselors may need to work individually with the various sides and if no other counselor is available, as could be the case in rural areas, the counselor will have to work especially hard to avoid being drawn into family battles through taking sides.

ISSUE 9: EXTENDED KINSHIP NETWORK

The term *metafamily system* has been applied to the family of the child of divorce and remarriage and includes all former extended family members of both spouses, the remarriage family itself, and other nonfamily members who have an impact on the family. Counselors need to see this extended network as possessing both negative and positive elements. The greater the number of newly acquired family members and family from the now dissolved family network, the more challenges await the child and parents.

Counselors also need to recognize the potential for good and bad to come from the changes in the family system. Children will be especially challenged by the need to remember and correctly place new members into the system already in memory and to emotionally balance those members with prior and possibly continuing members. Counselors should emphasize to the child the positive elements of adding new members such as extra gifts at Christmas and birthdays, more people to care for them in emergencies, and more people to pray for them. Children and teens may need help in finding and accepting their unique place in the new system. Both the parent and new stepparent should be encouraged to keep the additional family contact at a moderate level initially so the child or teen has time to adjust.[23]

ISSUE 10: SEXUAL CONFLICTS

Remarriage families face concerns over sexual boundaries not experienced by most intact families.[24] Child abuse allegations and subsequent investigations strongly suggest the frequent existence of a different standard of appropriate sexual interaction in stepfamilies when compared to intact families. The remarriage family is, at least in part, a nonbiological unit containing one parent who does not have blood ties to the children and has not had the experience of raising them from birth.[25] Allegations of sexual abuse are significantly higher in stepfamilies than intact families, and counselors must be aware of the greater potential for actual or alleged sexual misconduct by the stepparent.

Further, the newly married couple with children may behave in a sexual way with each other and be observed by the children. Children may, therefore, prematurely learn about sex and may resort to its use to attempt to get their way in the new family. The sexually charged atmosphere may lead to sexual fantasies and inappropriate sexual experimentation by family members leading to damage to the children and possible termination of the marriage. The possibility of sexual interactions between stepsiblings should also be considered. No issue in the remarried family cries out for biblical input more than this. Counselors should not hesitate to refer to the numerous passages teaching sexual responsibility under God while being bold in warning stepparents *and* biological parents of the dangers and temptations that exist. (See Matt. 26:41; 1 Cor. 10:13; James 1:14; 1 Pet. 1:6; 2 Pet. 2:9.)

ISSUE 11: EXIT AND ENTRY OF CHILDREN

Stability and consistency are among the most powerful needs of children entering a stepfamily situation. On a larger scale, entry and exit may apply to young adults leaving home to strike out on their own. This has relevance to the stepfamily, and the young person may be able to benefit from counseling intervention when the time to leave home arrives, but this scenario is many years away in most new stepfamilies.

The more immediate threat to stability and consistency in the stepfamily centers around problems of noncustodial parent visitation. Children can benefit in many ways if they are able to maintain contact with the noncustodial parent; however, they may also experience turmoil when leaving the primary home for days or weeks to spend time with the noncustodial parent. Counselors in the process of working with custodial parents frequently hear complaints that the child is wild or moody for days when they return from a parental visit. Children and teens going through this experience report feeling left out when they get home, feeling as if things had been happening in which they were not involved.

Time away is exaggerated because of time spent preparing to leave and time spent getting back into the swing of things upon return. While children and teens feel helpless and out of control,[26] research also indicates that youngsters are much better off having parental contact than not having the contact and being allowed to stay in the primary home all the time.[27] Counselors should work toward building the best possible relations between divorced spouses as a way of minimizing any negative impact from visits with noncustodial parents.

ISSUE 12: SOCIETY'S ATTITUDE TOWARD THE REMARRIED FAMILY

The prefix *step* continues to suggest a negative stereotype for most Americans, and the term *stepfamily* is considered abnormal, even deviant, by the majority of people.[28] Unfortunately, many people still view with suspicion any other form of family structure than the traditional two parents with their biological children. While attitudes are reported to be changing, members of stepfamilies continue to report feeling like they are in fact deviant in comparison to regular families.

Emily and John Visher, pioneers in the field of counseling stepfamilies, list several myths commonly held by and about stepfamilies, one of which is that anything negative that happens to the remarried family *must* be the result of being in a stepfamily.[29] They point out that both parents and children are prone to try to escape responsibility for family problems by blaming anything and everything on the fact that they all live in a stepfamily when, in fact, nuclear intact families have almost as many problems on average as stepfamilies.

Counseling intervention is directed primarily at remarried parents and focuses on helping them accept their new status as "another kind of normal" rather than deviant or abnormal. Others will tend to respond to stepfamilies the way the stepfamily responds to itself, and if parents can set the pattern of self-acceptance, the stepchildren as well as outsiders will be encouraged to accept their situation. Christians often report feeling especially ostracized by church people and may need special help with this important issue. As controversial as it may seem, moving to another, more accepting church may be the best answer for the family.

ISSUE 13: EFFECTS OF PARENTING ON THE NEW MARITAL RELATIONSHIP

Remarriage families are instant families, lacking time to adjust to marriage before being required to deal with children of many different ages. In the long run, satisfaction with the parent-child relationship is more important for the health of the marriage and family than the couple's relationship. In first and subsequent marriages, the presence of children tends to increase the statistical likelihood of the marriage surviving, *but only* when the parent-child/stepparent-stepchild relationships are satisfactory.

Counselors may need to help the married-again couple focus more on building bridges with the children while working on strengthening the marriage relationship. A difficult balance to establish perhaps, but if the marriage is to survive, an indispensable choice.[30]

ISSUE 14: FINANCIAL CONCERNS

The manner in which family finances are handled reflects both the level of financial sophistication of the remarried couple and their level of commitment to the marriage.[31] Acceptance of financial sharing and of providing equally for stepchildren compared to biological children are keys to eventual marital success. Children and teens have learned to gauge the love of a stepparent by the amount of money and things provided to meet their needs. Christians are accustomed to hearing "where your treasure is, there your heart will be also" (Matt. 6:21), and children and teens living with a stepparent instinctively know how to test stepparent commitment.

The counselor should not recommend or promote any particular financial arrangement but should help the new family develop a common-good approach to using family resources. Parent and stepparent should be reminded, outside the children's hearing, of the importance of financial sharing as a sign to the children of the commitment of their new stepparent. The family may benefit from a new evaluation of the issue of tithing and helping to support Christian ministries *as a family*.

ISSUE 15: CONFLICT AND COMPETITION

Most stepfamilies are the result of the divorce of one or both partners.[32] The potential for continued conflict is great because of the feelings left unresolved from previous marriages. Sadly, children are most likely to be sacrificed by divorced parents more intent on getting revenge than raising healthy children. The primary controlling factor seems to be the ability of the custodial parent and stepparent to accept the noncustodial biological parent as a part of the system that must be dealt with for the good of the children.

Post-divorce, post-remarriage conflict is often exacerbated by the refusal of the custodial parent to allow the noncustodial parent to have a role in the children's upbringing. Children suffer greatly when one parent, known to be willing to participate in their lives, is not allowed in.[33] Conflict and competition between custodial and noncustodial parents are worsened in direct proportion to the length of time between divorce and remarriage. The quicker the new marriage takes place, the greater (on average) the hostilities and the greater the damage to children.

Counselors can play a major role in educating all adults involved about the potential for harm to the children they all claim to love. Counselors can remind parents, custodial, step-, or noncustodial that true love means putting others before oneself. If this means sacrificing a need to get revenge or have the children know just how much of a bum the other parent is, then so be it! Both contact and conflict tend to decline over time, and so it will usually be the first five years that are the most troubling to a remarried couple with children.

The preceding list of fifteen problem issues is offered to encourage counselors to become or continue to be proactive when working with a remarried family. Familiarity with potential problems should raise the level of awareness for counselors and allow us all to do a better and more professional job of servicing this growing client population.

STEPMOTHERS

Approximately one in eight stepparents is a stepmother, a statistic reflective of the current reluctance of divorce courts to award custody to the father except under the most unusual circumstances. Whether this imbalance is good or bad will have to wait for further research, but the fact that there are far fewer stepmothers in America than stepfathers creates a situation where counselors have less information on what it is like to be a stepmother. We know that public perceptions of the stepmother tend to be less positive than for any other parental role. However, when people have contact with an actual stepmother, the negative index declines.[34] Other research has determined that stepmothers have a more difficult time than stepfathers, especially if adolescent stepdaughters are involved.[35]

To answer the seemingly common problems faced by stepmothers, it has been suggested that stepmothers choose one of three roles, discussed briefly in chapter 6. These three roles are:

• primary mother—when the children are very young at the time the stepmother enters the family,

• other mother—when the biological mother remains within the children's environment and has contact,

• friend—when the children are adolescent or older at the time the stepmother enters their lives.

The work of the counselor is to develop in the stepmother an acceptance of what may appear to be a less-than-complete parental role. If a strong bond continues to exist between the biological mother and children, problems will only be avoided when the stepmother is content with whatever level of relationship the children are willing to offer.[36] Frequently, the stepmother has emotional needs she is trying to meet through the stepchildren, and they may be having none of it! The stepmother then feels like a failure when, in fact, a more limited level of relationship might be the *only* type relationship possible in the near future. Tears may flow, but those stepmothers who make the best adjustment do so because they are willing to settle in the short term for what the children are willing to share.

STEPFATHERS

Stepfathers struggle with many concerns upon entering a family system that has survived without a father figure present in the home. The stepfather must come to understand that he is and may remain an outsider in the minds of the children, and as a result of nothing he has done. Studies have shown that the longer children reside in a single-parent home headed by a mother, the more difficult relationship building will be between stepfather and children.[37] Stepfathers are often uncertain about how much discipline to administer, how much affection to expect, and how to deal with the children's loyalty to their biological father. Stepfathers may be excluded simply because the children feel they would be betraying their real father if they liked the stepfather too much. Stepfathers are also viewed as competitors for mother's attention as well as an intruder who brings new rules and regulations into the family.[38]

In a positive sense, children (particularly younger children) may benefit from having another supportive adult available to them. Especially for boys, the arrival of a stepfather can be a true godsend. Stepfathers may be seen as the rescuers they often are and may actually be perceived by children as better than reality, a potential problem when reality arrives in the form of stepfather's lost temper or other failure.[39] Children may also benefit if the stepfather helps to reduce the mother's anxiety. Some have speculated that more adaptive mothers are those more likely to marry again in any case, thereby adding her personality strengths to the equation.[40]

Counseling implications include the following:

1. Stepfathers must be encouraged to exercise patience in building relationships with stepchildren.

2. Stepfathers must be forewarned about the risk of sexual encounters between themselves and stepdaughters, as well as the proclivity of some stepdaughters to use sexual flirtation as a way of controlling their mother.[41]

3. Stepfathers should avoid acceptance of the rescuer role. Downplaying his additions to family resources will give children time to accept stepfather in other than a Santa Claus role.

4. Stepfathers should be encouraged to consider the importance of the marriage commitment as primary over

commitment to the children. Typically, marriages outlast children living at home, and while this is less assured in remarriages, building the marital bond also strengthens the parental bond with stepchildren.

5. Stepfathers should be encouraged to present a bold but patient outlook on spiritual leadership in the home. As previously mentioned, the Bible has little to say on the modern phenomenon of a stepfamily, and stepfathers should be cautioned to balance expectations and assumptions with good counsel and individual prayer.

Stepfathers and stepmothers should be encouraged to consider the challenge God has placed before them, namely, to be the best substitute parent they can be for the glory of God and the good of the children. It is true that parenting days will pass and the marriage relationship will resume prominence, but if the stepparent-stepchild issues are not resolved, there may be no marriage left.

GROUP COUNSELING WITH STEPFAMILIES

A group therapy program has been developed for stepparents without children present and for stepfamilies as a unit.[42] The program involves six sessions of one-and-a-half to two hours and is limited to eight to ten people. The structure is as follows:

Session 1: Introduction. Explore the commonality of stepfamily problems. Stepparents typically have problems coping and tend to blame the children. Explain the myth of instant love.

Session 2: Roles and conflicting loyalties. Help families understand how conflicting loyalties generate problems in the stepfamily. Family alignments, past and present, should be highlighted and clarified.

Session 3: Communication skills. The process some have called the "stepparent disavowal syndrome" is discussed and clarified leading to a more open expression of feelings and attitudes. The stepparent disavowal syndrome occurs when the stepparent initially invests in the child and is then hurt when the child rejects him or her.

Session 4: Problems concerning the stepchild. Major issues of childrearing and discipline are dealt with focusing particularly on expressions of hostility by the child toward the stepparent and what that emotional expression may or may not mean. Children's feelings of insecurity, abandonment, jealousy, loyalty, resentment, and more are discussed.

Session 5: Problems in the marriage. Stepparents often feel the least cared for and the most exploited in the family. Natural parents commonly take the side of the child in a dispute, thereby undermining the already fragile authority of the stepparent.

Session 6: Problems of visitation and the ex-spouse. It is not unusual to hear stepparents say that they are most threatened at visitation time when the biological parent comes to visit or take the children away for a time. Visitation and feelings about the noncustodial parent *must* be clarified and resolved prior to the remarriage.

CONCLUSION

Christian counselors, pastors, and others who would help need to recognize and acknowledge the commonality of human sin as a force in every life and a causative factor in every marital dissolution. This will not change. Sin abounds, but grace much more abounds. As Christian professionals prepare to help the growing number of stepfamilies in their congregations and communities, we must acknowledge that we do not have the final answer on whether or not remarriage is always the best response to human needs following a divorce. We can be sure the issue of stepfamilies will not be disappearing.

Christians involved in ministry may want to consider the following recommendations when helping stepfamilies in the body of believers.[43]

1. We must acknowledge the existence of stepfamilies and accept them as valid members of the Body and suitable for ministry.

2. We must design programs and write literature especially for stepparents, remarried husbands and wives without stepchildren, and stepchildren.

3. We must understand, as leadership, the issues that confront reconstituted families.

4. We must be prepared to provide professional and lay services, as needed, to stepfamilies in the church. We must be both hospital and sanctuary.

5. We must train Christian lay people to provide the first line of ministry. The growing number and demands of this population will quickly exhaust clergy people working alone.

Those who work with remarried families invariably find themselves drawn back to the irreducible issue of children. Good people may disagree on the finer points of doctrine related to the question of divorce and remarriage, but many have come to the conclusion that it is the children's best interest that must remain predominate. Should children have a stepfather or stepmother? Should the needs of what some consider doctrinal purity be placed above the stated needs of children? Again, we return to the words of the Savior.

"But whoso shall offend one of these little ones which believe in me, it were better for him that a millstone were hanged about his neck, and that he were drowned in the depth of the sea. Woe unto the world because of offences! For it must needs be that offences come; but woe to that man by whom the offence cometh!" (Matt. 18:6–7 KJV).

NOTES

1. M. Coleman and L. H. Ganong, "Effect of Family Structure on Family Attitudes and Expectatations," *Family Relations* 33 (1984): 425–32.

2. J. M. Bernard and S. Nesbitt, "Divorce: An Unreliable Predictor of Children's Emotional Predispositions," *Journal of Divorce* 4, no. 4 (1981): 31–42.

3. D. Kalmuss and J. A. Seltzer, "Continuity of Marital Behavior in Remarriage: The Case of Spouse Abuse," *Journal of Marriage and the Family* 48 (1986): 113–20.

4. J. Bernard, *A Study of Marriage* (New York: Russell and Russell, 1956).

5. P. K. Knaub, S. L. Hanna, and N. Stinnet, "Strengths of Remarried Families," *Journal of Divorce* 7 (1984): 41–45.

6. A. I. Schwebel, M. A. Fine, and M. A. Renner, "A Study of Perceptions of the Stepparent Role," *Journal of Family Issues* 12, no. 1 (1991): 43–57.

7. B. E. Bernstein and S. K. Collins, "Remarriage Counseling: Lawyer and Therapist's Help with the Second Time Around," *Family Relations* 34 (1985): 387–91.

8. Schwebel, Fine, and Renner, "Stepparent Role," 49–51.

9. C. B. Reingold, *Remarriage* (New York: Harper and Row, 1976).

10. L. Messinger, "Remarriage Between Divorced People with Children from a Previous Marriage," *Journal of Marriage and Family Counseling* 2, no. 2 (1976): 193–200.

11. E. B. Visher and J. S. Visher, *Stepfamilies: A Guide to Working with Stepparents and Stepchildren* (New York: Brunner/Mazel, 1979).

12. W. M. Walsh, "Twenty Major Issues in Remarriage Counseling," *Journal of Counseling and Development* 70 (July/August 1992): 34–43.

13. P. R. Amato, "Family Process in One-Parent, Stepparent, and Intact Families: The Child's Point of View," *Journal of Marriage and the Family* 49 (1987): 327–37.

14. L. Tessman, *Children of Parting Parents* (New York: Aronson, 1978).

15. J. Kleinman, E. Rosenberg, and M. Whiteside, "Common Developmental Tasks in Forming Reconstituted Families," *Journal of Marriage and Family Therapy* 5 (1979): 79–86.

16. J. M. Theis, "Beyond Divorce: The Impact of Remarriage on Children," *Journal of Clinical Child Psychology* 6, no. 2 (1977): 59–61.

17. P. Skeen, R. B. Covi, and B. E. Robinson, "Stepfamilies: A Review of the Literature with Suggestions for Practitioners," *Journal of Counseling and Development* 64 (1985): 121–25.

18. F. Capaldi and B. McRae, *Stepfamilies: A Cooperative Responsibility* (New York: New Viewpoints/Vision Books, 1979).

19. S. K. Turnbull and J. M. Turnbull, "To Dream the Impossible Dream: An Agenda for Discussion with Stepparents," *Family Relations* 32 (1983): 227–30.

20. P. N. Stern, "Stepfather Families Integration around Child Discipline," *Issues in Mental Health Nursing* 1 (1978): 326–32.

21. Amato, "Family Process."

22. J. Bowlby, *Attachment and Loss*, vol. 3 (New York: Basic Books, 1980).

23. W. G. Clingempeel, "Quasi-Kin Relationships and Marital Quality in Stepfather Families," *Journal of Personality and Social Psychology* 41 (1981): 890–901.

24. Skeen, Covi, and Robinson, "Stepfamilies."

25. R. L. Hayes and B. A. Hayes, "Remarriage Families: Counseling Parents, Stepparents, and Their Children," *Counseling and Human Development* 18 (1986): 1–8.

26. E. B. Visher and J. S. Visher, "Stepfamilies in the 1980's," in *Therapy with Remarried Families*, ed. L. Messinger (Rockville, Md.: Aspen Systems Corp., 1982), 105–19.

27. P. Lutz, "The Stepfamily: An Adolescent Perspective," *Family Relations* 32 (1983): 367–75.

28. L. H. Ganong and M. Coleman, "The Effects of Remarriage on Children: A Review of the Empirical Literature," *Family Relations* 33 (1984): 389–406.

29. E. B. Visher and J. S. Visher, *Old Loyalties, New Ties: Therapeutic Strategies with Stepfamilies* (New York: Brunner/Mazel, 1988).

30. R. P. Rankin and J. S. Maneker, "The Duration of Marriage in a Divorcing Population: The Impact of Children," *Journal of Marriage and the Family* 47 (February 1985): 43–51.

31. B. Fishman, "The Economic Behavior of Stepfamilies," *Family Relations* 32 (1983): 359–66.

32. Turnbull and Turnbull, "Impossible Dream."

33. J. Strother and E. Jacobs, "Adolescent Stress as It Relates to Stepfamily Living: Implications for School Counselors," *The School Counselor* 32 (1984): 97–103.

34. M. A. Fine, "Perceptions of Stepparents: Variations in Stereotypes as a Function of Family Structure," *Journal of Marriage and the Family* 48 (1986): 537–43.

35. C. E. Bowerman and D. P. Irish, "Some Relationships of Stepchildren to Their Parents," *Marriage and Family Living* 24 (1970): 113–21.

36. M. Draughon, "Stepmother's Model of Identification in Relation to Mourning in the Child," *Psychological Reports* 36 (1975): 183–89.

37. M. J. Montgomery et al., "Patterns of Courtship for Remarriage: Implications for Child Adjustment and Parent-Child Relationships," *Journal of Marriage and the Family* 54 (1992): 686–98.

38. Amato, "Family Process."

39. L. E. Sauer and M. A. Fine, "Parent-Child Relationships in Stepparent Families," *Journal of Family Psychology* 1, no. 4 (1988): 434–51.

40. H. P. Oshman and M. Manosezitz, "Father Absence: Effects of Stepfathers upon Psychosocial Development in Males," *Developmental Psychology* 12 (1976): 379–480.

41. G. L. Schulman, "Myths That Intrude on the Adaptation of the Stepfamily," *Social Casework* 49 (1972): 131–39.

42. J. H. Nadler, "Effecting Change in Stepfamilies: A Psychodynamic/ Behavioral Group Approach," *American Journal of Psychotherapy* 37, no. 1 (1983): 100–112.

43. D. A. Thompson, *Counseling and Divorce* (Dallas, Tex.: Word, 1989), 139.

Chapter 12

Future Family— What Works!

A happy family is but an earlier heaven.
Sir John Bowring, 1792–1872

Final chapters are always difficult to write—there is so much left unsaid, so much that might help single parents and family members, so much that perhaps could have been better said. But here we are at the point when a look to the future awaits us and the single parents to whom we want to minister. The ongoing changes in the American family demand our attention and help. Things are steadily worsening, and we have no reason to think that the need for counselor and other helper intervention will diminish. As the divorce rate has risen 111 percent since 1970, 111 percent more counseling help is needed. With 79 percent of divorced men and 75 percent of divorced women remarrying, an equal or greater need for counseling is created. With 60 percent of remarried people being parents, counselor intervention is more and more required.[1] Counselors working with single parents and stepparents will not be unemployed!

WHAT WORKS IN COUNSELING

Counselors working with single parents and stepparents spend a great deal of their time dealing with concrete, palpable, impact-laden problems. By the time single parents or stepparents make the first counseling appointment, they have reached the end of the rope and are slipping fast. Consequently, the single-parent and stepparent client population requires an immediate shot of encouragement during that first visit, or they will probably not return for the second. Single parents and stepparents are stressed-out, stretched thin, overworked, underpayed, overwrought, and ready to go nuclear! This population is in no mood for anything short of optimism and practical answers from a counselor who knows what he or she is doing and is ready to get on with it. For this population, time is "a-wasting."

GOOD WILL

Single-parent and stepparent clients expect to meet with a counselor who cares about them independent of what has gone on in their lives already. It is no secret that some mistakes have been made. Clients want their counselor to like them and express that liking up front. This cannot be faked, of course. Good will by the counselor is one of those transparent qualities that counselor trainers look for in applicants to graduate programs. Good will is a somewhat uncommon quality, however, and can only be encouraged and strengthened, not taught. Good will expresses an attitude about people that was probably acquired at one's parent's knees in the first five years of life. Counselors have good will, or they are not counselors at all. Good will can only be enhanced, not created.

PRESENCE

Stressed-out clients require a counselor's full attention. Distractions must be set aside or appointments rescheduled. If the counselor has had a fender bender on the way to the office and is unable to calm down, he or she should explain the situation to the client and reschedule. If an argument preceded the counselor's leaving for the office and his or her emotional state remains unsettled, reschedule! If a teenage son or daughter announced last night that plans were complete for moving into an apartment with seven friends and the counselor-parent has not returned to equilibrium, reschedule that appointment. At times like these it is unethical and unworkable to try to press on through a counseling session.

Counselor presence also involves paying careful attention to the client for the full counseling session. Paying attention must be communicated through counselor behavior. Body language such as leaning forward slightly, making comfortable eye contact, preventing distractions such as phone calls, sitting face-to-face with the client, and maintaining an alert but relaxed posture all communicate to the client that the counselor is earning his or her fee. Presence also assumes genuine interest in the client even though the topic of the session and the conversation at the moment might be terminally boring. Presence means the counselor *wants* to pay attention, no matter what is being shared by the client.

ACKNOWLEDGING ONE'S PERSONAL POWER AS A COUNSELOR

Clients do not appreciate a patronizing attitude on the part of the counselor. Christian counselors especially seem prone to down playing their credentials and training in an attempt to make the client feel accepted. In fact, what clients want is to feel reassured that their counselor knows what he or she is doing. Counselors should hang those diplomas, certificates, and licenses on the wall for clients to look at. Clients are paying for professional services with time, money, or both and do not mind being told, through the symbols of power, that they have made the right decision. Clients go through the same process as new car buyers. Once the money is paid, the purchaser spends considerable energy finding ways to prove to themselves that they have spent their money wisely. Display your credentials!

VULNERABILITY AND OPENNESS

Counseling can be a risky occupation. A counselor never knows when a client will ask that embarrassing question causing an awkward silence or an even more awkward explanation of why the question cannot be answered. Counselors faced with this unpleasant situation usually respond with a rationale that to answer the question would violate someone else's privacy or in some other way cause havoc to reign in the surrounding environment.

While counselors certainly have a right to determine what is or is not appropriate to share with a client, counselor reluctance will often be interpreted as a failure to trust the client. The dilemma for the counselor is obvious: How can he or she ask the client to be open and share when the counselor is not willing to do so? And, of course, the answer is they cannot. Counselors must allow themselves to experience a certain level of vulnerability through being open with the client. Risky? Of course. But indispensable too!

SELF-APPRECIATION

Stressed clients are prone to wear their emotions on their sleeves. This thin emotional skin typical of clients experiencing trauma surfaces in tears and anger and sometimes in challenges to the counselor. Counselors must be able to combine transparent sensitivity with elephant hide, impenetrable to the slings and arrows of outrageous clients.

I had had three sessions with Bill and Lucille Sommers. They initially came in for marriage problems, and we had just passed through the initial phases of intake and counseling when they canceled their fourth appointment. Then they canceled again! I sensed something was happening, and I assumed that they had made a decision either to end their marriage or to get on with building it back up, in either case no longer needing a counselor.

Then their name appeared on the schedule book again, and I was thoroughly uncertain of what I was going to hear from them. They sat down as I closed the office door and began to shoot glances back and forth, as if asking each other, "Do you want to tell him, or should I?"

"Come on, out with it," I said with a smile, really curious now.

"Well," Lucille said with an uncomfortable squirm in her seat, "I need to tell you that we would like another counselor. You see, I don't like you!"

She doesn't like me? Me? Me, the experienced counselor who tries to be nice to everyone? Me, the counselor who has spent years training for this work? Me? She doesn't like me?

I laughed out loud when I finally knew why they were so uneasy. Sure it was okay, I told them. Things like this are bound to happen once in a while, and I would be happy to refer them to another counselor if they wished. They wished!

The point is, I had to have a sufficiently secure self-concept so that this affront to my self-esteem could pass by with only minor impact. Counselors have to be so sure that they are doing a good job that when they confront the occasional Lucille, it is not a problem. Professionalism means being able to accept a request for a second opinion, even a second counseling opinion. Only when we feel sufficiently secure in ourselves and what God has called us to do will we be able to truly accept negative feedback and challenges from clients for what they are, expressions of their own concerns.

WILLINGNESS TO SERVE AS AN EXAMPLE FOR CLIENTS

There is no escape from the modeling role for counselors. Some try to fool themselves into thinking that clients are not interested in the way they conduct their lives, but clients care very much what we do, either as an encouragement for them as they try to reorganize some or all of their lives or because they want to use a counselor as an excuse to continue what they have been doing.

I tell my students that Christian counselors are more vulnerable to loss of testimony than anyone, including pastors. Leaders such as pastors can have a moral setback, obtain forgiveness, and go through the process of being recovered and brought back into the ministry. But when Christian counselors fail, we are not so much sinners as stupid. Pastors and others can recover from a moral failure, but counselors (experts in the eyes of most clients) have lost their expertise permanently, at least with the current client population.

Therefore, we must be extra vigilant as we conduct ourselves in the community. We must work hard to have a good marriage, and while we cannot hope to have perfect children, we must not be careless in how we deal with adolescent rebellion and such matters because we know that a client will, sooner or later, ask *us* how we did when our children/teenagers/husband/wife had a problem. We are transparent people as Christian counselors, and there is no escaping the power we play as role models for our clients.

WILLINGNESS TO RISK MAKING MISTAKES

Christian counselors serve as conduits for the Holy Spirit to convict, correct, rehabilitate, and encourage believers struggling with a personal problem. In this sense, there are no chances to be taken in counseling because we know that we are not in complete control of what is happening. We serve as pipelines of ministry for clients, and what we do we do in prayer and under the guidance of the Bible and the Holy Spirit.

We must also recognize, however, that we will often not know what God wants for a client, and in this sense and this sense only, counselors must be willing to strike out into the unknown and become risk-takers. A Christian counselor may be conservative theologically and even politically but rarely therapeutically. There is too much that counselors will never be 100 percent certain about, and this uncertainty forces the most reticent of counselors to take steps into the darkness while looking for the light that will best help the client. Successful counselors must be comfortable with being wrong once in a while, just as successful business people will have a short list of failures to accompany their longer list of successes. There are no risks with God, but we may not always have a clear sense of his guidance. However, such uncertainty of what God's plan might be cannot prevent counselors from acting to help the client.

SENSE OF HUMOR

Clients are not looking for a stand-up comedian as their counselor. However, they *are* looking for a counselor to help break the pressure they feel, and a humorous comment or brief story can help to break the tension. Counselors in general need to have a good sense of humor as a way of coping with what they are hearing hourly in the office. A humorous mind-set prevents burnout and prolongs ministry. A minor point, some would say, but I will suggest that the absence of a sense of humor probably accounts for more counselors leaving the profession than any other single factor.

COMMITMENT TO BIBLICAL AUTHORITY

Christian counselors must exercise care in determining how they express themselves on the issue of the Bible in counseling. Christian clients have a right to expect that an acknowledged Christian counselor will in fact be a *Christian* counselor. I want my clients to know that I accept the Bible as inerrant (though my ability to understand the Bible is far from inerrant) and will defer to God's principles each and every time an opportunity arises.

However, Christian counselors do not want to present the issue of biblical authority in such a way that clients may see their counselor as just a preacher who happens to be sitting down while he preaches. We want to employ the Bible as much as possible *and* build a health-giving relationship at the same time. "Earning the right to help" is a phrase that fits well with Christian counseling.

WHAT WORKS IN THE FAMILY (ANY FAMILY!)

Experience and good research reveals several qualities or characteristics found in functional families. These "traits of excellence" are found across the board in rich and poor families of every ethnic background and geographic origin and in every generation. Functional families are those that get the job done, no matter if the family is remarried, single-parent, adoptive, or intact and traditional. Characteristics we will be examining briefly are not limited to Christian families but are always found in the best of Christian families. The following qualities are indispensable to family success.

COMMUNICATION

Healthy families are known for open communication wherein children of all ages feel free to respectfully speak to Mom or Dad about anything. Such healthy, functional families practice clear communication that is easy to understand and that leaves the hearer and the speaker feeling better for the interchange. Healthy families speak the truth in love, and parents and other older family members are willing to listen to the words spoken by "mere children."

Communication is sometimes overworked in trying to understand pathological family patterns, but it remains true that there is no better reflection of a family's condition than the way family members speak and listen to each other. Counselors should try to arrange situations during which the family can be observed talking with each other. The Craig family did not fit the stereotype because Ron and Sue did have open and easy communication with each other and the children. Even though their marriage ended, continuance of this communication pattern will serve the children well as they grow and deal with their new family structures.

RELATIONSHIPS

Healthy, functional families develop family relationships characterized as affiliative, trusting, positive and optimistic, warm, unconditionally accepting, and relaxed. *Affiliation* simply means the family members enjoy one another's presence. *Trusting* implies assuming the best rather than the worst of each family member, even when there may be some doubt. Being positive and optimistic conveys the message to children that the glass, though not full, is more full than empty and needs to be appreciated for what is there. Warmth is an emotional feeling, a "warm fuzzy" common in better families and of tremendous benefit to children and parents. To be unconditionally accepting is to model the mind of Christ and to live a life of grace-full acceptance of others, flaws and all. When parents are relaxed, children relax, and everyone feels better.

Additionally, the most healthy families are led by true parenting partnerships that exhibit leadership but not dominance by father or stepfather. Feelings about the marriage tend to be more positive in fully functional families where responsibilities of all sorts are shared willingly. Family members are happy to be in the family and do not mind if people know it.

POWER

Healthy, fully functioning families are powerful families led by powerful parents. Not necessarily power as the world knows power; not necessarily the kind of power shown by government leaders, sports heroes, and financial overlords, but the power of confidence in what the family is doing and where the family is heading. Power exhibited by a Christian family is based on the power of God in their day-to-day life and is relatively independent of circumstances.

Power is exhibited in better families when Mom and Dad are able to share parenting power and do not feel threatened when the other takes over for a while. Parents manifest power when they share parental authority rather than have it held by only one parent. Children learn about good power when they see their parents equally discuss decisions and reach a joint decision that has been negotiated. Power is shown in the respect families have for the viewpoints of others. Nothing demonstrates confidence and power more than parents trusting God when it comes to dealing with the world.

ROLE DIFFERENTIATION

The most dysfunctional, unhealthy families are *always* characterized by blurred boundaries or no boundaries at all. Healthy families, on the other hand, exhibit clear lines of demarcation between parents, children, teenagers, and even grown children. Robert Frost wrote a poem that includes the line, "Good fences make good neighbors." The same truism applies to families: Good boundaries make good families. Not walls or barriers, but clear markers between Mom, Dad, and the children.

In better families these boundaries are well understood and easily accepted by everyone. Such boundaries make children feel secure in their individual role in the family and allow them to respect, without envy, the roles occupied by others. Jealousy is rare in these families. Individual uniqueness is valued, and children are not pressed into a family mold to make the parents feel better. There are no cookie-cutter kids in the healthiest families. Children are not seen as possessions of the parents and are not treated as though their role was to make parents happier and more fulfilled.

EMOTIONAL EXPRESSION

Expression of emotion is a frequent issue in counseling. Probably no other variable of family interaction is so impacted by family tradition and culture as is emotional expression. Some cultures require men to cry at funerals and women to be silent while other cultures demand exactly the opposite. As we discuss this issue, we want to remember the importance of culture as we determine what is healthy or dysfunctional.

In healthy families, emotions can be expressed without fear. Sons are not afraid to cry in their father's presence. Daughters are not afraid to be strong and independent emotionally when mother is around. Emotions are what they are! In fully functional families emotional expression is viewed as just another aspect of living and is neither good nor bad on its own. Healthy families demonstrate a more realistic acceptance of stressors that in other families might cause disruption. Most importantly, healthy families are characterized by members who lean on each other for emotional support when a crisis does occur. Functional families come together in times of stress; dysfunctional families pull away and face the crisis alone.

PROBLEM SOLVING

Simply stated, functional families find a way to solve their problems, less functional or dysfunctional do not. In healthy families, parents are seen to be problem solvers using their combined wisdom and experience. Children come to value parents as people they can always turn to and who will help them come up with a solution to what is bothering them.

Healthy families are led by parents willing to use outside resources such as pastor and expert friends while at the same time accepting full responsibility for the decision reached. Functional families demonstrate effective problem solving for the children, knowing that children learn to be adults by watching their parents. If parents appear ineffective in problem solving, children will lose confidence in them and will not want to be like them. A successful family life *must* employ effective problem solving as one of its support pillars.

This is what works! We know from good research and much experience what characterizes good counseling and good parenting. You might have noticed that the characteristics that make a good counselor could be transposed onto the image of a good parent. We have also seen that the needs of single parents and stepparents differ only in degree, not in kind, when compared to intact families. I believe God expects the best from Christian single parents as any other type or version of parent. God's principles for parenting are not limited by the circumstances in which we live.

THE CRAIG FAMILY

At this writing the members of the Craig family are experiencing differing degrees of recovery from the divorce. Alicia, the youngest, seems to be doing the best, and while she clings to her mother more than most children, we think this behavior will diminish with time and reassurance that her mother will be there for her. Kevin, their youngest son, is still having problems in school. Teachers worry about his aggressiveness, but as I have shared with his mother, Sue, some of that aggressiveness could be growing out of Kevin's personality rather than stemming exclusively from the divorce trauma as we originally thought. We will have to wait and see with Kevin. The fact that his dad is still involved in his life is a major advantage for Kevin as for the other children.

The older children seem to be adjusting well. Emily, the oldest, has become almost a sister to her mother and each feels very good about their relationship. Emily will be graduating from high school next year and plans to go away to college, probably a Christian college, to study nursing. Emily's leaving home will probably present Sue with a new challenge. Scott, now a sophomore in high school, struggles with his father's explanation of the need to divorce. Scott knows that from a Christian perspective, his dad's claim that he "knew" it was the right thing to do does not hold water. But he remains close and loyal to his father even while defensive of his mother.

Scott told me in one session that he and his father no longer talk much about their pre-divorce experiences and keep the conversation on a current and somewhat surface level.

Sue has moved from depression and hurt to anger and is making good progress in the grieving she needs to do for the dead marriage. It has been much easier, she told me, to be the offended partner *and* the one who forced Ron to make a decision. Even though Sue sometimes questions the correctness of demanding that Ron choose who he wanted to be his wife, she feels somewhat vindicated. She is able to attend church regularly now without embarrassment, even though she feels snubbed by some of her former friends and acquaintances in the church. She is determined to continue her Christian life and testimony and be the best mother she can be for the children. She has not, as yet, considered beginning to date. Sue has done a good job of forcing herself to be patient and let her emotional processes work for her. Sue will be fine.

Ron is really struggling at this point. I do not counsel with Ron, but the town we live in is not large and stories get around. Ron and his new wife seem happy and much in love, but Ron has started to drink socially, something that is totally inconsistent with his pre-divorce lifestyle. He struggles, too, with the issue of divided loyalties between his two families. He has shared with mutual friends how guilty he feels anytime he does something with his stepchildren and not his "real" children. Those of us who have known Ron for some time are worried about his emotional state, especially the risk for excessive drinking to relieve his apparent guilt. We will have to wait and see with Ron. The future for him is cloudy at this point.

Counseling continues with Sue and her three youngest children. Emily slowly stopped coming because, as she said, her school schedule was too heavy. Emily was doing well at the point she terminated counseling, and we will continue to work with the other members of the family. Sue and Kevin will probably need the most long-term help, but we expect all to come through this trauma well.

As I talked with Sue and the children individually, I was struck with their need to be reminded of God's love and grace for living. A portion of Scripture that became our key verse is: "Have I not commanded you? Be strong and courageous. Do not be terrified; do not be discouraged, for the LORD your God will be with you wherever you go" (Josh. 1:9). The Craig family has seen this promise fulfilled and will continue to trust in God's grace in the days to come. They will be all right.

NOTES

1. E. B. Visher and J. S. Visher, *Old Loyalties, New Ties: Therapeutic Strategies with Stepfamilies* (New York: Brunner/Mazel, 1988), ix.

Bibliography

Abelsohn, D. and G. S. Saayman. "Adolescent Adjustment to Parental Divorce: An Investigation from the Perspective of Basic Dimensions of Structural Family Therapy Theory." *Family Process* 30 (1991): 177–91.

Acock, A. C., and K. J. Kiecolt. "Is It Family Structure or Socioeconomic Status? Family Structure during Adolescence and Adult Adjustment." *Social Forces* 68 (1989): 553–71.

Adams, M. "Kids and Divorce: No Long-Term Harm." *USA Today*, 20 December, 1984, 1, 5D.

Albers, L. J., J. A. Doane, and J. Mintz. "Social Competence and Family Environment: A 15-year Follow-Up of Disturbed Adolescents." *Family Process* 25 (1986): 379–89.

Allen, S. F., C. D. Stoltenberg, and C. K. Rosko. "Perceived Separation of Older Adolescents and Young Adults from Their Parents: A Comparison of Divorced Versus Intact Families." *Journal of Counseling and Development* 89 (September-October 1990): 57–61.

Alpert-Gillis, L. J., J. L. Pedro-Carroll, and E. L. Cowen. "The Children of Divorce Intervention Program: Development, Implementation, and Evaluation of a Program for Young Urban Children." *Journal of Consulting and Clinical Psychology* 57, no. 5 (1989): 583–89.

Amato, P. R. "Family Process in One-Parent, Stepparent, and Intact Families: The Child's Point of View." *Journal of Marriage and the Family* 49 (1987): 327–37.

————. "Parental Divorce and Attitudes toward Marriage and Family Life." *Journal of Marriage and the Family* 48 (1986): 453–61.

————. "Parental Divorce and Attitudes toward Marriage and Family Life." *Journal of Marriage and the Family* 50 (1988): 453–61.

Amato, P. R., and A. Booth. "Consequences of Parental Divorce and Marital Unhappiness for Adult Well-Being." *Social Forces* 69, no. 3 (1991): 895–914.

American Psychological Association, Division of Counseling Psychology, Committee on Definition. *American Psychologist* 11 (1986): 282–85.

Andersen, T. Z., and G. D. White. "An Empirical Investigation of Interaction and Relationship Patterns in Functional and Dysfunctional Nuclear Families and Stepfamilies." *Family Process* (1986): 407–22.

Asmussen, L., and R. Larson. "The Quality of Family Time among Young Adolescents in Single-Parent and Married-Parent Families." *Journal of Marriage and the Family* 53 (1991): 1021–30.

Atlas, S. *The Parents without Partners Source Book.* Philadelphia, Pa: Running Press, 1984.

Awad, G. A., and R. Parry. "Access Following Marital Separation." *Canadian Journal of Psychiatry* 25, no. 5 (1980): 357–65.

Bales, J. "Parent's Divorce Has Major Impact on College Students." *APA Monitor* 15, no. 8 (1984): 13.

Bane, M. J. "Marital Disruption and the Lives of Children." *Journal of Social Issues* 52, no. 1 (1976): 103–17.

Bay, R. C., and S. L. Braver. "Perceived Control of the Divorce Settlement Process and Interparental Conflict." *Family Relations* 39 (1990): 382–87.

Bayrakal, S., and T. M. Kope. "Dysfunction in the Single-Parent and Only-Child Family." *Adolescence* 25, no. 97 (1990): 1–7.

Benedek, E. P. "Child Custody Laws: Their Psychiatric Implications." *American Journal of Psychiatry* 129 (1972): 326–28.

Benedek, R. S., and E. P. Benedek. "Post-Divorce Visitation." *Journal of the American Academy of Child Psychiatry* 16 (1977): 256–71.

Berman, W. H. "The Role of Attachment in the Post-Divorce Experience." *Journal of Personality and Social Psychology* 54, no. 3 (1988): 496–503.

Bernard, J. *A Study of Marriage.* New York: Russell and Russell, 1956.

———. *Remarriage: A Study of Marriage* 2nd ed. New York: Russell and Russell, 1971.

Bernard, J. M., and S. Nesbitt. "Divorce: An Unreliable Predictor of Children's Emotional Predispositions." *Journal of Divorce* 4, no. 4 (1981): 31–42.

Bernstein, B. E., and S. K. Collins. "Remarriage Counseling: Lawyer and Therapist's Help with the Second Time Around." *Family Relations* 34 (1985): 387–91.

Biller, H. B. "Father Absence, Divorce, and Personality Development." In *The Role of Father in Child Development*, 2nd ed., ed. M. E. Lamb. New York: Wiley, 1981.

Blechman, E. A., and M. Manning. "A Reward-Cost Analysis of the Single-Parent Family." In *Behavior Modification and Families*, ed. E. J. Mash, L. A. Hamerlynck, and L. C. Handy. New York: Brunner/Mazel, 1976.

Bloom, B. L., S. J. Asher, and S. W. White. "Marital Disruption as a Stressor: A Review and Analysis." *Psychological Bulletin* 85 (1978): 867–99.

Bloom, B. L., and K. R. Kindle. "Demographic Factors in the Continuing Relationships Between Former Spouses." *Family Relations* 34 (1985): 375–81.

Bohannon, P. *Divorce and After.* Garden City, N.Y.: Doubleday, 1970.

Bonkowski, S. E. "Lingering Sadness: Young Adult's Response to Parental Divorce." *Social Casework* (April 1989): 219–23.

Bonkowski, S. E., S. Q. Bequette, and S. Boomhower. "A Group Design to Help Children Adjust to Parental Divorce." *The Journal of Contemporary Social Work* (1984): 131–39.

Bonkowski, S. E., S. J. Boomhower, and S. Q. Bequette. "What You Don't Know Can Hurt You: Unexpressed Fears and Feelings of Children from Divorcing Families." *Journal of Divorce* 91 (1985): 33–45.

Booth, A., D. B. Brinkerhoff, and L. K. White. "The Impact of Parental Divorce on Courtship." *Journal of Marriage and the Family* 65, no. 4 (1984): 85–94.

Booth, A., and J. N. Edwards. "Age at Marriage and Marital Stability." *Journal of Marriage and the Family* (February 1985): 67–75.

Borrine, M. L., P. J. Handal, N. Y. Brown, and H. R. Searight. "Family Conflict and Adolescent Adjustment in Intact, Divorced, and Blended Families." *Journal of Consulting and Clinical Psychology* 59, no. 5 (1991): 753–55.

Bowerman, C. E., and D. P. Irish. "Some Relationships of Stepchildren to Their Parents." *Marriage and Family Living* 24 (1970): 113–21.

Bowlby, J. *Attachment and Loss: Separation.* New York: Basic Books, 1973.

———. *Attachment and Loss.* Vol. 3. New York: Basic Books, 1980.

Bradford, A., R. S. Moore, B. Enwall, J. Tayler, S. B. Cooper, and C. G. Williams. *Parting: A Counselor's Guide for Children of Separated Parents.* Columbia, S. C.: South Carolina Department of Education, 1982.

Brevino, M. M. "The 87 Percent Factor." *The Delta Kappa Gamma Bulletin* 54, no. 3 (1988): 9–16.

Brown, D. G. "Divorce and Family Mediation: History, Review, and Future Directions." *Conciliation Courts Review* 20, no. 2 (1982): 1–44.

Brown, J. H., P. R. Portes, and D. A. Christensen. "Understanding Divorce Stress on Children: Implications for Research and Practice." *The American Journal of Family Therapy* 17, no. 4 (1989): 315–25.

Bruce, M. L., and K. M. Kim. "Differences in the Effects of Divorce on Major Depression in Men and Women." *American Journal of Psychiatry* 149, no. 7 (1992): 914–17.

Buchanan, C. M., E. E. Maccoby, and S. M. Dornbusch. "Caught between Parents: Adolescents' Experiences in Divorced Homes." *Child Development* 62 (1991): 1008–29.

Buehler, C. "Initiator Status and the Divorce Transition." *Family Relations* 36 (1987): 82–86.

Bundy, M. L., and P. N. White. "Parents as Sexuality Educators: A Parent Training Program." *Journal of Counseling and Development* 68 (January/February 1990): 321–23.

Bursik, K. "Adaptation to Divorce and Ego Development in Adult Women." *Journal of Personality and Social Psychology* 60, no. 2 (1991): 300–306.

Camiletti, Y. "Anticipatory Counseling for Adolescents of Divorced Parents." *The School Guidance Worker* 39, no. 1 (1983): 20–23.

Canfield, J. "Self-Esteem in Adolescents." Handout for the Fourth National Conference of Advances in Testing Survivors of Sexual Abuse, *U.S. Journal Training*, 3–6 March 1993).

Capaldi, F., and B. McRae. *Stepfamilies: A Cooperative Responsibility*. New York: New Viewpoints/Vision Books, 1979.

Charnas, J. F. "Practive Trends in Divorce Related Child Custody." *Journal of Divorce* 4, no. 4 (1981): 57–67.

Chasin, R., and H. Grunebaum. "A Model for Evaluation in Child Custody Disputes." *American Journal of Family Therapy* 9, no. 1 (1981): 43–49.

Chiriboga, D., L. Catron, and P. Weiler. "Childhood Distress and Adult Functioning during Marital Separation." *Family Relations* 36 (1987): 163–67.

Clingempeel, W. G. "Quasi-Kin Relationships and Marital Quality in Stepfather Families." *Journal of Personality and Social Psychology* 41 (1981): 890–901.

Coffman, S. G. "Conflict-Resolution Strategy for Adolescents with Divorced Parents." *The School Counselor* 38 (1988): 61–66.

Coffman, S. S., and A. E. Roark. "Likely Candidates for Group Counseling: Adolescents with Divorced Parents." *The School Counselor* (March 1988): 246–52.

Coleman, M., and L. H. Ganong. "Effect of Family Structure on Family Attitudes and Expectations." *Family Relations* 33 (1984): 425–32.

Coogler, O. J. *Structured Mediation in Divorce Settlement: A Handbook for Marital Mediators.* Lexington, Mass.: Lexington Books, 1978.

Copeland, A. P. "Individual Differences in Children's Reactions to Divorce." *Journal of Clinical Child Psychology* 14, no. 1 (1985): 11–19.

Craddock, A. E. "Family Structure and Sex-Role Orientation." *The American Journal of Family Therapy* 18, no. 4 (1990): 355–62.

Dawson, D. A. "Family Structure and Children's Health and Well-Being: Data from the National Health Interview Survey of Child Health." *Journal of Marriage and the Family* (1991): 573–84.

Devall, E., Z. Stoneman, and G. Brody. "The Impact of Divorce and Maternal Employment on Pre-Adolescent Children." *Family Relations* 35 (1986): 153–59.

Dishon, M. "Psychological Aspects and Factors in Planning Visitation." *Family Law News* 8, no. 3 (1985): 36–39.

Doherty, W. J., and R. H. Needle. "Psychological Adjustment and Substance Use among Adolescents Before and After a Parental Divorce." *Child Development* 62 (1991): 328–37.

Drake, E. A. "Helping Children Cope with Divorce: The Role of the School." In *Children of Separation and Divorce: Management and Treatment,* ed. I. R. Stuart and L. E. Abt. New York: Van Nostrand Reinhold, 1981.

Draughon, M. "Stepmother's Model of Identification in Relation to Mourning in the Child." *Psychological Reports* 36 (1975): 183–89.

Dudley, J. R. "Increasing Our Understanding of Divorced Fathers Who Have Infrequent Contact with Their Children." *Family Relations* 40 (1991): 279–85.

Dyer, W., and J. Vriend. *Group Counseling for Personal Mastery.* New York: Sovereign Books, 1980.

Eggebeen, D. J. "Determinants of Maternal Employment: White Preschool Children: 1960–1980." *Journal of Marriage and the Family* (1988): 149–59.

Elkin, M. "Joint Custody: Affirming That Parents and Families Are Forever." *Social Work* (January/February 1987): 18–25.

Evans, A., and J. Neel. "School Behaviors of Children from One-Parent and Two-Parent Homes." *Principal* 60, no. 1 (1980): 38–39.

Farber, S. S., R. D. Felner, and J. Primavera. "Parental Separation/Divorce and Adolescents: An Examination of Factors Mediating Adaptation." *American Journal of Community Psychology* 13, no. 2 (1985): 171–84.

Farber, S. S., J. Primavera, and R. D. Felner. "Older Adolescents and Parental Divorce: Adjustment Problems and Mediators of Coping." *Journal of Divorce* 7, no. 2 (1983): 59–74.

Felner, R. D., A. Stolberg, and E. L. Cowen. "Crisis Events and School Mental Health Referral Patterns of Young Children." *Journal of Consulting and Clinical Psychology* 43 (1975): 305–10.

Feri, E. *Growing Up in a One-Parent Family: A Long-Term Study of Child Development.* Windsor, Berkshire, England: NFER Publishing, 1976.

Fine, M. A. "Perceptions of Stepparents: Variations in Stereotypes as a Function of Family Structure." *Journal of Marriage and the Family* 48 (1986): 537–43.

Fine, M. A., J. R. Moreland, and A. I. Schwebel. "Long-Term Effects of Divorce on Parent-Child Relationships." *Developmental Psychology* 19, no. 5 (1983): 703–13.

Fisher, B. *Rebuilding: When Your Relationship Ends.* San Luis Obispo, Calif.: Impact Publishers, 1981.

Fishman, B. "The Economic Behavior of Stepfamilies." *Family Relations* 32 (1983): 359–66.

Flewelling, R. L., and K. E. Bauman. "Family Structure and Initial Substance Use in Early Adolescence." *Journal of Marriage and the Family* 52 (1990): 171–82.

Flynn, T. "Single Parenthood." *The Sunday Denver Post,* Contemporary, 25 March 1984.

Forehand, R., K. Middleton, and N. Long. "Adolescent Functioning as a Consequence of Recent Parental Divorce and the Parent-Adolescent Relationship." *Journal of Applied Developmental Psychology* 8 (1987): 305–15.

Forehand, R., A. M. Thomas, M. Wierson, G. Brody, and R. Fauber. "Role of Maternal Functioning and Parenting Skills in Adolescent Functioning Following Parental Divorce." *Journal of Abnormal Psychology* 99, no. 3 (1990): 278–83.

Forehand, R., M. Wierson, L. Armistead, T. Kempton, and R. Fauber. "Interparental Conflict and Paternal Visitation

Following Divorce: The Interactive Effect on Adolescent Competence." *Child Study Journal* 20, no. 3 (1990): 193–202.

Foster, H. H., and D. J. Freed. "Life with Father." *Family Law Quarterly* 1, no. 40 (1978): 321–42.

Freeman, R., and B. Couchman. "Coping with Family Change: A Model for Therapeutic Group Counseling with Children and Adolescents." *School Guidance Worker* 40, no. 5 (1985): 44–50.

Freese, A. *Help for Your Grief*. New York: Schoken, 1977.

Frentz, C., F. M. Gresham, and S. N. Elliott. "Popular, Controversial, Neglected, and Rejected Adolescents: Contrasts of Social Competence and Achievement Differences." *Journal of School Psychology* 29 (1991): 109–20.

Furstenberg, F. F., and C. W. Nord. "Parenting Apart: Patterns of Childrearing after Marital Disruption." *Journal of Marriage and the Family* (November 1985): 893–906.

Furstenberg, F. F., C .W. Nord, J. L. Petersen, and N. Zill. "The Life Course of Children of Divorce: Marital Disruption and Parental Contact." *American Sociological Review* 48 (1983): 656–68.

Futterman, E. H. "After the Civilized Divorce." *Journal of Child Psychiatry* 19 (1980): 525–30.

Ganong, L. H., and M. Coleman. "The Effects of Remarriage on Children: A Review of the Empirical Literature." *Family Relations* 33 (1984): 389–406.

Garbarino, J., and F. Stott. *What Children Can Tell Us*. San Francisco: Jossey-Bass, 1989.

Gelbich, J. A., and E. K. Hare. "The Effects of Single Parenthood on School Achievement in a Gifted Population." *Gifted Child Quarterly* 53, no. 3 (1989): 115–17.

Gerler, E., N. Drew, and P. Mohr. "Succeeding in Middle School: A Multimodal Approach." *Elementary School Guidance and Counseling* 24 (1990): 263–71.

Girdner, L. K. "Adjudication and Mediation: A Comparison of Custody Decision-Making Processes Involving Third Parties." *Journal of Divorce* 8 (March-April 1985): 33–47.

Glenn, N. D. "The Recent Trend in Marital Success in the United States." *Journal of Marriage and the Family* 53 (1991): 261–70.

Glenn, N. D., and K. B. Kramer. "The Marriages and Divorces of the Children of Divorce." *Journal of Marriage and the Family* 49 (1987): 811–25.

Glenn, N. D., and C. N. Weaver. "The Marital Happiness of Remarried Divorced Persons." *Journal of Marriage and the Family* 39, no. 2 (1977): 331–37.

Glenwick, D. S., and J. D. Mowrey. "When Parent Becomes Peer: Loss of Intergenerational Boundaries in Single-Parent Families." *Family Relations* 35 (1986): 57–62.

Glosoff, H., and C. Kopowicz. *Children Achieving Potential: An Introduction to Elementary School Counseling and State-Level Policies.* Alexandria, Va.: American Association for Counseling and Development, 1990.

Goetting, A. "Divorce Outcome Research: Issues and Perspectives." *Journal of Family Issues* 2 (1981): 350–78.

Goldstein, J., A. Freud, and A. Solnit. *Beyond the Best Interests of the Child.* New York: Free Press, 1973.

Goldstein, S., and A. J. Solnit. *Divorce and Your Child.* New Haven: Yale University Press, 1984.

Grief, G. L. "Single Fathers Rearing Children." *Journal of Marriage and the Family* (February 1985).

Grief, G. L., and A. DeMaris. "Single Fathers with Custody." *The Journal of Contemporary Human Services* 71, no. 5 (1990): 259–66.

Grief, G. L., and F. Emad. "A Longitudinal Examination of Mothers without Custody: Implications for Treatment." *The American Journal of Family Therapy* 17, no. 2 (1989):155–63.

Grunlan, S. A. *Marriage and the Family: A Christian Perspective.* Grand Rapids, Mich.: Academic Books, 1984.

Grych, J. H., and F. D. Fincham. "Marital Conflict and Children's Adjustment: A Cognitive-Contextual Framework." *Psychological Bulletin* 108, no. 2 (1990): 267–90.

Guidubaldi, J., and H. D. Clemenshaw. "Divorce, Family Health, and Child Adjustment." *Family Relations* 34 (1985): 35–41.

Guidubaldi, J., H. D. Clemenshaw, J. D. Perry, and C. S. McLoughlin. "The Impact of Parental Divorce on Children: Report of the Nationwide NASP Study." *School Psychology Review* 12 (1983): 300–323.

Guidubaldi, J., and J. D. Perry. "Divorce and Mental Health Sequelae for Children: A Two-Year Follow-Up of a National Sample." *Journal of the American Academy of Child Psychiatry* 24 (1985): 531–37.

Guttman, J., N. Geva, and S. Gefen. "Teacher's and School Children's Stereotypic Perception of the 'Child of Divorce.'" *American Educational Research Journal* 25, no. 4 (1988): 555–71.

Hancock, E. "The Dimensions of Meaning and Belonging in the Process of Divorce." *American Journal of Orthopsychiatry* 50, no. 1 (1980): 18–27.

Hansen, C. M. "The Effects of Interparental Conflict on the Adjustment of the Preschool Child to Divorce." Ph.D. diss., University of Colorado, 1982.

Hayes, R. L., and B. A. Hayes. "Remarriage Families: Counseling Parents, Stepparents, and Their Children." *Counseling and Human Development* 18 (1986): 1–8.

Heider, F. *The Psychology of Interpersonal Relations.* New York: Wiley, 1958.

Hepworth, J., R. S. Ryder, and A. S. Dreyer. "The Effects of Parental Loss on the Formation of Intimate Relationships." *Journal of Marriage and the Family* 10, no. 1 (1984): 73–82.

Herlihy, B., and L. B. Golden. *Ethical Standards Casebook.* Alexandria, Va.: American Association for Counseling and Development, 1990 .

Hetherington, E. M., M. Cox, and R. Cox. "The Aftermath of Divorce." In *Mother-Child, Father-Child Relations,* ed. J. H. Stevens, Jr., and M. Matthews. Washington, D.C.: National Association for the Education of Young Children, 1977.

Hodges, W. F. *Interventions for Children of Divorce: Custody, Access, and Psychotherapy.* New York: Wiley, 1986.

Hodges, W. F., C. W. Tierney, and H. K. Buschbaum. "The Cumulative Effect of Stress on Preschool Children of Divorced and Intact Families." *Journal of Marriage and the Family* 46 (1984): 611–17.

Hodges, W. F., R. C. Wechsler, and C. Ballantine. "Divorce and the Preschool Child." *Journal of Divorce* 3 (1979): 55–69.

Hoyt, L. A., E. L. Cowen, J. L. Pedro-Carroll, and L. J. Alpert-Gillis. "Anxiety and Depression in Young Children of Divorce." *Journal of Clinical and Child Psychology* 19, no. 1 (1990): 26–32.

Irving, H. H. *Divorce Mediation: The Rational Alternative.* Toronto: Personal Library, 1980.

Isaacs, M. B. "Helping Mom Fail: A Case of Stalemated Divorcing Process." *Family Process* 21 (1982): 225–34.

Isaacs, M. B., G. H. Leon, and M. Kline. "When Is a Parent Out of the Picture? Different Custody, Different Perceptions." *Family Process* 26 (1987): 101–10.

Johnson, B. H. "Single Mothers Following Separation and Divorce: Making It on Your Own." *Family Relations* 36 (1986): 189–97.

Johnson, C. L. "Postdivorce Reorganization of Relationships between Divorcing Children and Their Parents." *Journal of Marriage and the Family* 50 (1988): 221–31.

Johnson, D., and F. Johnson. *Joining Together: Group Theory and Group Skills.* 3rd ed. Englewood Cliffs, N.J.: Prentice-Hall, 1987.

Johnson, H. C. "Working with Stepfamilies: Principles and Practice." *Social Work* 25 (1980): 304–8.

Johnston, J. R. "Role Diffusion and Role Reversal: Structural Variations in Divorced Families and Children's Functioning." *Family Relations* 39 (1990): 405–13.

Johnston, J. R., L. E. G. Campbell, and S. S. Mayes. "Latency Children in Post-Separation and Divorce Disputes." *Journal of the American Academy of Child Psychiatry* 24, no. 5 (1985).

Kalmuss, D., and J. A. Seltzer. "Continuity of Marital Behavior in Remarriage: The Case of Spouse Abuse." *Journal of Marriage and the Family* 48 (1986): 113–20.

Kalter, N. "Long-Term Effects of Divorce on Children: A Developmental Vulnerability Model." *American Journal of Orthopsychiatry* 57, no. 4 (1987): 587–600.

Kalter, N., D. Alpern, R. Spence, and J. W. Plunkett. "Locus of Control of Children of Divorce." *Journal of Personality Assessment* 48 (1984): 410–14.

Kalter, N., J. Pickar, and M. Lesowitz. "School-Based Developmental Facilitation Groups for Children of Divorce." *American Journal of Orthopsychiatry* 54 (1984): 613–23.

Kaseman, C. M. "The Single-Parent Family." *Perspectives in Psychiatric Care* 12 (1974): 113–18.

Kaslow, N. J., L. P. Rehm, S. L. Pollack, and A. W. Siegel. "Depression and Perception of Family Functioning in Children and Their Parents." *The American Journal of Family Therapy* 18, no. 3 (1990): 227–35.

Kavanaugh, R. *Facing Death.* Baltimore: Penguin Books, 1974.

Keat, D. "Change in Multimodal Counseling." *Elementary School Guidance and Counseling* 24 (1990): 248–62.

Keith, V. M., and B. Finlay. "The Impact of Parental Divorce on Children's Educational Attainment, Marital Timing, and Likelihood of Divorce." *Journal of Marriage and the Family* 50 (1988): 797–809.

Kelly, E. W., and T. J. Sweeney. "Typical Faulty Goals of Adolescents: A Base for Counseling." *The School Counselor* 29 (March 1979): 236–46.

Kempton, T., L. Armistead, M. Wierson, and R. Forehand. "Presence of a Sibling as a Potential Buffer Following Parental Divorce: An Examination of Young Adolescents." *Journal of Clinical Child Psychology* 20, no. 4 (1991): 434–38.

Kinnaird, K. L., and M. Gerrard. "Premarital Sexual Behavior and Attitudes toward Marriage and Divorce among Young Women as a Function of Their Mother's Marital Status." *Journal of Marriage and the Family* 48 (November 1986): 757–65.

Kitson, G. C., and L. A. Morgan. "The Multiple Consequences of Divorce." *Journal of Marriage and the Family* 52 (1990): 913–24.

Kleinman, J., E. Rosenberg, and M. Whiteside. "Common Developmental Tasks in Forming Reconstituted Families." *Journal of Marriage and Family Therapy* 5 (1979): 79–86.

Knaub, P. K., S. L. Hanna, and N. Stinnet. "Strengths of Remarried Families." *Journal of Divorce* 7 (1984): 41–45.

Koch, M. A., and C. R. Lowery. "Visitation and the Noncustodial Father." *Journal of Divorce* 8, no. 2 (1984): 47–65.

Kompara, D. R. "Difficulties in the Socialization Process of Stepparenting." *Family Relations* 29 (1980): 69–73.

Kupisch, S. "Children and Stepfamilies." In *Children's Needs: Psychological Perspectives,* ed. A. Thomas and J. Grimes. Washington, D.C.: National Association of Psychologists, 1987.

Kubler-Ross, E. *On Death and Dying.* New York: MacMillan, 1969.

Kurdek, L. A., ed. *Children and Divorce.* San Francisco: Jossey-Bass, 1983.

————. "The Relationship between Reported Well-Being and Divorce History, Availability of a Proximate Adult, and Gender." *Journal of Marriage and the Family* 53 (1991): 71–78.

Lazarus, A. "Multimodal Applications and Research: A Brief Overview and Update." *Elementary School Guidance and Counseling* 24 (1990): 243–47.

Lewis, H. C. *All About Families: The Second Time Around.* Atlanta, Ga.: Peachtree, 1980.

Lopez, F. G. "The Impact of Parental Divorce on College Student Development." *Journal of Counseling and Development* 65 (1987): 484–86.

Lopez, F. G., V. L. Campbell, and C. E. Watkins. "The Relation of Parental Divorce to College Student Development." *Journal of Divorce* 12, no. 1 (1988): 83–98.

Lowery, C. R., and S. A. Settle. "Effects of Divorce on Children: Differential Impact of Custody and Visitation Patterns." *Family Relations* 34 (1985): 455–63.

Lutz, P. "The Stepfamily: An Adolescent Perspective." *Family Relations* 32 (1983): 367–75.

McCombs, A., and R. Forehand. "Adolescent School Performance Following Parental Divorce: Are There Family Factors That Can Enhance Success?" *Adolescence* 24, no. 96 (1989): 871–79.

McGoldrick, M., and E. A. Carter. "Forming a Remarried Family." In *The Family Life Cycle: A Framework for Family Therapy*, edited by E. A. Carter and M. McGoldrick. New York: Gardner Press, 1980.

McLoughlin, D., and R. Whitfield. "Adolescents and Their Experiences of Parental Divorce." *Journal of Adolescence* 7 (1984): 155–70.

Machida, S., and S. D. Holloway. "The Relationship between Divorced Mothers' Perceived Control over Child Rearing and Children's Post-Divorce Development." *Family Relations* 40 (1991): 272–79.

Mauldon, J. "The Effect of Marital Disruption on Children's Health." *Demography* 27, no. 3 (1990): 431–46.

Mechanic, D., and S. Hansel. "Divorce, Family Conflict, and Adolescents' Well-Being." *Journal of Health and Social Behavior* 30 (1989): 105–16.

Menaghan, E. G., and M. A. Lieberman. "Changes in Depression Following Divorce: A Panel Study." *Journal of Marriage and the Family* 48 (1986): 319–28.

Mendes, H. A. "Single Fatherhood." *Social Work* 21 (1976): 308–12.

Messinger, L. "Remarriage between Divorced People with Children from a Previous Marriage." *Journal of Marriage and Family Counseling* 2, no. 2 (1976): 193–200.

Montgomery, M. J., E. R. Anderson, E. M. Hetherington, and W. G. Clingempeel. "Patterns of Courtship for Remarriage: Implications for Child Adjustment and Parent-Child Relationships." *Journal of Marriage and the Family* 54 (1992): 686–98.

Morawetz, A., and G. Walker. *Brief Therapy with Single-Parent Families.* New York: Brunner/Mazel, 1984.

Mueller, D. P., and P. W. Cooper. "Children of Single-Parent Families: How They Fare as Young Adults." *Family Relations* 35 (1986): 169–76.

Nadler, J. H. "Effecting Change in Stepfamilies: A Psychodynamic/Behavioral Group Approach." *American Journal of Psychotherapy* 37, no. 1 (1983): 100–112.

National Association of Elementary School Principals Report. "One-Parent Families and Their Children." *Principal* 60, no. 1 (1980): 31–37.

National Center for Health Statistics. *American Demographics Magazine*, April 1991.

Needle, R. H., S. S. Su, and W. J. Doherty. "Divorce, Remarriage, and Adolescent Substance Use: A Prospective Longitudinal Study." *Journal of Marriage and the Family* 52 (1990): 157–69.

Oshman, H. P., and M. Manosezitz. "Father Absence: Effects of Stepfathers upon Psychosocial Development in Males." *Developmental Psychology* 12 (1976): 379–480.

Papernow, P. L. "The Stepfamily Cycle: An Experimental Model of Stepfamily Development." *Family Relations* 33 (1984): 355–63.

Parish, T. S. "Ratings of Self and Parents by Youth: Are They Affected by Family Status, Gender, and Birth Order?" *Adolescence* 26, no. 101 (1991): 105–12.

Parish, T. S., and S. E. Wigle. "A Longitudinal Study of the Impact of Parental Divorce on Adolescents' Evaluations of Self and Parents." *Adolescence* 20, no. 77 (1985): 239–44.

Pasley, K. "Stepfathers." In *Dimensions of Fatherhood*, ed. S. M. Hanson and F. W. Mozett. Beverly Hills, Calif.: Sage, 1985.

Peres, Y., and R. Pasternak. "To What Extent Can the School
    Reduce the Gaps between Children Raised by Divorced
    and Intact Families?" *Journal of Divorce and Remarriage* 15,
    (March-April 1991): 143–50.
Peterson, J. L., and N. Zill. "Marital Disruption, Parent-Child
    Relationships, and Behavior Problems in Children." *Jour-
    nal of Marriage and the Family* 48 (1986): 295–307.
Phelps, D. W. "Parental Attitudes toward Family Life and
    Child Behavior of Mothers in Two-Parent and One-Par-
    ent Families." *Journal of School Health* 39 (1969): 43–46.
Popenoe, D. *Disturbing the Nest.* New York: Aldine De Gruyter, 1988.
Ramos, S. *The Complete Book of Child Custody.* New York:
    Putnam, 1979.
Rankin, R. P., and J. S. Maneker. "The Duration of Marriage in
    a Divorcing Population: The Impact of Children." *Journal
    of Marriage and the Family* 47 (February 1985): 43–51.
Raphael, B., J. Cubis, M. Dunne, T. Lewin, and B. Kelly. "The
    Impact of Parental Loss on Adolescents' Psychological
    Characteristics." *Adolescence* 24, no. 99 (1990): 689–700.
Rekers, G. A. *Counseling Families.* Waco, Tex.: Word, 1988.
Reid, W. J., and A. Crisafulli. "Marital Discord and Child Be-
    havior Problems: A Meta-Analysis." *Journal of Abnormal
    Child Psychology* 18, no. 1 (1990): 105–17.
Reingold, C. B. *Remarriage.* New York: Harper and Row, 1976.
Repucci, N. D. "The Wisdom of Solomon: Issues in Child Cus-
    tody Determination." In *Children, Mental Health, and the
    Law,* ed. N. D. Repucci, L. A. Weithron, E. P. Mulvey, and
    J. Monohan. Beverly Hills, Calif.: Sage, 1984.
Richards, C. A., and I. Goldenberg. "Fathers with Joint Physi-
    cal Custody of Young Children: A Preliminary Look." *The
    American Journal of Family Therapy* 14, no. 2 (1986): 154–62.
Risman, B. J. "Can Men 'Mother'? Life as a Single Father." *Fam-
    ily Relations* 35 (1986): 95–102.
Robson, B. E. "School-Based Groups for Children and Adoles-
    cents of Divorce." *Canadian Home Economics Journal* 36, no.
    1 (1986): 13–22.
Rogers, C. "The Underlying Theory: Drawn from Experiences
    with Individuals and Groups." *Counseling and Values* 32
    (1987): 38–45.

Roseby, V., and R. Deutsch. "Children of Separation and Divorce: Effects of a Social Role-Taking Group Intervention on Fourth and Fifth Graders." *Journal of Clinical Child Psychology* 14, no. 10 (1985): 55–60.

Runyon, N., and P. L. Jackson. "Divorce: Its Impact on Children." *Perspectives in Psychiatric Care* 3, no. 4 (1988): 101–5.

Rutter, M. *Maternal Deprivation Reassessed*. Baltimore: Penguin, 1972.

Sanik, M. M., and T. Mauldin. "Single- Versus Two-Parent Families: A Comparison of Mothers' Time." *Family Relations* 35 (1986): 53–56.

Santrock, J. W. "Relation of Type and Onset of Father Absence to Cognitive Development." *Child Development* 43 (1972): 455–69.

Santrock, J. W., and R. A. Warshak. "Father Custody and Social Development in Boys and Girls." *Journal of Social Issues* 35 (1979): 12–15.

Sauer, L. E., and M. A. Fine. "Parent-Child Relationships in Stepparent Families." *Journal of Family Psychology* 1, no. 4 (1988): 434–51.

Scherman, A., and L. Lepak. "Children's Perceptions of the Divorce Process." *Elementary School Guidance and Counseling* (October 1986): 29–35.

Schlesinger, B. "Children's Viewpoints of Living in a One-Parent Family." *Journal of Divorce* 5 (1982): 1–23.

Schulman, G. L. "Myths That Intrude on the Adaptation of the Stepfamily." *Social Casework* 49 (1972): 131–39.

Schwebel, A. I., M. A. Fine, and M. A. Renner. "A Study of Perceptions of the Stepparent Role." *Journal of Family Issues* 12, no. 1 (1991): 43–57.

Sears, R. R., E. E. Maccoby, and H. Levin. *Patterns of Child Rearing*. Evanston, Ill.: Row, Peterson and Co., 1957.

Seltzer, J. A. "Legal Custody Arrangements and Children's Welfare." *American Journal of Sociology* 9, no. 4 (1991): 895–929.

———. "Relationship between Fathers and Children Who Live Apart: The Father's Role after Separation." *Journal of Marriage and the Family* 53 (1991): 79–101.

Seltzer, J. A., N. C. Schaeffer, and H. W. Charng. "Family Ties After Divorce: The Relationship between Visiting and

Paying Child Support." *Journal of Marriage and the Family* 51 (1989): 1013–32.

Simmons, R. C., F. Rosenberg, and M. Rosenberg. "Disturbance in the Self-Image of Adolescence." *American Sociological Review* 38 (1973): 553–68.

Skafte, D. *Child Custody Evaluations.* Beverly Hills, Calif.: Sage, 1985.

Skeen, P., R. B. Covi, and B. E. Robinson. "Stepfamilies: A Review of the Literature with Suggestions for Practitioners." *Journal of Counseling and Development* 64 (1985): 121–25.

Smith, R. M. "The Impact of Fathers on Delinquent Children." *Dissertation Abstracts International* 35, no. 10-A (1976): 6487–88.

Smith, T. E. "Parental Separation and the Academic Self-Concepts of Adolescents." *Journal of Marriage and the Family* 52 (1990): 107–18.

Sorosky, A. D. "The Psychological Effect of Divorce on Adolescents." *Adolescence* 12 (1977): 123–36.

Stack, S. "New Micro-Level Data on the Impact of Divorce on Suicide, 1959–1980: A Test of Two Theories." *Journal of Marriage and the Family* 52 (1990): 119–27.

Stanley, B. K., W. J. Weikel, and J. Wilson. "The Effects of Father Absence on Interpersonal Problem-Solving Skills of Nursery School Children." *Journal of Counseling and Development* 64 (February 1986): 383–85.

Stellway, R. J. *Christiantown USA.* New York: The Haworth Press, 1990.

Stern, P. N. "Stepfather Families Integration around Child Discipline." *Issues in Mental Health Nursing* 1 (1978): 326–32.

Stohlberg, A. L., and J. P. Bush. "A Path Analysis of Factors Predicting Children's Divorce Adjustment." *Journal of Clinical Child Psychology* 14 (1985): 49–54.

Strother, J., and E. Jacobs. "Adolescent Stress as It Relates to Stepfamily Living: Implications for School Counselors." *The School Counselor* 32 (1984): 97–103.

Tessman, L. *Children of Parting Parents.* New York: Aronson, 1978.

Theis, J. M. "Beyond Divorce: The Impact of Remarriage on Children." *Journal of Clinical Child Psychology* 6, no. 2 (1977): 59–61.

Thompson, C. L., and L. B. Rudolph. *Counseling Children.* Pacific Grove, Calif.: Brooks/Cole, 1992.

Thompson, D. A. *Counseling and Divorce.* Dallas, Tex.: Word, 1989

Thornton, A., and D. Camburn. "Religious Participation and Adolescent Sexual Behavior and Attitudes." *Journal of Marriage and the Family* 51 (1989): 641–53.

Trovato, F. "A Longitudinal Analysis of Divorce and Suicide in Canada." *Journal of Marriage and the Family* 49 (1987): 193–203.

Tschann, J. M., J. R. Johnston, M. Kline, and J. Wallerstein. "Family Process and Children's Functioning during Divorce." *Journal of Marriage and the Family* 51 (1989): 431–44.

Turnbull, S. K., and J. M. Turnbull. "To Dream the Impossible Dream: An Agenda for Discussion with Stepparents." *Family Relations* 32 (1983): 227–30.

Udry, J. R. "Biological Predispositions and Social Control in Adolescent Sexual Behavior." *American Sociological Review,* 53 (1988): 709–22.

Visher, E. B., and J. S. Visher. *Stepfamilies: A Guide to Working with Stepparents and Stepchildren.* New York: Brunner/Mazel, 1979.

—————. "Stepfamilies in the 1980's." In *Therapy With Remarried Families,* ed. L. Messinger. Rockville, Md.: Aspen Systems Corp., 1982.

—————. *Old Loyalties, New Ties: Therapeutic Strategies with Stepfamilies.* New York: Brunner/Mazel, 1988.

Wallerstein, J. S. "Children of Divorce: Preliminary Report of a Ten-Year Follow-Up of Young Children." *American Journal of Orthopsychiatry* 54, no. 3 (1984): 444–58.

—————. "The Overburdened Child: Some Long-Term Consequences of Divorce." *Social Work* (March/April 1985): 116–24.

Wallerstein, J. S., and S. Blakeslee. *Second Chances.* New York: Ticknor and Fields, 1989.

Wallerstein, J. S., and J. B. Kelly. "Responses of the Preschool Child to Divorce: Those Who Cope." In *Child Psychiatry: Treatment and Research,* ed. M. F. McMillan and S. Henao. New York: Brunner/Mazel, 1974.

————. "The Effects of Parental Divorce: Experiences of the Preschool Child." *Journal of the American Academy of Child Psychiatry* 14 (1975): 600–616.

————. "The Effects of Parental Divorce." *American Journal of Orthopsychiatry* 46, no. 2 (1976): 255–69.

————. "Divorce Counseling: A Community Service for Families in the Midst of Divorce." *American Journal of Orthopsychiatry* 47, no. 1 (1977): 4–22.

Walsh, W. M. "Twenty Major Issues in Remarriage Counseling." *Journal of Counseling and Development* 70 (July/August 1992): 34–43.

Wasserman, I. M. "A Longitudinal Analysis of the Linkage between Suicide, Unemployment, and Marital Dissolution." *Journal of Marriage and the Family* 46, no. 4 (1984): 853–59.

Webster-Stratton, C. "The Relationship of Marital Support, Conflict, and Divorce to Parent Perceptions, Behaviors, and Childhood Conduct Problems." *Journal of Marriage and the Family* 51 (1989): 417–30.

Weiss, R. S. "Issues in the Adjudication of Custody When Parents Separate." In *Divorce and Separation: Context, Causes, and Consequences,* ed. G. Levinger and O. C. Moles. New York: Basic Books, 1979.

Westberg, G. *Good Grief.* Phildelphia: Fortress Press, 1962.

Westoff, L. A. "Two-Time Winners." *New York Times Magazine,* 10 August 1975, 10–13.

"Where Have All the Children Gone?" *Business Week,* 29 June 1992.

Wierson, M., R. Forehand, R. Fauber, and A. McCombs. "Buffering Young Male Adolescents against Negative Parental Divorce Influences: The Role of Good-Parent-Adolescent Relations." *Child Study Journal* 19, no. 2 (1989): 101–14.

Wilbur, J. R., and M. Wilbur. "The Noncustodial Parent: Dilemmas and Interventions." *Journal of Counseling and Development* 66 (May 1988): 434–37.

Wolchik, S. A., S. L. Braver, and I. N. Sandler. "Maternal Versus Joint Custody: Postseparation Experiences and Adjustment." *Journal of Clinical Child Psychology* 14, no. 1 (1985): 5–10.

Youngs, G. A., R. Rathge, R. Mullis, and A. Mullis. "Adolescent Stress and Self-Esteem." *Adolescence* XXV, no. 98 (1990): 333–41.

Subject Index

45, 63, 116, 134, 137, 208, 249

Homemaking, 102
Humor, sense of, 20, 267–77
Hypermaturity, 190–91

Illness, 25
Independence, 79–82, 188
Intellectualism, 84–85
Individuation, 71–72
Instant love, 246
Interview(s), 14–17, 46–48
Ireland, 2

James, book of, 251
Jesus Christ, 22, 46, 116, 163
John, book of, 25

Kinship network, 250
Kubler-Ross, 37–38

Legalistic rigidity, 201
Loss, 37–38, 86–87
Lutheran, 12

Malachi, book of, 116, 137,
Marriage myths, 242–43
Matthew, Gospel of, 116, 137,
    163, 181, 251
Mark, Gospel of, 181
Maturity, 39–40
Media, 10
Mother, working, 4
Moses, 8

National Association of
    Elementary School
    Principals, 26

National Asscoiation of
    Evangelicals, 4
National Institute for Mental
    Health, 55–56, 162
Neighborhood, 13–14
Nostalgia, 9

Peter, 1 and 2, books of, 251
Piaget, Jean, 69–71
Popularity, 78
Problem-solving, 271–72
Pornography, 7
Proverbs, book of, 63
Psalms, book of, 25, 63
Psychological tasks and
    divorce, 167–72

Rejection, 56
Relationships, family, 269–70
Religious activity, 85–86
Remarriage
    Remarriage, 113–34,
    Remarrriage myths, 243
    Remarriage pitfalls, 128–32
Resatellization, 187–88
Rogers, Carl, 195–97
Role differentiation, 270–71
Romans, book of, 139

Satir, Virginia, 90
Satellization, 185–86
School achievement, 52–53,
    56, 76
Self-Esteem, 75, 224
Separation
    Separation, 71
    Separation anxiety, 50
    Separation tasks, adoles-
    cents, 191–92

About the Author

Dr. David Miller is the Professor of Counselor Education at Liberty University in Lynchburg, Virginia. He also serves as a licensed professional counselor and conducts workshops around the country for parents of teenagers and for single parents. Dr. Miller has an M.Ed. from Wayne State University and a Ph.D. in counselor education from the University of South Carolina. Other books published by the author include *Parent Power, A Parent's Guide to Adolescence, Single Moms/Single Dads,* and *Breaking Free.*

Dr. Miller and his wife, Linda, have three children. They reside in Lynchburg, Virginia.